Children Welcome!
Family Holiday & Days Out Guide

**Family Friendly Pubs
Britain's Blue Flag
& Seaside Award Beaches**

For Contents see page 3

Index of towns/ counties see page 189

© FHG Guides Ltd, 2007
ISBN 1 85055 393 9
978 1 85055 393 9

Maps: ©MAPS IN MINUTES™ 2006. ©Crown Copyright,
Ordnance Survey Northen Ireland 2006 Permit No. NI 1675.

Typeset by FHG Guides Ltd, Paisley.
Printed and bound in Malaysia by Imago.

Distribution. Book Trade: ORCA Book Services, Stanley House,
3 Fleets Lane, Poole, Dorset BH15 3AJ
(Tel: 01202 665432; Fax: 01202 666219)
e-mail: mail@orcabookservices.co.uk
Published by FHG Guides Ltd., Abbey Mill Business Centre,
Seedhill, Paisley PA1 ITJ (Tel: 0141-887 0428 Fax: 0141-889 7204).
e-mail: admin@fhguides.co.uk

Children Welcome! Family Holidays & Days Out Guide is published by FHG Guides Ltd,
part of Kuperard Group.

Cover design:	FHG Guides
Cover Pictures:	Higher Bamham Farm, Launceston, Cornwall
	Essex Development and Regeneration Agency
	Hampshire County Council

Acknowledgements

Our thanks for pictures courtesy of:
Essex Development and Regeneration Agency (p7)
Teignbridge District Council (p39), N.E. Lincolnshire Council (p42),
Devon County Council (p56, 63), Hampshire County Council (p74, 75),
Eastbourne Borough Council (p84, 86), Herefordshire Council (p105),
N.E. Lincolnshire Council (p110), Blackpool Borough Council Tourism (p117),
VisitScotland Aberdeen and Grampian (p124), VisitScotland Perthshire (p127),
Bridgend County Borough Council (p137).

Contents

How to use this Guide	7
Readers' Offer Vouchers	9-38
Good Beach Guide	39-44
CORNWALL	45
SOUTH DEVON	52
NORTH DEVON	61
SOMERSET AND WILTSHIRE	68
HAMPSHIRE AND DORSET	72
ISLE OF WIGHT	79
SUSSEX	84
KENT	89
LONDON & HOME COUNTIES	94
EAST ANGLIA	99
(Bedfordshire, Cambridgeshire, Essex, Hertfordshire, Norfolk, Suffolk)	
MIDLANDS	105
(Derbyshire, Gloucestershire Herefordshire, Leicestershire, Lincolnshire, Northamptonshire, Nottinghamshire, Oxfordshire, Shropshire, Staffordshire, Warwickshire, West Midlands, Worcestershire)	
NORTH EAST ENGLAND	110
(Durham, Northumberland, Tyne & Wear, Yorkshire)	
NORTH WEST ENGLAND	117
(Cheshire, Cumbria, Greater Manchester, Lancashire, Merseyside)	
SCOTLAND	124
WALES	133
Classified Accommodation Listings	141-149
Family Friendly Pubs, Inns and Hotels	150-154
Website Directory	155-188
Index of Towns/Regions	189

Ratings & Awards

For the first time ever the AA, VisitBritain, VisitScotland, and the Wales Tourist Board will use a single method of assessing and rating serviced accommodation. Irrespective of which organisation inspects an establishment the rating awarded will be the same, using a common set of standards, giving a clear guide of what to expect. The RAC is no longer operating an Hotel inspection and accreditation business.

Accommodation Standards: Star Grading Scheme

Using a scale of 1-5 stars the objective quality ratings give a clear indication of accommodation standard, cleanliness, ambience, hospitality, service and food, This shows the full range of standards suitable for every budget and preference, and allows visitors to distinguish between the quality of accommodation and facilities on offer in different establishments. All types of board and self-catering accommodation are covered, including hotels, B&Bs, holiday parks, campus accommodation, hostels, caravans and camping, and boats.

VisitBritain and the regional tourist boards, **enjoyEngland.com**, **VisitScotland** and **VisitWales**, and the **AA** have full details of the grading system on their websites

enjoy**England**.com

visit**Scotland**.com

visit**Wales**.com

the **AA**.com

The more stars, the higher level of quality

★★★★★
exceptional quality, with a degree of luxury

★★★★
excellent standard throughout

★★★
very good level of quality and comfort

★★
good quality, well presented and well run

★
acceptable quality; simple, practical, no frills

National Accessible Scheme

If you have particular mobility, visual or hearing needs, look out for the National Accessible Scheme. You can be confident of finding accommodation or attractions that meet your needs by looking for the following symbols.

- Typically suitable for a person with sufficient mobility to climb a flight of steps but would benefit from fixtures and fittings to aid balance

- Typically suitable for a person with restricted walking ability and for those that may need to use a wheelchair some of the time and can negotiate a maximum of three steps

- Typically suitable for a person who depends on the use of a wheelchair and transfers unaided to and from the wheelchair in a seated position. This person may be an independent traveller

- Typically suitable for a person who depends on the use of a wheelchair in a seated position. This person also requires personal or mechanical assistance (eg carer, hoist).

holidays for all sizes

The widest choice of family lodges and holiday parks. Indoor and outdoor pools, kids clubs, restaurants and entertainment. Short breaks available. With our Lowest Price Guarantee you can feel free knowing that we won't be beaten on price. See our web site for details **hoseasons.co.uk/cw1** or call **0870 900 9011**. Quote H0019

Hoseasons
holiday lodges & parks

feel free

Looking for Holiday Accommodation?

for details of hundreds of properties throughout the UK visit our website

www.holidayguides.com

Children Welcome!
Family Holiday & Days Out Guide

How To Use This Guide

The guide offers information on good beaches, resorts and visits, plus comprehensive coverage of Family Holiday Accommodation.

The order is geographical, starting with Cornwall and working eastwards through Devon, Somerset, Dorset and around the South Coast to London before moving northwards to Scotland, and then to Wales.

For 2007 we have once again included our Vouchers with FREE and REDUCED RATE entry to holiday attractions throughout the country. See pages 9-38.

Detailed page references are provided on contents page 3.

Starting from page 141 are the summarised accommodation listings, classified in the same county order as the main guide and with detailed information in symbol form. This easy reference guide will help you to make preliminary selections, if you wish, of the kind of accommodation and facilities which you feel are most suitable.

On pages 150-154 we once again include the supplement, "Family Friendly Pubs, Inns and Hotels", a brief list of some establishments which have indicated that they particularly welcome children. Please note that not all the hotels/inns featured here have advertisements in this Guide.

A useful index of towns and the sections in which they appear is featured on page 189

ENGLAND and WALES Counties

NORTH WALES
1. Denbighshire
2. Flintshire
3. Wrexham

SOUTH WALES
4. Swansea
5. Neath and Port Talbot
6. Bridgend
7. Rhondda Cynon Taff
8. Merthyr Tydfil
9. Vale of Glamorgan
10. Cardiff
11. Caerphilly
12. Blaenau Gwent
13. Torfaen
14. Newport
15. Monmouthshire

©MAPS IN MINUTES™ 2006

FHG KUPERARD READERS' OFFER 2007

LEIGHTON BUZZARD RAILWAY
Page's Park Station, Billington Road,
Leighton Buzzard, Bedfordshire LU7 4TN
Tel: 01525 373888
e-mail: info@buzzrail.co.uk
www.buzzrail.co.uk

One FREE adult/child with full-fare adult ticket
Valid 11/3/2007 - 28/10/2007

NOT TO BE USED IN CONJUNCTION WITH ANY OTHER OFFER

FHG KUPERARD READERS' OFFER 2007

BEKONSCOT MODEL VILLAGE & RAILWAY
Warwick Road, Beaconsfield,
Buckinghamshire HP9 2PL
Tel: 01494 672919
e-mail: info@bekonscot.co.uk
www.bekonscot.com

Bekonscot Model Village & Railway

One child FREE when accompanied by full-paying adult
Valid February to October 2007

NOT TO BE USED IN CONJUNCTION WITH ANY OTHER OFFER

FHG KUPERARD READERS' OFFER 2007

BUCKINGHAMSHIRE RAILWAY CENTRE
Quainton Road Station, Quainton,
Aylesbury HP22 4BY
Tel & Fax: 01296 655720
e-mail: bucksrailcentre@btopenworld.com
www.bucksrailcentre.org

One child FREE with each full-paying adult
Not valid for Special Events

NOT TO BE USED IN CONJUNCTION WITH ANY OTHER OFFER

FHG KUPERARD READERS' OFFER 2007

THE RAPTOR FOUNDATION
The Heath, St Ives Road,
Woodhurst, Huntingdon, Cambs PE28 3BT
Tel: 01487 741140 • Fax: 01487 841140
e-mail: heleowl@aol.com
www.raptorfoundation.org.uk

TWO for the price of ONE
Valid until end 2007 (not Bank Holidays)

NOT TO BE USED IN CONJUNCTION WITH ANY OTHER OFFER

A 70-minute journey into the lost world of the English narrow gauge light railway. Features historic steam locomotives from many countries. **PETS MUST BE KEPT UNDER CONTROL AND NOT ALLOWED ON TRACKS**	**Open:** Sundays and Bank Holiday weekends 11 March to 28 October. Additional days in summer. **Directions:** on A4146 towards Hemel Hempstead, close to roundabout junction with A505.

FHG GUIDES, ABBEY MILL BUSINESS CENTRE, PAISLEY PA1 1TJ • www.holidayguides.com

Be a giant in a magical miniature world of make-believe depicting rural England in the 1930s. "A little piece of history that is forever England."	**Open:** 10am-5pm daily mid February to end October. **Directions:** Junction 16 M25, Junction 2 M40.

FHG GUIDES, ABBEY MILL BUSINESS CENTRE, PAISLEY PA1 1TJ • www.holidayguides.com

A working steam railway centre. Steam train rides, miniature railway rides, large collection of historic preserved steam locomotives, carriages and wagons.	**Open:** Sundays and Bank Holidays April to October, plus Wednesdays in school holidays 10.30am to 5.30pm. **Directions:** off A41 Aylesbury to Bicester Road, 6 miles north west of Aylesbury.

FHG GUIDES, ABBEY MILL BUSINESS CENTRE, PAISLEY PA1 1TJ • www.holidayguides.com

Birds of Prey Centre offering audience participation in flying displays which are held 3 times daily. Tours, picnic area, gift shop, tearoom, craft shop.	**Open:** 10am-5pm all year except Christmas and New Year. **Directions:** follow brown tourist signs from B1040.

FHG GUIDES, ABBEY MILL BUSINESS CENTRE, PAISLEY PA1 1TJ • www.holidayguides.com

FHG
·K·U·P·E·R·A·R·D·
READERS' OFFER 2007

SACREWELL FARM & COUNTRY CENTRE
Sacrewell, Thornhaugh,
Peterborough PE8 6HJ
Tel: 01780 782254
e-mail: info@sacrewell.fsnet.co.uk
www.sacrewell.org.uk

One child FREE with one full paying adult
Valid from March 1st to October 1st 2007

NOT TO BE USED IN CONJUNCTION WITH ANY OTHER OFFER

FHG
·K·U·P·E·R·A·R·D·
READERS' OFFER 2007

GEEVOR TIN MINE
Pendeen, Penzance,
Cornwall TR19 7EW
Tel: 01736 788662 • Fax: 01736 786059
e-mail: bookings@geevor.com
www.geevor.com

TWO for the price of ONE or £3.75 off a family ticket
Valid 02/01/2007 to 20/12/2007

NOT TO BE USED IN CONJUNCTION WITH ANY OTHER OFFER

FHG
·K·U·P·E·R·A·R·D·
READERS' OFFER 2007

TAMAR VALLEY DONKEY PARK
St Ann's Chapel, Gunnislake,
Cornwall PL18 9HW
Tel: 01822 834072
e-mail: info@donkeypark.com
www.donkeypark.com

50p OFF per person, up to 6 persons
Valid from Easter until end October 2007

NOT TO BE USED IN CONJUNCTION WITH ANY OTHER OFFER

FHG
·K·U·P·E·R·A·R·D·
READERS' OFFER 2007

NATIONAL SEAL SANCTUARY
Gweek, Helston,
Cornwall TR12 6UG
Tel: 01326 221361
e-mail: seals@sealsanctuary.co.uk
www.sealsanctuary.co.uk

TWO for ONE - on purchase of another ticket of
equal or greater value. Valid until December 2007.

NOT TO BE USED IN CONJUNCTION WITH ANY OTHER OFFER

Farm animals, 18th century watermill and farmhouse, farm artifacts, caravan and camping, children's play areas. Restaurant and gift shop.	**Open:** all year. 9.30am to 5pm 1st March -30th Sept 10am-4pm 1st Oct to 28th Feb **Directions:** signposted off both A47 and A1.

FHG GUIDES, ABBEY MILL BUSINESS CENTRE, PAISLEY PA1 1TJ • www.holidayguides.com

Geevor is the largest mining history site in the UK in a spectacular setting on Cornwall's Atlantic coast. Guided underground tour, many surface buildings, museum, cafe, gift shop. Free parking.	**Open:** daily except Saturdays 10am to 4pm **Directions:** 7 miles from Penzance beside the B3306 Land's End to St Ives coast road

FHG GUIDES, ABBEY MILL BUSINESS CENTRE, PAISLEY PA1 1TJ • www.holidayguides.com

Cornwall's only Donkey Sanctuary set in 14 acres overlooking the beautiful Tamar Valley. Donkey rides, rabbit warren, goat hill, children's playgrounds, cafe and picnic area. New all-weather play barn.	**Open:** Easter to end Oct: daily 10am to 5.30pm. Nov to March: weekends and all school holidays 10.30am to 4.30pm **Directions:** just off A390 between Callington and Gunnislake at St Ann's Chapel.

FHG GUIDES, ABBEY MILL BUSINESS CENTRE, PAISLEY PA1 1TJ • www.holidayguides.com

Britain's leading grey seal rescue centre	**Open:** daily (except Christmas Day) from 10am **Directions:** from A30 follow signs to Helston, then brown tourist signs to Seal Sanctuary.

FHG GUIDES, ABBEY MILL BUSINESS CENTRE, PAISLEY PA1 1TJ • www.holidayguides.com

FHG K·U·P·E·R·A·R·D
READERS' OFFER 2007

CARS OF THE STARS MOTOR MUSEUM
Standish Street, Keswick,
Cumbria CA12 5HH
Tel: 017687 73757
e-mail: cotsmm@aol.com
www.carsofthestars.com

One child free with two paying adults
Valid during 2007

NOT TO BE USED IN CONJUNCTION WITH ANY OTHER OFFER

FHG K·U·P·E·R·A·R·D
READERS' OFFER 2007

ESKDALE HISTORIC WATER MILL
Mill Cottage, Boot, Eskdale,
Cumbria CA19 1TG
Tel: 019467 23335
e-mail: david.king403@tesco.net
www.eskdale.info

Two children FREE with two adults
Valid during 2007

NOT TO BE USED IN CONJUNCTION WITH ANY OTHER OFFER

FHG K·U·P·E·R·A·R·D
READERS' OFFER 2007

CRICH TRAMWAY VILLAGE
Crich, Matlock
Derbyshire DE4 5DP
Tel: 01773 854321 • Fax: 01773 854320
e-mail: enquiry@tramway.co.uk
www.tramway.co.uk

One child FREE with every full-paying adult
Valid during 2007

NOT TO BE USED IN CONJUNCTION WITH ANY OTHER OFFER

FHG K·U·P·E·R·A·R·D
READERS' OFFER 2007

THE BIG SHEEP
Abbotsham, Bideford,
Devon EX39 5AP
Tel: 01237 472366
e-mail: info@thebigsheep.co.uk
www.thebigsheep.co.uk

Admit one child FREE with each paying adult
Valid during 2007

NOT TO BE USED IN CONJUNCTION WITH ANY OTHER OFFER

A collection of cars from film and TV, including Chitty Chitty Bang Bang, James Bond's Aston Martin, Del Boy's van, Fab1 and many more. **PETS MUST BE KEPT ON LEAD**	**Open:** daily 10am-5pm. Open February half term, lst April to end November, also weekends in December. **Directions:** in centre of Keswick close to car park.

FHG GUIDES, ABBEY MILL BUSINESS CENTRE, PAISLEY PA1 1TJ • www.holidayguides.com

The oldest working mill in England with 18th century oatmeal machinery running daily. **DOGS ON LEADS**	**Open:** 11am to 5pm April to Sept. (may be closed Saturdays). **Directions:** near inland terminus of Ravenglass & Eskdale Railway or over Hardknott Pass.

FHG GUIDES, ABBEY MILL BUSINESS CENTRE, PAISLEY PA1 1TJ • www.holidayguides.com

A superb family day out in the atmosphere of a bygone era. Explore the recreated period street and fascinating exhibitions. Unlimited tram rides are free with entry. Play areas, woodland walk and sculpture trail, shops, tea rooms, pub, restaurant and lots more.	**Open:** daily April to October 10 am to 5.30pm, weekends in winter. **Directions:** eight miles from M1 Junction 28, follow brown and white signs for "Tramway Museum".

FHG GUIDES, ABBEY MILL BUSINESS CENTRE, PAISLEY PA1 1TJ • www.holidayguides.com

"England for Excellence" award-winning family entertainment park. Highlights: hilarious shows including the famous sheep-racing and the duck trials; the awesome Ewetopia indoor adventure playground for adults and children; brewery; mountain boarding; great local food.	**Open:** daily, 10am to 6pm April - Oct Phone for Winter opening times and details. **Directions:** on A39 North Devon link road, two miles west of Bideford Bridge.

FHG GUIDES, ABBEY MILL BUSINESS CENTRE, PAISLEY PA1 1TJ • www.holidayguides.com

FHG
·K·U·P·E·R·A·R·D·
READERS' OFFER 2007

DEVONSHIRE COLLECTION OF PERIOD COSTUME
Totnes Costume Museum,
Bogan House, 43 High Street,
Totnes,
Devon TQ9 5NP

FREE child with a paying adult with voucher
Valid from Spring Bank Holiday to end of Sept 2007

NOT TO BE USED IN CONJUNCTION WITH ANY OTHER OFFER

FHG
·K·U·P·E·R·A·R·D·
READERS' OFFER 2007

CREALY ADVENTURE PARK
Sidmouth Road, Clyst St Mary, Exeter,
Devon EX5 1DR
Tel: 0870 116 3333 • Fax: 01395 233211
e-mail: fun@crealy.co.uk
www.crealy.co.uk

FREE superkart race or panning for gold.
Height restrictions apply. Valid until 31/10/07.
Photocopies not accepted. One voucher per person.

NOT TO BE USED IN CONJUNCTION WITH ANY OTHER OFFER

FHG
·K·U·P·E·R·A·R·D·
READERS' OFFER 2007

KILLHOPE LEAD MINING MUSEUM
Cowshill, Upper Weardale,
Co. Durham DL13 1AR
Tel: 01388 537505
e-mail: killhope@durham.gov.uk
www.durham.gov.uk/killhope

One child FREE with full-paying adult
Valid April to October 2007 (not Park Level Mine)

NOT TO BE USED IN CONJUNCTION WITH ANY OTHER OFFER

FHG
·K·U·P·E·R·A·R·D·
READERS' OFFER 2007

AVON VALLEY RAILWAY
Bitton Station, Bath Road, Bitton,
Bristol BS30 6HD
Tel: 0117 932 5538
e-mail: info@avonvalleyrailway.org
www.avonvalleyrailway.org

One FREE child with every fare-paying adult
Valid May - Oct 2007 (not 'Day Out with Thomas' events)

NOT TO BE USED IN CONJUNCTION WITH ANY OTHER OFFER

Themed exhibition, changed annually, based in a Tudor house. Collection contains items of dress for women, men and children from 17th century to 1980s, from high fashion to everyday wear.	**Open:** Open from Spring Bank Holiday to end September. 11am to 5pm Tuesday to Friday. **Directions:** centre of town, opposite Market Square. Mini bus up High Street stops outside.

FHG GUIDES, ABBEY MILL BUSINESS CENTRE, PAISLEY PA1 1TJ • www.holidayguides.com

Maximum fun, magic and adventure. An unforgettable family experience, with Tidal Wave log flume, rollercoaster, Queen Bess pirate ship, techno race karts, bumper boats, Vicorian carousel, animal handling, and huge indoor and outdoor play areas. The South-West's favourite family attraction!	**Open:** Summer: daily 10am to 5pm High season: daily 10am to 7pm Winter (Nov-March): Wed-Sun 10am -5pm **Directions:** minutes from M5 J30 on the A3052 Sidmouth road, near Exeter

FHG GUIDES, ABBEY MILL BUSINESS CENTRE, PAISLEY PA1 1TJ • www.holidayguides.com

Voted 'Most Family-Friendly Museum 2004' and 'Most Welcome Experience 2005', Killhope is Britain's best preserved lead mining site, with lots to see and do. Underground Experience is something not to be missed.	**Open:** April 1st to October 31st 10.30am to 5pm daily. **Directions:** alongside A689, midway between Stanhope and Alston in the heart of the North Pennines.

FHG GUIDES, ABBEY MILL BUSINESS CENTRE, PAISLEY PA1 1TJ • www.holidayguides.com

The Avon Valley Railway offers a whole new experience for some, and a nostalgic memory for others. **PETS MUST BE KEPT ON LEADS AND OFF TRAIN SEATS**	**Open:** Steam trains operate every Sunday, Easter to October, plus Bank Holidays and Christmas. **Directions:** on the A431 midway between Bristol and Bath at Bitton.

FHG GUIDES, ABBEY MILL BUSINESS CENTRE, PAISLEY PA1 1TJ • www.holidayguides.com

FHG
·K·U·P·E·R·A·R·D·
READERS' OFFER 2007

NOAH'S ARK ZOO FARM
Failand Road, Wraxall,
Bristol BS48 1PG
Tel: 01275 852606 • Fax: 01275 857080
e-mail: info@noahsarkzoofarm.co.uk
www.noahsarkzoofarm.co.uk

One FREE child for each group of 4 or more persons
Valid until October 2007 (closed in winter)

NOT TO BE USED IN CONJUNCTION WITH ANY OTHER OFFER

FHG
·K·U·P·E·R·A·R·D·
READERS' OFFER 2007

CIDER MUSEUM & KING OFFA DISTILLERY
21 Ryelands Street,
Hereford HR4 0LW
Tel: 01432 354207 • Fax: 01432 371641
e-mail: enquiries@cidermuseum.co.uk
www.cidermuseum.co.uk

50p reduction on entry fee
Valid during 2007

NOT TO BE USED IN CONJUNCTION WITH ANY OTHER OFFER

FHG
·K·U·P·E·R·A·R·D·
READERS' OFFER 2007

MUSEUM OF KENT LIFE
Lock Lane, Sandling, Maidstone,
Kent ME14 3AU
Tel: 01622 763936 • Fax: 01622 662024
e-mail: enquiries@museum-kentlife.co.uk
www.museum-kentlife.co.uk

Two tickets for the price of one (cheapest ticket FREE)
Valid from March to November 2007

NOT TO BE USED IN CONJUNCTION WITH ANY OTHER OFFER

FHG
·K·U·P·E·R·A·R·D·
READERS' OFFER 2007

QUEX MUSEUM, HOUSE & GARDENS
Quex Park,
Birchington
Kent CT7 0BH
Tel: 01843 842168 • Fax: 01843 846661
e-mail: pcmuseum@btconnect.com

One adult FREE with each full-paying adult on
presentation of voucher. Valid until 31 December 2007

NOT TO BE USED IN CONJUNCTION WITH ANY OTHER OFFER

Fantastic 'hands-on' adventure zoo farm for all ages and all weathers. 80 different species from chicks and lambs to camels and rhinos. New indoor and outdoor mazes (longest in world and educational). Family-friendly cafe and shop.	**Open:** from February half-term to end October 10.30am to 5pm Mon to Sat. Check open days on website **Directions:** on B3128 between Bristol and Clevedon or Exit 19/20 M5

FHG GUIDES, ABBEY MILL BUSINESS CENTRE, PAISLEY PA1 1TJ • www.holidayguides.com

Discover the fascinating history of cider making. There is a programme of temporary exhibitions and events plus free samples of Hereford cider brandy.	**Open:** April to Oct 10am to 5pm ; Nov to March 11am to 3pm. Closed Sun and Mon excluding Bank Holiday weekends. **Directions:** situated west of Hereford off the A438 Hereford to Brecon road.

FHG GUIDES, ABBEY MILL BUSINESS CENTRE, PAISLEY PA1 1TJ • www.holidayguides.com

Kent's award-winning open air museum is home to a collection of historic buildings which house interactive exhibitions on life over the last 150 years.	**Open:** seven days a week from February to start November, 10am to 5pm. **Directions:** Junction 6 off M20, follow signs to Aylesford.

FHG GUIDES, ABBEY MILL BUSINESS CENTRE, PAISLEY PA1 1TJ • www.holidayguides.com

World-ranking Museum incorporating Kent's finest Regency house. Gardens with peacocks, woodland walk, walled garden, maze and fountains. Children's activities and full events programme. Tearoom and gift shop. Full events programme.	**Open:** mid-March-Nov: Sun-Thurs 11am-5pm (House opens 2pm). Winter: Sundays 1-3.30pm (Museum and Gardens only). **Directions:** A2 to Margate, on entering Birchington turn right at church into Park Lane; Powell-Cotton Museum signposted.

FHG GUIDES, ABBEY MILL BUSINESS CENTRE, PAISLEY PA1 1TJ • www.holidayguides.com

FHG
K·U·P·E·R·A·R·D
READERS' OFFER 2007

DOCKER PARK FARM
Arkholme, Carnforth,
Lancashire LA6 1AR
Tel & Fax: 015242 21331
e-mail: info@dockerparkfarm.co.uk
www.dockerparkfarm.co.uk

One FREE child per one paying adult (one voucher per child)
Valid from January to December 2007

NOT TO BE USED IN CONJUNCTION WITH ANY OTHER OFFER

FHG
K·U·P·E·R·A·R·D
READERS' OFFER 2007

NATIONAL FISHING HERITAGE CENTRE
Alexandra Dock, Grimsby
N.E. Lincs DN31 1UZ
Tel: 01472 323345 • Fax: 01472 323555
nfhc@nelincs.gov.uk
www.nelincs.gov.uk

One child FREE with every paying adult.
Valid until August 2007 (not Bank Holidays)

NOT TO BE USED IN CONJUNCTION WITH ANY OTHER OFFER

FHG
K·U·P·E·R·A·R·D
READERS' OFFER 2007

SKEGNESS NATURELAND SEAL SANCTUARY
North Parade, Skegness,
Lincolnshire PE25 1DB
Tel: 01754 764345
e-mail: natureland@fsbdial.co.uk
www.skegnessnatureland.co.uk

Natureland Seal Sanctuary

Free entry for one child when accompanied by
full-paying adult. Valid during 2007.

NOT TO BE USED IN CONJUNCTION WITH ANY OTHER OFFER

FHG
K·U·P·E·R·A·R·D
READERS' OFFER 2007

DINOSAUR ADVENTURE PARK
Weston Park, Lenwade, Norwich,
Norfolk NR9 5JW
Tel: 01603 876310 • Fax: 01603 876315
e-mail: info@dinosaurpark.co.uk
www.dinosaurpark.co.uk

Dinosaur Adventure Park

50p off standard admission prices for up to six people
Valid until end of October 2007

NOT TO BE USED IN CONJUNCTION WITH ANY OTHER OFFER

We are a working farm, with lots of animals to see and touch. Enjoy a walk round the Nature Trail or refreshments in the tearoom. Lots of activities during school holidays.	**Open:** Summer: daily 10.30am- 5pm. Winter: weekends only 10.30am-4pm. **Directions:** Junction 35 off M6, take B6254 towards Kirkby Lonsdale, then follow the brown signs.

FHG GUIDES, ABBEY MILL BUSINESS CENTRE, PAISLEY PA1 1TJ • www.holidayguides.com

Sign on as a crew member for an incredible journey of discovery that will take you to the edge of disaster and the extremes of the elements to witness at first hand the depths of human endurance. Plot your course, take the wheel in the Skipper's Wheelhouse, study maps and charts, try the radio, send a Morse Code message - and lots more.	**Open:** Apr-Oct: Mon-Fri 10am to 5pm, Sat-Sun 10.30am-5.30pm. Please phone for winter opening hours. **Directions:** A180 Corporation Road towards Sainsbury's.

FHG GUIDES, ABBEY MILL BUSINESS CENTRE, PAISLEY PA1 1TJ • www.holidayguides.com

Well known for rescuing and rehabilitating orphaned and injured seal pups found washed ashore on Lincolnshire beaches. Also: penguins, aquarium, pets' corner, reptiles, Floral Palace (tropical birds and butterflies etc).	**Open:** daily from 10am. Closed Christmas/Boxing/New Year's Days. **Directions:** at the north end of Skegness seafront.

FHG GUIDES, ABBEY MILL BUSINESS CENTRE, PAISLEY PA1 1TJ • www.holidayguides.com

It's time you came-n-saurus for a monster day out of discovery, adventure and fun. Enjoy the adventure play areas, dinosaur trail, secret animal garden and lots more.	**Open:** Please call for specific opening times or see our website. **Directions:** 9 miles from Norwich, follow the brown signs to Weston Park from the A47 or A1067

FHG GUIDES, ABBEY MILL BUSINESS CENTRE, PAISLEY PA1 1TJ • www.holidayguides.com

21

FHG
K·U·P·E·R·A·R·D
READERS' OFFER 2007

THE COLLECTORS WORLD OF ERIC ST JOHN-FOTI
Hermitage Hall, Downham Market,
Norfolk PE38 0AU
Tel: 01366 383185 • Fax: 01366 386519
www.collectors-world.org

50p off adult admission - 25p off child admission
Valid during 2007

NOT TO BE USED IN CONJUNCTION WITH ANY OTHER OFFER

FHG
K·U·P·E·R·A·R·D
READERS' OFFER 2007

THE TALES OF ROBIN HOOD
30 - 38 Maid Marian Way,
Nottingham NG1 6GF
Tel: 0115 9483284 • Fax: 0115 9501536
e-mail: robinhoodcentre@mail.com
www.robinhood.uk.com

One FREE child with full paying adult per voucher
Valid from January to December 2007

NOT TO BE USED IN CONJUNCTION WITH ANY OTHER OFFER

FHG
K·U·P·E·R·A·R·D
READERS' OFFER 2007

NEWARK AIR MUSEUM
The Airfield, Winthorpe, Newark,
Nottinghamshire NG24 2NY
Tel: 01636 707170
e-mail: newarkair@onetel.com
www.newarkairmuseum.co.uk

Party rate discount for every voucher (50p per person off normal admission). Valid during 2007.

NOT TO BE USED IN CONJUNCTION WITH ANY OTHER OFFER

FHG
K·U·P·E·R·A·R·D
READERS' OFFER 2007

DIDCOT RAILWAY CENTRE
Didcot,
Oxfordshire OX11 7NJ
Tel: 01235 817200 • Fax: 01235 510621
e-mail: didrlyc@globalnet.co.uk
www.didcotrailwaycentre.org.uk

One child FREE when accompanied by full-paying adult
Valid until end 2007 except during Day Out With Thomas events

NOT TO BE USED IN CONJUNCTION WITH ANY OTHER OFFER

The collections of local eccentric Eric St John-Foti (Mr Norfolk Punch himself!) on view and the Magical Dickens Experience. Two amazing attractions for the price of one. Somewhere totally different, unique and interesting.	**Open:** 11am to 5pm (last entry 4pm) Open all year. **Directions:** one mile from town centre on the A1122 Downham/Wisbech Road.

FHG GUIDES, ABBEY MILL BUSINESS CENTRE, PAISLEY PA1 1TJ • www.holidayguides.com

Travel back in time with Robin Hood and his merry men on an adventure-packed theme tour, exploring the intriguing and mysterious story of their legendary tales of Medieval England. Enjoy film shows, live performances, adventure rides and even try archery! Are you brave enough to join Robin on his quest for good against evil?	**Open:** 10am-5.30pm, last admission 4.30pm. **Directions:** follow the brown and white tourist information signs whilst heading towards the city centre.

FHG GUIDES, ABBEY MILL BUSINESS CENTRE, PAISLEY PA1 1TJ • www.holidayguides.com

A collection of 70 aircraft and cockpit sections from across the history of aviation. Extensive aero engine and artefact displays.	**Open:** daily from 10am (closed Christmas period and New Year's Day). **Directions:** follow brown and white signs from A1, A46, A17 and A1133.

FHG GUIDES, ABBEY MILL BUSINESS CENTRE, PAISLEY PA1 1TJ • www.holidayguides.com

See the steam trains from the golden age of the Great Western Railway. Steam locomotives in the original engine shed, a reconstructed country branch line, and a re-creation of Brunel's original broad gauge railway. On Steam Days there are rides in the 1930s carriages.	**Open:** Sat/Sun all year; daily 23 June to 2 Sept + school holidays. 10am-5pm weekends and Steam Days, 10am-4pm other days and in winter. **Directions:** at Didcot Parkway rail station; on A4130, signposted from M4 (Junction 13) and A34

FHG GUIDES, ABBEY MILL BUSINESS CENTRE, PAISLEY PA1 1TJ • www.holidayguides.com

FHG KUPERARD READERS' OFFER 2007

ANIMAL FARM ADVENTURE PARK
Red Road, Berrow, Burnham-on-Sea
Somerset TA8 2RW
Tel: 01278 751628 • Fax: 01278 751633
info@afap.fsnet.co.uk
www.animal-farm.co.uk

*TWO admissions for the price of ONE.
Valid until end 2007*

NOT TO BE USED IN CONJUNCTION WITH ANY OTHER OFFER

FHG KUPERARD READERS' OFFER 2007

PARADISE PARK & GARDENS
Avis Road, Newhaven,
East Sussex BN9 0DH
Tel: 01273 512123 • Fax: 01273 616000
e-mail: enquiries@paradisepark.co.uk
www.paradisepark.co.uk

*Admit one FREE adult or child with one adult
paying full entrance price. Valid during 2007*

NOT TO BE USED IN CONJUNCTION WITH ANY OTHER OFFER

FHG KUPERARD READERS' OFFER 2007

YESTERDAY'S WORLD
High Street, Battle, E. Sussex TN33 0AQ
Tel: 01424 775378 (24hr info)
Enquiries/bookings: 01424 893938
e-mail: info@yesterdaysworld.co.uk
www.yesterdaysworld.co.uk

*One child FREE when accompanied by one
full-paying adult. Valid until end 2007*

NOT TO BE USED IN CONJUNCTION WITH ANY OTHER OFFER

FHG KUPERARD READERS' OFFER 2007

AMERICAN ADVENTURE GOLF
Fort Fun, Royal Parade,
Eastbourne, East Sussex BN22 7LU
Tel: 01323 642833
e-mail: fortfuneb@aol.com
www.fortfun.co.uk

*One FREE game of golf with every full-paying customer
(value £3). Valid April-Oct 2007 before 12 noon only*

NOT TO BE USED IN CONJUNCTION WITH ANY OTHER OFFER

Stay and play all day at Somerset's top all-weather family day out. Cuddle pets and baby animals, mega playbarn with 3 levels of fun and exciting giant slides! Acres of friendly animals to meet and feed, farm walks, massive play park with trampolines, free train rides and lots, lots more! See website for event days.	**Open:** 10am-5.30pm daily all year except 24-26 December. **Directions:** from M5 J22 head for Berrow/Brean; follow Animal Farm signs.

FHG GUIDES, ABBEY MILL BUSINESS CENTRE, PAISLEY PA1 1TJ • www.holidayguides.com

Discover 'Planet Earth' for an unforgettable experience. A unique Museum of Life, Dinosaur Safari, beautiful Water Gardens with fish and wildfowl, plant houses, themed gardens, Heritage Trail, miniature railway. Playzone includes crazy golf and adventure play areas. Garden Centre and Terrace Cafe.	**Open:** open daily, except Christmas Day and Boxing Day. **Directions:** signposted off A26 and A259.

FHG GUIDES, ABBEY MILL BUSINESS CENTRE, PAISLEY PA1 1TJ • www.holidayguides.com

The past is brought to life at one of the South East's best loved family attractions. 100,000+ nostalgic artefacts, set in a charming 15th century house and country garden. New attractions and tearooms.	**Open:** 9.30am to 6pm (last admission 4.45pm, one hour earlier in winter). Closing times may vary – phone or check website. **Directions:** just off A21 in Battle High Street opposite the Abbey.

FHG GUIDES, ABBEY MILL BUSINESS CENTRE, PAISLEY PA1 1TJ • www.holidayguides.com

18-hole American Adventure Golf set in ⅓ acre landscaped surroundings. Played on different levels including water features.	**Open:** April until end October 10am until dusk. **Directions:** on the seafront ¼ mile east of Eastbourne Pier.

FHG GUIDES, ABBEY MILL BUSINESS CENTRE, PAISLEY PA1 1TJ • www.holidayguides.com

FHG ·K·U·P·E·R·A·R·D·
READERS' OFFER 2007

WILDERNESS WOOD
Hadlow Down, Near Uckfield,
East Sussex TN22 4HJ
Tel: 01825 830509 • Fax: 01825 830977
e-mail: enquiries@wildernesswood.co.uk
www.wildernesswood.co.uk

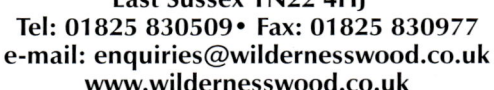

one FREE admission with a full-paying adult
Valid during 2007 (not for Special Events)

NOT TO BE USED IN CONJUNCTION WITH ANY OTHER OFFER

FHG ·K·U·P·E·R·A·R·D·
READERS' OFFER 2007

WASHINGTON WETLAND CENTRE
Pattinson, Washington,
Tyne & Wear NE38 8LE
Tel: 0191 416 5454
e-mail: info.washington@wwt.org.uk
www.wwt.org.uk

One FREE admission with full-paying adult
Valid from 1st Jan to 30th Sept 2007

NOT TO BE USED IN CONJUNCTION WITH ANY OTHER OFFER

FHG ·K·U·P·E·R·A·R·D·
READERS' OFFER 2007

HATTON COUNTRY WORLD FARM VILLAGE
Dark Lane, Hatton, Near Warwick,
Warwickshire CV35 8XA
Tel: 01926 843411
e-mail: hatton@hattonworld.com
www.hattonworld.com

Admit one child FREE with one full-paying adult day ticket.
Admission into Shopping Village free. Valid during 2007

NOT TO BE USED IN CONJUNCTION WITH ANY OTHER OFFER

FHG ·K·U·P·E·R·A·R·D·
READERS' OFFER 2007

STRATFORD BUTTERFLY FARM
Swan's Nest Lane, Stratford-upon-Avon
Warwickshire CV37 7LS
Tel: 01789 299288 • Fax: 01789 415878
e-mail: sales@butterflyfarm.co.uk
www.butterflyfarm.co.uk

Admit TWO for the price of ONE
Valid until 31/12/2007

NOT TO BE USED IN CONJUNCTION WITH ANY OTHER OFFER

Wilderness Wood is a unique family-run working woodland in the Sussex High Weald. Explore trails and footpaths, enjoy local cakes and ices, try the adventure playground. Many special events and activities. Parties catered for.

Open: daily 10am to 5.30pm or dusk if earlier.

Directions: on the south side of the A272 in the village of Hadlow Down. Signposted with a brown tourist sign.

FHG GUIDES, ABBEY MILL BUSINESS CENTRE, PAISLEY PA1 1TJ • www.holidayguides.com

---

Conservation site with 100 acres of stunning wetland and woodland, home to rare wildlife. Waterside cafe, play area, gift shop.

Open: every day except Christmas Day

Directions: signposted from A19, A195, A1231 and A182.

FHG GUIDES, ABBEY MILL BUSINESS CENTRE, PAISLEY PA1 1TJ • www.holidayguides.com

---

Two attractions side-by-side. Hatton Farm Village has fun for the whole family, with animals, demonstrations and adventure play. Hatton Shopping Village has 25 craft and gift shops, an antiques centre, a factory-style store, and two restaurants. Free parking.

Open: daily 10am to 5pm. Open until 4pm Christmas Eve; 11am-4pm 27 Dec-1st Jan incl; closed Christmas Day & Boxing Day.

Directions: 5 minutes from M40 (J15), A46 towards Coventry, then just off A4177 (follow brown tourist signs).

FHG GUIDES, ABBEY MILL BUSINESS CENTRE, PAISLEY PA1 1TJ • www.holidayguides.com

---

Wander through a tropical rainforest with a myriad of multicoloured butterflies, sunbirds and koi carp. See fascinating animals in Insect City and view deadly spiders in perfect safety in Arachnoland.

Open: daily except Christmas Day. 10am-6pm summer, 10am-dusk winter.

Directions: on south bank of River Avon opposite Royal Shakespeare Theatre. Easily accessible from town centre, 5 minutes' walk.

FHG GUIDES, ABBEY MILL BUSINESS CENTRE, PAISLEY PA1 1TJ • www.holidayguides.com

27

FHG READERS' OFFER 2007

AVONCROFT MUSEUM
Stoke Heath,
Bromsgrove,
Worcestershire B60 4JR
Tel: 01527 831363 • Fax: 01527 876934
www.avoncroft.org.uk

*One FREE child with one full-paying adult
Valid from March to November 2007*

NOT TO BE USED IN CONJUNCTION WITH ANY OTHER OFFER

FHG READERS' OFFER 2007

YORKSHIRE DALES FALCONRY & WILDLIFE CONSERVATION CENTRE
Crow's Nest, Giggleswick, Near Settle LA2 8AS
Tel: 01729 822832• Fax: 01729 825160
e-mail: info@falconryandwildlife.com
www.falconryandwildlife.com

*One child FREE with two full-paying adults
Valid until end 2007*

NOT TO BE USED IN CONJUNCTION WITH ANY OTHER OFFER

FHG READERS' OFFER 2007

WORLD OF JAMES HERRIOT
23 Kirkgate, Thirsk,
North Yorkshire YO7 1PL
Tel: 01845 524234
Fax: 01845 525333
www.worldofjamesherriot.org

Admit TWO for the price of ONE (one voucher per transaction only). Valid until October 2007

NOT TO BE USED IN CONJUNCTION WITH ANY OTHER OFFER

FHG READERS' OFFER 2007

EMBSAY & BOLTON ABBEY STEAM RAILWAY
Bolton Abbey Station, Skipton,
North Yorkshire BD23 6AF
Tel: 01756 710614
e-mail: embsay.steam@btinternet.com
www.embsayboltonabbeyrailway.org.uk

One adult travels FREE when accompanied by a full fare paying adult (does not include Special Event days). Valid during 2007.

NOT TO BE USED IN CONJUNCTION WITH ANY OTHER OFFER

A fascinating world of historic buildings covering 7 centuries, rescued and rebuilt on an open-air site in the heart of the Worcestershire countryside. **PETS ON LEADS ONLY**	**Open:** July and August all week. March to November varying times, please telephone for details. **Directions:** A38 south of Bromsgrove, near Junction 1 of M42, Junction 5 of M5.

All types of birds of prey exhibited here, from owls and kestrels to eagles and vultures. Special flying displays 12 noon, 1.30pm and 3pm. Bird handling courses arranged for either half or full days. **GUIDE DOGS ONLY**	**Open:** 10am to 4.30pm summer 10am to 4pm winter **Directions:** on main A65 trunk road outside Settle. Follow brown direction signs.

Visit James Herriot's original house recreated as it was in the 1940s. Television sets used in the series 'All Creatures Great and Small'. There is a children's interactive gallery with life-size model farm animals and three rooms dedicated to the history of veterinary medicine.	**Open:** daily. Easter-Oct 10am-5pm; Nov-Easter 11am to 4pm **Directions:** follow signs off A1 or A19 to Thirsk, then A168, off Thirsk market place

Steam trains operate over a 4½ mile line from Bolton Abbey Station to Embsay Station. Many family events including Thomas the Tank Engine take place during major Bank Holidays.	**Open:** steam trains run every Sunday throughout the year and up to 7 days a week in summer. 10.30am to 4.30pm **Directions:** Embsay Station signposted from the A59 Skipton by-pass; Bolton Abbey Station signposted from the A59 at Bolton Abbey.

FHG
·K·U·P·E·R·A·R·D·
READERS' OFFER 2007

THE GRASSIC GIBBON CENTRE
Arbuthnott, Laurencekirk,
Aberdeenshire AB30 1PB
Tel: 01561 361668
e-mail: lgginfo@grassicgibbon.com
www.grassicgibbon.com

The Grassic Gibbon Centre

TWO for the price of ONE entry to exhibition (based on full adult rate only). Valid during 2007 (not groups)

NOT TO BE USED IN CONJUNCTION WITH ANY OTHER OFFER

FHG
·K·U·P·E·R·A·R·D·
READERS' OFFER 2007

STORYBOOK GLEN
Maryculter,
Aberdeen
Aberdeenshire AB12 5FT
Tel: 01224 732941
www.storybookglenaberdeen.co.uk

Visit Storybook Glen

*10% discount on all admissions
Valid until end 2007*

NOT TO BE USED IN CONJUNCTION WITH ANY OTHER OFFER

FHG
·K·U·P·E·R·A·R·D·
READERS' OFFER 2007

OBAN RARE BREEDS FARM PARK
Glencruitten, Oban,
Argyll PA34 4QB
Tel: 01631 770608
e-mail: info@obanrarebreeds.com
www.obanrarebreeds.com

Oban Rare Breeds Farm Park

*20% DISCOUNT on all admissions
Valid during 2007*

NOT TO BE USED IN CONJUNCTION WITH ANY OTHER OFFER

FHG
·K·U·P·E·R·A·R·D·
READERS' OFFER 2007

INVERARAY JAIL
Church Square, Inveraray,
Argyll PA32 8TX
Tel: 01499 302381 • Fax: 01499 302195
e-mail: info@inverarayjail.co.uk
www.inverarayjail.co.uk

INVERARAY JAIL

*One child FREE with one full-paying adult
Valid until end 2007*

NOT TO BE USED IN CONJUNCTION WITH ANY OTHER OFFER

Visitor Centre dedicated to the much-loved Scottish writer Lewis Grassic Gibbon. Exhibition, cafe, gift shop. Outdoor children's play area. Disabled access throughout.

Open: daily April to October 10am to 4.30pm. Groups by appointment including evenings.

Directions: on the B967, accessible and signposted from both A90 and A92.

FHG GUIDES, ABBEY MILL BUSINESS CENTRE, PAISLEY PA1 1TJ • www.holidayguides.com

---

28-acre theme park with over 100 nursery rhyme characters, set in beautifully landscaped gardens. Shop and restaurant on site.

Open: 1st March to 31st October: daily 10am to 6pm; 1st Nov to end Feb: Sat/Sun only 11am to 4pm

Directions: 6 miles west of Aberdeen off B9077

FHG GUIDES, ABBEY MILL BUSINESS CENTRE, PAISLEY PA1 1TJ • www.holidayguides.com

---

Rare breeds of farm animals, pets' corner, conservation groups, tea room, woodland walk in beautiful location

Open: 10am to 6pm mid-March to end October

Directions: two-and-a-half miles from Oban along Glencruitten road

---

FHG GUIDES, ABBEY MILL BUSINESS CENTRE, PAISLEY PA1 1TJ • www.holidayguides.com

---

19th century prison with fully restored 1820 courtroom and two prisons. Guides in uniform as warders, prisoners and matron. Remember your camera!

Open: April to October 9.30am-6pm (last admission 5pm); November to March 10am-5pm (last admission 4pm)

Directions: A83 to Campbeltown

FHG GUIDES, ABBEY MILL BUSINESS CENTRE, PAISLEY PA1 1TJ • www.holidayguides.com

FHG READERS' OFFER 2007
K·U·P·E·R·A·R·D

SCOTTISH MARITIME MUSEUM
Harbourside, Irvine,
Ayrshire KA12 8QE
Tel: 01294 278283
Fax: 01294 313211
www.scottishmaritimemuseum.org

TWO for the price of ONE
Valid from April to October 2007

NOT TO BE USED IN CONJUNCTION WITH ANY OTHER OFFER

FHG READERS' OFFER 2007
K·U·P·E·R·A·R·D

JEDFOREST DEER & FARM PARK
Mervinslaw Estate, Camptown, Jedburgh,
Borders TD8 6PL
Tel: 01835 840364
e-mail: mervinslaw@ecosse.net
www.aboutscotland.com/jedforest

One FREE child with two full-paying adults
Valid May/June and Sept/Oct 2007

NOT TO BE USED IN CONJUNCTION WITH ANY OTHER OFFER

FHG READERS' OFFER 2007
K·U·P·E·R·A·R·D

SCOTTISH SEABIRD CENTRE
The Harbour, North Berwick,
East Lothian EH39 4SS
Tel: 01620 890202 • Fax: 01620 890222
e-mail: info@seabird.org
www.seabird.org

20% OFF any admission
Valid until 1st October 2007

NOT TO BE USED IN CONJUNCTION WITH ANY OTHER OFFER

FHG READERS' OFFER 2007
K·U·P·E·R·A·R·D

THE SCOTTISH MINING MUSEUM
Lady Victoria Colliery, Newtongrange,
Midlothian EH22 4QN
Tel: 0131-663 7519 • Fax: 0131-654 0952
visitorservices@scottishminingmuseum.com
www.scottishminingmuseum.com

One child FREE with full-paying adult
Valid January to December 2007

NOT TO BE USED IN CONJUNCTION WITH ANY OTHER OFFER

Scotland's seafaring heritage is among the world's richest and you can relive the heyday of Scottish shipping at the Maritime Museum.

Open: 1st April to 31st October - 10am-5pm

Directions: situated on Irvine harbourside and only a 10 minute walk from Irvine train station.

FHG GUIDES, ABBEY MILL BUSINESS CENTRE, PAISLEY PA1 1TJ • www.holidayguides.com

---

Working farm with visitor centre showing rare breeds, deer herds, ranger-led activities, and walks. Birds of prey displays and tuition. Corporate activities. Shop and cafe.

Open: daily Easter to August 10am to 5.30pm; Sept/Oct 11am to 4.30pm.

Directions: 5 miles south of Jedburgh on A68.

FHG GUIDES, ABBEY MILL BUSINESS CENTRE, PAISLEY PA1 1TJ • www.holidayguides.com

---

Get close to Nature with a visit to this award-winning Centre. With panoramic views across islands and sandy beaches, the area is a haven for wildlife. Live cameras zoom in close to see wildlife including gannets, puffins and seals. Wildlife boat safaris, new Environmental Zone and Flyway.

Open: daily from 10am

Directions: from A1 take road for North Berwick; near the harbour; Centre signposted.

FHG GUIDES, ABBEY MILL BUSINESS CENTRE, PAISLEY PA1 1TJ • www.holidayguides.com

---

visitscotland 5-Star Attraction with two floors of interactive exhibitions, a 'Magic Helmet' tour of the pithead, re-created coal road and coal face, and new Big Stuff tour. Largest working winding engine in Britain.

Open: daily. Summer: 10am to 5pm (last tour 3.30pm). Winter: 10am to 4pm (last tour 2.30pm)

Directions: 5 minutes from Sherrifhall Roundabout on Edinburgh City Bypass on A7 south

FHG GUIDES, ABBEY MILL BUSINESS CENTRE, PAISLEY PA1 1TJ • www.holidayguides.com

FHG READERS' OFFER 2007

BO'NESS & KINNEIL RAILWAY
Bo'ness Station, Union Street,
Bo'ness, West Lothian EH51 9AQ
Tel: 01506 822298
e-mail: enquiries.railway@srps.org.uk
www.srps.org.uk

FREE child train fare with one paying adult/concession. Valid 31st March-31st Oct 2007. Not Thomas events or Santa Steam trains

NOT TO BE USED IN CONJUNCTION WITH ANY OTHER OFFER

FHG READERS' OFFER 2007

MYRETON MOTOR MUSEUM
Aberlady,
East Lothian
EH32 0PZ
Tel: 01875 870288

*One child FREE with each paying adult
Valid during 2007*

NOT TO BE USED IN CONJUNCTION WITH ANY OTHER OFFER

FHG READERS' OFFER 2007

GLASGOW SCIENCE CENTRE
50 Pacific Quay
Glasgow
G51 1EA
Tel: 0871 540 1000
www.glasgowsciencecentre.org

£1 off entry to Science Mall or IMAX Cinema (not valid for feature-length films; not with group tickets). Valid until 30/5/2007

NOT TO BE USED IN CONJUNCTION WITH ANY OTHER OFFER

FHG READERS' OFFER 2007

SPEYSIDE HEATHER GARDEN & VISITOR CENTRE
Speyside Heather Centre, Dulnain Bridge,
Inverness-shire PH26 3PA
Tel: 01479 851359 • Fax: 01479 851396
e-mail: enquiries@heathercentre.com
www.heathercentre.com

*FREE entry to 'Heather Story' exhibition
Valid during 2007*

NOT TO BE USED IN CONJUNCTION WITH ANY OTHER OFFER

Steam and heritage diesel passenger trains from Bo'ness to Birkhill for guided tours of Birkhill fireclay mines. Explore the history of Scotland's railways in the Scottish Railway Exhibition. Coffee shop and souvenir shop.	**Open:** weekends April to October, daily July and August. **Directions:** in the town of Bo'ness. Leave M9 at Junction 3 or 5, then follow brown tourist signs.

FHG GUIDES, ABBEY MILL BUSINESS CENTRE, PAISLEY PA1 1TJ • www.holidayguides.com

On show is a large collection, from 1899, of cars, bicycles, motor cycles and commercials. There is also a large collection of period advertising, posters and enamel signs.	**Open:** March-November - open daily 11am to 4pm. December-February - weekends 11am to 3pm or by special appointment. **Directions:** off A198 near Aberlady. Two miles from A1.

FHG GUIDES, ABBEY MILL BUSINESS CENTRE, PAISLEY PA1 1TJ • www.holidayguides.com

Hundreds of interactive exhibits, live science shows and Scotland's only IMAX cinema - a great day out whatever the weather!	**Open:** 10am-6pm 7 days until 28/10/06. From 29/10/06 to 30/3/2007 open 10am-6pm Tues-Sun. **Directions:** J24 M8, J21 M77. Nearest Underground: Cessnock. Train - Exhibition Centre.

FHG GUIDES, ABBEY MILL BUSINESS CENTRE, PAISLEY PA1 1TJ • www.holidayguides.com

Award-winning attraction with unique 'Heather Story' exhibition, gallery, giftshop, large garden centre selling 300 different heathers, antique shop, children's play area and famous Clootie Dumpling restaurant.	**Open:** all year except Christmas Day. **Directions:** just off A95 between Aviemore and Grantown-on-Spey.

FHG GUIDES, ABBEY MILL BUSINESS CENTRE, PAISLEY PA1 1TJ • www.holidayguides.com

FHG READERS' OFFER 2007 · K·U·P·E·R·A·R·D

NEW LANARK WORLD HERITAGE SITE
New Lanark Mills, Lanark,
Lanarkshire ML11 9DB
Tel: 01555 661345 • Fax: 01555 665738
e-mail: visit@newlanark.org
www.newlanark.org

One FREE child with one full price adult
Valid until 31st October 2007

NOT TO BE USED IN CONJUNCTION WITH ANY OTHER OFFER

FHG READERS' OFFER 2007 · K·U·P·E·R·A·R·D

LLANBERIS LAKE RAILWAY
Gilfach Ddu, Llanberis,
Gwynedd LL55 4TY
Tel: 01286 870549
e-mail: info@lake-railway.co.uk
www.lake-railway.co.uk

One pet travels FREE with each full fare paying adult
Valid Easter to October 2007

NOT TO BE USED IN CONJUNCTION WITH ANY OTHER OFFER

FHG READERS' OFFER 2007 · K·U·P·E·R·A·R·D

PILI PALAS - BUTTERFLY PALACE & NATURE WORLD
Menai Bridge
Isle of Anglesey LL59 5RP
Tel: 01248 712474
e-mail: info@pilipalas.co.uk
www.pilipalas.co.uk

One child FREE with two adults paying full entry price
Valid March to October 2007

NOT TO BE USED IN CONJUNCTION WITH ANY OTHER OFFER

FHG READERS' OFFER 2007 · K·U·P·E·R·A·R·D

FELINWYNT RAINFOREST CENTRE
Felinwynt, Cardigan,
Ceredigion SA43 1RT
Tel: 01239 810882/810250
e-mail: dandjdevereux@btinternet.com
www.butterflycentre.co.uk

TWO for the price of ONE (one voucher per party only)
Valid until end October 2007

NOT TO BE USED IN CONJUNCTION WITH ANY OTHER OFFER

A beautifully restored cotton mill village close to the Falls of Clyde. Explore the fascinating history of the village, try the 'Millennium Experience', a magical ride which takes you back in time to discover what life used to be like.

Open: 11am-5pm daily. June-August 10.30am-5pm daily. Closed Christmas Day and New Year's Day.

Directions: 25 miles from Glasgow and 35 miles from Edinburgh; well signposted on all major routes.

FHG GUIDES, ABBEY MILL BUSINESS CENTRE, PAISLEY PA1 1TJ • www.holidayguides.com

---

A 60-minute ride along the shores of beautiful Padarn Lake behind a quaint historic steam engine. Magnificent views of the mountains from lakeside picnic spots.

DOGS MUST BE KEPT ON LEAD AT ALL TIMES ON TRAIN

Open: most days Easter to October. Free timetable leaflet on request.

Directions: just off A4086 Caernarfon to Capel Curig road at Llanberis; follow 'Country Park' signs.

FHG GUIDES, ABBEY MILL BUSINESS CENTRE, PAISLEY PA1 1TJ • www.holidayguides.com

---

Visit Wales' top Butterfly House, with Bird House, Snake House, Ant Avenue, Tropical Hide, shop, cafe, adventure playground, indoor play area, picnic area, nature trail etc.

Open: March to end Oct: 10am - 5.30pm daily; Nov/Dec 11am-3pm

Directions: follow brown and white signs when crossing to Anglesey; one-and-a- half miles from Bridge

FHG GUIDES, ABBEY MILL BUSINESS CENTRE, PAISLEY PA1 1TJ • www.holidayguides.com

---

Mini-rainforest full of tropical plants and exotic butterflies. Personal attention of the owner, Mr John Devereux. Gift shop, cafe, video room, exhibition. Suitable for disabled visitors. WTB Quality Assured Visitor Attraction.

PETS NOT ALLOWED IN TROPICAL HOUSE ONLY

Open: daily Easter to end October 10.30am to 5pm

Directions: West Wales, 7 miles north of Cardigan off Aberystwyth road. Follow brown tourist signs on A487.

FHG GUIDES, ABBEY MILL BUSINESS CENTRE, PAISLEY PA1 1TJ • www.holidayguides.com

FHG
·K·U·P·E·R·A·R·D·
READERS' OFFER 2007

NATIONAL CYCLE COLLECTION
Automobile Palace, Temple Street,
Llandrindod Wells, Powys LD1 5DL
Tel: 01597 825531
e-mail: cycle.museum@powys.org.uk
www.cyclemuseum.org.uk

TWO for the price of ONE
Valid during 2007 except Special Event days

NOT TO BE USED IN CONJUNCTION WITH ANY OTHER OFFER

FHG
·K·U·P·E·R·A·R·D·
READERS' OFFER 2007

RHONDDA HERITAGE PARK
Lewis Merthyr Colliery, Coed Cae Road,
Trehafod, Near Pontypridd CF37 7NP
Tel: 01443 682036
e-mail: info@rhonddaheritagepark.com
www.rhonddaheritagepark.com

Two adults or children for the price of one when accompanied by a full paying adult. Valid until end 2007 for full tours only. Not valid on special event days/themed tours.

NOT TO BE USED IN CONJUNCTION WITH ANY OTHER OFFER

Looking for Holiday Accommodation?

FHG
·K·U·P·E·R·A·R·D·

for details of hundreds of
properties throughout the UK
visit our website on

www.holidayguides.com

Journey through the lanes of cycle history and see bicycles from Boneshakers and Penny Farthings up to modern Raleigh cycles. Over 250 machines on display

PETS MUST BE KEPT ON LEADS

Open: 1st March to 1st November daily 10am onwards.

Directions: brown signs to car park. Town centre attraction.

FHG GUIDES, ABBEY MILL BUSINESS CENTRE, PAISLEY PA1 1TJ • www.holidayguides.com

---

Make a pit stop whatever the weather! Join an ex-miner on a tour of discovery, ride the cage to pit bottom and take a thrilling ride back to the surface. Multi-media presentations, period village street, children's adventure play area, restaurant and gift shop. Disabled access with assistance.

Open: Open daily 10am to 6pm (last tour 4pm). Closed Mondays Oct - Easter, also Dec 25th to 2nd Jan incl.

Directions: Exit Junction 32 M4, signposted from A470 Pontypridd. Trehafod is located between Pontypridd and Porth.

FHG GUIDES, ABBEY MILL BUSINESS CENTRE, PAISLEY PA1 1TJ • www.holidayguides.com

---

FHG Guides 2007

- Recommended COUNTRY HOTELS
- Recommended INNS & PUBS
- BED & BREAKFAST STOPS • CHILDREN WELCOME!
- The Original FHG Guide to COAST & COUNTRY HOLIDAYS
- CARAVAN & CAMPING HOLIDAYS GUIDE
- BRITAIN'S BEST Leisure & Relaxation Holidays
- THE GOLF GUIDE Where to Play / Where to Stay
- PETS WELCOME!
- Recommended SHORT BREAK HOLIDAYS in Britain
- SELF CATERING HOLIDAYS in Britain

Available from bookshops or larger newsagents

FHG Guides Ltd.
Abbey Mill Business Centre,
Seedhill, Paisley PAI ITJ
www.holidayguides.com

Guide to Good Beaches

Public awareness of the quality of beaches and more determined efforts by officialdom to tackle pollution and other seaside problems have grown apace in the last few years as environmental issues become of more general interest rather than the preserve of a minority. 'Clean' beaches are about more than litter and dog dirt. They are about more than water quality and oil spillage, or rotting seaweed and life-saving. Indeed they are about a whole range of considerations and any attempt at classification must take different aspects into account. At present we can refer to three main organisations and sets of standards in compiling our own easy reference summary of beaches which have received some accepted sign of approval.

Started in 1987 as part of the EEC's Year of the Environment, the **BLUE FLAG** campaign aims not only to encourage and reward high standards of beach management at coastal resorts, but also to promote improved quality of bathing water. It is awarded in over 23 countries in Europe and South Africa for resort beaches and marinas with high standards of environmental management.

To win a Blue Flag, therefore, water quality is judged along with cleanliness and beach facilities, with a final decision by a European jury in Brussels. A dog ban during the summer is an absolute requirement and only beaches regularly used by the public, and resorts with safe bathing all year round may enter the competition. In 2006 120 beaches in Britain were awarded the coveted Blue Flag award. ENCAMS co-ordinates the Blue Flag in the UK on behalf of the FEEE (The Foundation for Environmental Education in Europe).

Guide to Good Beaches

ENCAMS (Environmental Campaigns) is a part-government funded charity working for the improvement of local environments. Its aims are to encourage individual, corporate and community responsibility for care of the environment through a variety of campaigns and programmes. All of the Seaside Award beaches have met very strict criteria, which include meeting the EC requirements for bathing water, providing good beach safety and supervision, putting in place good beach management (including dog controls and facilities for disabled visitors) and providing the public with clear information. A large database of UK beaches is maintained, with information on water quality, access, safety, cleanliness, dog control, first aid provision and conservation management. Beaches are split into two types, resort and rural.

SEASIDE AWARD RESORT BEACHES are usually found near towns, and are easy to reach by public transport. You would expect to find a cafe or restaurant, toilets and a variety of things to do. To gain a Seaside Award, resort beaches have to pass 29 different checks.

SEASIDE AWARD RURAL BEACHES are usually quieter, and enjoyed for their scenery rather than their facilities. Because of their rural nature, they may be more difficult to reach by public transport. To gain a Seaside Award rural beaches have to pass 13 different checks. Dogs may be allowed on some of these beaches.

The Marine Conservation Society, with the support of the Crown Estate, publishes **THE GOOD BEACH GUIDE** on the internet.

www.goodbeachguide.co.uk

giving up-to-date, independently monitored information on the quality of Britain's bathing waters. The beaches that are recommended in this guide have achieved the highest water quality standards and are not affected by inadequately treated sewage.

The information is also available in print as a pocket booklet – please send a stamped addressed A5 envelope (+62p postage) to the address below:

MARINE CONSERVATION SOCIETY
Unit 3, Wolf Business Park,
Alton Road, Ross-on-Wye HR9 5NB
Tel: 01989 566017
Fax: 01989 567815
e-mail: info@mcsuk.org
www.mcsuk.org

ENCAMS
Elizabeth House,
The Pier, Wigan WN3 4EX
Tel: 01942 612621
Fax: 01942 824778
e-mail: enquiries@encams.org
www.encams.org

EUROPEAN BLUE FLAG 2006 Beaches
in Britain and Northern Ireland

Scotland
- Dundee & Angus
- Fife
- Highlands

Northern Ireland
- Co. Londonderry
- Co. Antrim
- Co. Down

North East England
- Tyne & Wear
- East Yorkshire
- North Yorkshire

North West England
- Merseyside

Midlands
- Lincolnshire

Wales
- Anglesey
- Gwynedd
- North Wales
- Carmarthenshire
- Ceredigion
- Pembrokeshire
- South Wales

East England
- Norfolk
- Suffolk
- Essex

South West England
- Cornwall
- Dorset
- Devon

South East England
- Kent
- East Sussex
- West Sussex
- Isle of Wight

©MAPS IN MINUTES™ 2006

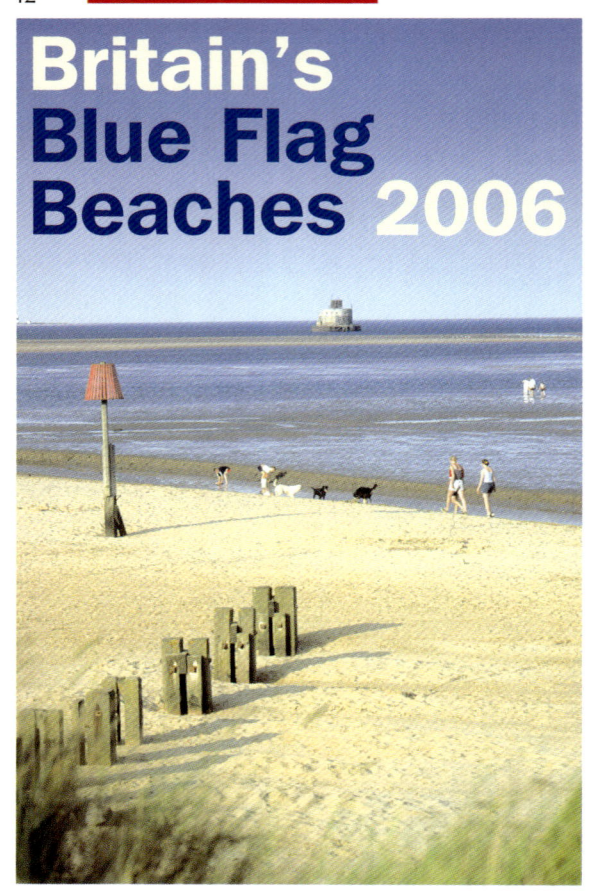

Britain's Blue Flag Beaches 2006

Cornwall
Gyllyngvase
Porthtowan
Polzeath
Sennen Cove
Carbis Bay
Marazion
Porthmeor
Porthminster

North Devon
Woolacombe Sands
Croyde Bay
Westward Ho!
Ilfracombe Tunnels

South Devon
Bigbury on Sea
Blackpool Sands
Challaborough
Dawlish Warren
Torbay
  Breakwater
  Broadsands
  Preston
  Meadfoot
  Oddicombe

Dorset
Poole
  Canford Cliffs
  Branksome Chine
  Sandbanks
  Shore Road
Bournemouth
  Fisherman's Walk
  Alum Chine
  Durley Chine
  Southbourne
Swanage Central

Sussex
Bognor Regis
Littlehampton
Eastbourne
West Wittering

Kent
Birchington Minnis Bay
Leysdown
Sheerness Beach Street
West Bay Westgate
St Mildred's Bay
Viking Bay
Westbrook Margate
Margate Walpole Bay
Margate Main Sands

Isle of Wight
Sandown
Shanklin

Norfolk
Great Yarmouth Gorleston
Great Yarmouth Central
Cromer
Hunstanton
Mundesley
Sea Palling
Sheringham

Guide to Good Beaches

Essex
Southend Jubilee
Southend Three Shells
Shoebury Common
Shoeburyness
Brightlingsea
Dovercourt

Suffolk
Felixstowe South
Lowestoft North
Lowestoft South
Southwold Pier

Lincolnshire
Cleethorpes

Tyne & Wear
Whitley Bay South
Tynemouth
  King Edwards Bay
  Longsands South
Roker
Seaburn

East Yorkshire
Hornsea
Withernsea

North Yorkshire
Scarborough North
Filey
Whitby

Merseyside
Ainsdale Beach

WALES

Gwynedd
Pwllheli
Fairbourne
Tywyn
Abersoch
Criccieth
Aberdyfi
Dinas Dinlle
Barmouth Abermaw

Anglesey
Benllech
Llanddona
Llanddwyn
Porth Dafarch
Trearddur Bay

North Wales
Llandudno North Shore
Llandudno West Shore
Penmaenmawr

Ceredigion
Aberporth
Borth
Llangrannog
New Quay
Tresaith
Aberystwyth North
Aberystwyth South

Carmarthenshire
Pembrey Country Park

Pembrokeshire
Dale
Amroth
Broadhaven North
Lydstep
Newgale
Poppit Sands
Saundersfoot
St Davids Whitesands
Tenby Castle
Tenby North
Tenby South

South Wales
Porthcawl Rest Bay
Barry Whitmore Bay
Bracelet Bay
Caswell Bay
Langland Bay
Port Eynon
Trecco Bay
Southerndown

SCOTLAND

Dundee & Angus
Montrose
Broughty Ferry

Fife
Aberdour Silver Sands
Burntisland
Elie Harbour
St Andrews West
St Andrews East

Highlands
Nairn Central

NORTHERN IRELAND

Ballycastle
Cranfield
Downhill
Magilligan/Benone Strand
Portrush West
Portrush White Rocks
Portstewart
Tyrella

action-packed parks

The widest choice of self-catering family holidays. Indoor and outdoor pool complexes, kids' clubs, bars and restaurants. Seaside & countryside. Pets welcome at over 200 parks. Call for your free brochure on **0870 900 9011** Quote H0020 or book on-line at **hoseasons.co.uk/cw2**

Hoseasons feel free

Looking for Holiday Accommodation?

FHG
K·U·P·E·R·A·R·D

for details of hundreds of properties throughout the UK visit our website on

www.holidayguides.com

Publisher's note

While every effort is made to ensure accuracy, we regret that FHG Guides cannot accept responsibility for errors, misrepresentations or omissions in our entries or any consequences thereof. Prices in particular should be checked.

We will follow up complaints but cannot act as arbiters or agents for either party.

CORNWALL

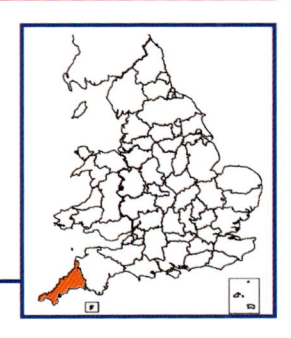

Best Beaches

ENCAMS (Environmental Campaigns) runs the Keep Britain Tidy Campaign whose annual Seaside Awards acknowledge those beaches which are visited and enjoyed for their intrinsic qualities, and where local interest and management maintains a clean environment whilst at the same time promoting considerate use by visitors. Cornwall's beaches are well represented in the 2006 awards, for both resort and rural beaches. Several beaches which meet the strict criteria of the European Foundation for Environmental Education have been awarded a prestigious Blue Flag.

BLUE FLAG BEACHES 2006
- *Polzeath*
- *Carbis Bay*
- *Marazion*
- *St Ives Porthmeor*
- *St Ives Porthminster*
- *Sennen Cove*
- *Gyllyngvase*
- *Porthtowan*

South West Tourism
(Bristol & Bath, Cornwall, Devon, Dorset, Gloucestershire & The Cotswolds, Somerset, Wiltshire).

- Tel: 0870 442 0880
- Fax: 0870 442 0881
- e-mail: post@swtourism.co.uk
- www.westcountrynow.com
- www.visitsouthwest.co.uk

The Classified Listing Section on pages 141-149 is a quick, easy to use summary of the facilities offered by the accommodation featured in this guide.

Cornwall

BUDE

Family Fun Activities: Seawater swimming pool on Summerleaze beach • Tropical Leisure Pool, including flume and wave machine, fitness suite, 10-pin bowling, roller blading rink and indoor adventure play area • Adventure centres offering tuition in various sports • Sports hall, multi-gym and activities • Sustrans cycle route • Bude Canal Wharf area • Heritage Trail • Museum • Mini-golf, putting, golf, bowls, squash, table tennis, cricket, tennis, sea and canal angling.

Special Events: May: Model Boat Festival; re-enactment of Battle of Stamford Hill. **May-September:** events, shows, fetes and revels. **July:** Bude festival of Music, Downhill Classic Triathlon. **August:** arts & crafts exhibitions; Bude Carnival Week; Lifeboat Week; 8-day Bude Jazz Festival. **September:** Quadrathon. **October:** canoe sprint.

Bude Visitor Centre, The Crescent, Bude EX23 8LE • 01288 354240
e-mail: budetic@visitbude.info
www.visitbude.info

Beaches

- **SUMMERLEAZE BEACH.** Level access via car park. *Safety and maintenance:* lifeguards during summer months. *Beach facilities:* beach huts, deck chairs etc for hire; mini-golf and go karts; open sea pool; cafe, shop and restaurant; RNLI centre/shop. Toilets, & access. *Dog restrictions:* none, but they must be kept under proper control.

- **CROOKLETS BEACH.** Sandy, with level access. Car park adjoining. *Safety and maintenance:* lifeguards on duty during June/July/August. *Beach facilities:* deckchairs, beach huts, windbreaks etc for hire; snack bar and beach shop; toilets (disabled facilities for members of National Radar Key Scheme). *Dog restrictions:* banned from beach area from Good Friday to 1st October.

- **SANDY MOUTH BEACH.** Beach owned by National Trust. *Safety and maintenance:* lifeguards during summer months. *Beach facilities:* cafe owned by NT. Toilets but no & facilities. *Dog restrictions:* none.

NEWQUAY

Family Fun Activities: Tunnels Through Time • Dairyland • Cornwall Pearl • Trerice Manor • Trenance Park with Water World fun pool and Newquay Zoo • Blue Reef Aquarium • Tennis, golf, pitch and putt, miniature railway, lakeside cafe, boating, sailing, surfing (Fistral Beach), angling, golf course • Discos, nightclubs.

Special Events: June: Newquay Surf Triathlon. **July:** Surf Festival, Newquay Harbour Sports. **August:** British Surfing Championships. Gig racing.

Tourist Information Centre, Marcus Hill, Newquay • 01637 854020
www.newquay.org.uk

Beaches

- **HARBOUR BEACH.** Sandy and naturally sheltered; promenade and limited parking. *Safety and maintenance:* cleaned daily. *Beach facilities:* pleasure craft; fishing and shark trips; ice cream kiosk; restaurant; toilets with & access.

- **TOWAN BEACH.** 400 yards long, sandy with rock pools, naturally sheltered promenade. & access. Parking 5 minutes' walk. *Safety and maintenance:* flagged, warning signs, lifeguards; cleaned daily. *Beach facilities:* deck chairs, windbreaks, wet suits; ice-cream kiosk, snack bar.

- **GREAT WESTERN BEACH.** 200 yards long, sandy with rock pools and cliffs; parking 5 minutes' walk. *Safety and maintenance:* flagged, warning signs, lifeguards; cleaned daily. *Beach facilities:* deck chairs, windbreaks, surfboards; ice cream and snack bar; toilets with & access.

Cornwall

- **TOLCARNE BEACH.** 500 yards long, sandy. Access down cliff steps, also path to beach. Parking 6 minutes' walk. *Safety and maintenance:* flagged, warning signs; cleaned daily. *Beach facilities:* deck chairs, surfboards, beach huts, trampolines; ice-cream kiosks, cafeteria, beach shop, barbecues; toilets.
- **LUSTY GLAZE BEACH.** 200 yards long; sandy with cliffs and rock pools, access via steps. *Safety and maintenance:* flagged, warning signs, lifeguards; cleaned daily. *Beach facilities*: deck chairs, surf boards, beach huts; ice-cream kiosk, cafe/takeaway, pub/restaurant and beach shop; showers and toilets; outdoor adventure centre. *Dog restrictions:* banned between 8am and 7pm.
- **PORTH BEACH.** 300 yards long, sandy and naturally sheltered with rock pools. Good parking. *Safety and maintenance*: flagged, warning signs, lifeguards; cleaned daily. *Beach facilities:* deck chairs, boogie boards, windbreaks; ice-cream kiosks, snack bars, restaurant and pub. *Dog restrictions:* banned from Easter to end September.
- **WHIPSIDERRY BEACH.** 200 yards long; sandy with cliffs and steps. *Safety and maintenance:* warning signs; cut off by tidal seas around cliffs.
- **WATERGATE BEACH.** Two miles long, sandy; good parking. *Safety and maintenance:* flagged, warning signs, lifeguards; cleaned daily. *Beach facilities:* surfboards; surf school and power kite school; bistro and takeaway, shops; toilets.
- **CRANTOCK BEACH.** Approx. one mile long, naturally sheltered with sandy dunes; good parking. *Safety and maintenance:* flagged, warning signs, lifeguards; Gannel tidal estuary very dangerous when tide going out. Beach owned and cleaned by NT. *Beach facilities:* deck chairs, surf boards; ice-cream kiosks, snack bars; toilets.
- **FISTRAL BEACH.** Approx. one mile long, sandy with dunes; good parking. *Safety and maintenance:* flagged, warning signs, lifeguards; cleaned daily. *Beach facilities:* deck chairs and windbreaks; wetsuit and surfboard hire; restaurant, cafe and takeaway, shops; toilets with ♿ access.

PENZANCE

Family Fun Activities: Water sports area at Marazion • Sea water swimming pool, indoor swimming pool, children's playground, boating lake, amusement arcade • Riding, tennis, bowls, putting, go-karting • Shark fishing, sailing, sub-aqua, sea and fresh water angling • Rock climbing • Cinema, arts theatre, dance halls and discos, clubs and pub entertainment nightly.

☆ **Special Events:** **April**: British Funboard Cup, Hockey Festival. **June:** Golowan Festival. **August:** Newlyn Fish Festival. **September:** Michaelmas Fair.

Tourist Information Centre, Station Road, Penzance TR18 2NF
01736 362207
www.go-cornwall.com

ST IVES

Family Fun Activities: Boat trips, sea angling, sailing, surfing, parascending, tennis, bowling, squash, putting • Leisure centre with swimming pool and gym • Museum, art galleries (Tate St Ives).

Tourist Information Centre, The Guildhall, St Ives TR26 2DS
01736 796297
www.stives-cornwall.co.uk

Beaches

- **PORTHMEOR BEACH.** One km long, sand backed by low cliffs. Good surfing beach. Limited parking. *Safety and maintenance:* area for use of surfboards marked with buoys, lifeguards in summer months; cleaned daily during holiday season. *Beach facilities:* deck chairs, surf boards, beach huts for hire; boat trips around bay; beach shop and cafe on promenade; toilets. *Dog restrictions:* banned from Easter to 1st October.

★ Fun for all the Family ★

◆ **Colliford Lake Park, Bolventnor, Bodmin (01208 821469)**. Set amidst 50 acres of moorland beauty, rare breeds of animals and birds, craft demonstrations, adventure play areas. New '4 in 1' attraction.
www.collifordlakepark.com

◆ **Eden Project, near St Austell (01726 811911)**. The world's largest greenhouse in a breathtaking location. Two gigantic geodesic conservatories set amidst landscaped outdoor terraces.
www.edenproject.com

◆ **Goonhilly Satellite Earth Station, near Helston (0800 679593)**. The fascinating world of satellite communications - see global TV live as it happens. Audio-visual show, conducted tours; shop, restaurant.
www.goonhilly.bt.com

◆ **Lappa Valley Railway and Leisure Park, St Newlyn East, Newquay (01872 510317)**. Two-mile ride on steam train, plus leisure area with crazy golf, adventure playground, boating lake, picnic areas, woodland walks.
www.lappavalley.co.uk

◆ **The Monkey Sanctuary, near Looe (01503 262532)**. Breeding colony of "Woolly" monkeys that enjoy the company of visitors!
www.monkeysanctuary.org

◆ **Land of Legend and Model Village, The Old Forge, Polperro (01503 272378)**. Exciting animated Land of Legend show detailing Cornish life; also model village.

◆ **Newquay Zoo, Trenance Leisure Park, Newquay (01637 873342)**. A wealth of wildlife including Tropical House, Children's Zoo, walk in Rabbit Warren; play areas; park with leisure facilities.
www.newquayzoo.co.uk

◆ **Paradise Park, near St Ives (01736 751020)**. Cornwall's conservation theme park which keeps and breeds endangered species.
www.paradisepark.org.uk

◆ **Poldark Mine and Heritage Complex, Wendron, Helston (01326 573173)**. An 18th century Cornish tin mine at 125 feet below ground level. Guided tours and working models; restaurant.
www.poldark-mine.co.uk

◆ **Shire Horse Farm and Carriage Museum, Treskillard, Redruth (01209 713606)**. See the shires at work on the farm and visit the blacksmith's shop. Guided tours, wagon rides; picnic area.

◆ **Tamar Otter Sanctuary, near Launceston (01566 785646)**. Enjoy a close encounter with these shy but playful creatures; also deer, owls and golden pheasants. Nature trail, tearoom and shop. No dogs.

◆ **Trinity House National Lighthouse Museum, Penzance (01736 360077)**. The world's finest collection of light house apparatus, illustrating their history and the lives of the keepers.
www.trinityhouse.co.uk

◆ **Tunnels Through Time, Newquay (01637 873379)**. More than 70 amazingly realistic characters re-create the stories and legends of Cornwall. Open Easter to October.
www.tunnelsthroughtime.co.uk

◆ **Wheal Martyn China Clay Heritage Centre, near St Austell (01726 850362)**. Restored 19th century clay works with working water wheels; nature trail and adventure trail.
www.wheal-martyn.com

Cornwall

TRENONA FARM
Ruan High Lanes, Truro, Cornwall TR2 5JS

Enjoy a relaxing stay on this mixed farm, on the unspoilt Roseland Peninsula midway between Truro and the Eden Project at St Austell.
B&B in the Victorian farmhouse in double/family rooms, either en suite or with private bathroom. 
Self-catering in two renovated barns, each sleeping 6, both well equipped and furnished. Ample parking with room for boats and trailers.
Pets welcome by arrangement. Wheelchair access.

Tel: 01872 501339 • e-mail: info@trenonafarmholidays.co.uk • www.trenonafarmholidays.co.uk

---

Tregea Hotel ~PADSTOW~

In the old quiet part of Padstow and close to harbour, beaches and walks. A beautiful small family-run hotel with personal friendly service and comfortable accommodation of a very high standard. Non-smoking. Eight en suite bedrooms. Off-street parking. Credit/debit cards accepted.

Tregea Hotel
16-18 High Street, Padstow, Cornwall PL28 8BB
Tel: 0871 871 2686 • Fax: 0871 871 2687
e-mail: enquiries@tregea.co.uk • www.tregea.co.uk

Wringford Down

Family friendly hotel set in 4 acres of Cornish countryside

Located on the Rame peninsula in an Area of Outstanding Natural Beauty with tiny Cornish fishing villages, dramatic cliff top walks and secluded sandy bays.

Great facilities for all ages:

- Family suites
- Bar & restaurant
- Covered, heated pool
- Tennis court
- Indoor & outdoor play areas
- Ball pool, bouncy castle
- Pool & table tennis
- Childcare on-site
- Shetland ponies & other animals

Tel: 01752 822287   www.cornwallholidays.co.uk

ROCKLANDS

"Rocklands" is situated overlooking part of Cornwall's superb coastline and enjoys uninterrupted sea views. The Lizard is well known for its lovely picturesque scenery, coastal walks and enchanting coves and beaches, as well as the famous Serpentine Stone which is quarried and sold locally. Open Easter to October. Generations of the Hill family have been catering for visitors on the Lizard since the 1850s. Three bedrooms with sea views, two en suite, tea/coffee making facilities and electric heaters; sittingroom with TV and video; sun lounge; diningroom with separate tables. Children and well trained pets welcome.

Bed and Breakfast £23pppn, en suite £25pppn; reductions for children under 10 years.

Mrs D. J. Hill, "Rocklands", The Lizard, Near Helston TR12 7NX • Tel: 01326 290339

Cornwall

CORNISH HOLIDAY COTTAGES

Calamansac, Heathercroft, Rose Cottages, Seagulls

Charming Cottages and Country Houses in Du Maurier country – Frenchman's Creek, Helford River and Falmouth, including launching dinghies and moorings. Surrounded by National Trust gardens and spectacular scenery. A selection of the finest cottages available, supervised personally by our helpful staff, some with waterside gardens, some at Port Pendennis, Falmouth.
From £175 to £1,650 per week.
Open all year.

Contact Emily/Chris, Cornish Holiday Cottages, Killibrae, West Bay, Maenporth, Falmouth, Cornwall TR11 5HP •• Telephone/Fax: (01326) 250339
e-mail: info@cornishholidaycottages.net •• website: www.cornishholidaycottages.net

Fowey Harbour Cottages

We are a small Agency offering a selection of cottages and flats situated around the beautiful Fowey Harbour on the South Cornish Coast. Different properties accommodate from two to six persons and vary in their decor and facilities so that hopefully there will be something we can offer to suit anyone. All properties are registered with VisitBritain and are personally vetted by us.

Short Breaks and weekend bookings accepted subject to availability (mainly out of peak season but sometimes available at "last minute" in season).

Brochure and details from W. J. B. Hill & Son,
3 Fore Street, Fowey PL23 1AH
Tel: 01726 832211 • Fax: 01726 832901
e-mail: hillandson@talk21.com
www.foweyharbourcottages.co.uk

ST IVES BAY HOLIDAY PARK

CALL OUR 24hr BROCHURE LINE **0800 317713**

The park on the beach

CHALETS • CARAVANS • CAMPING

St Ives Bay Holiday Park is set in sand dunes which run down to its own sandy beach. Many units have superb sea views. There is a large indoor pool and 2 clubs with FREE entertainment on the Park.

www.stivesbay.co.uk

BAMHAM FARM COTTAGES
Higher Bamham Farm, Launceston PL15 9LD

Eight individually designed cottages, one mile from Launceston, the historic capital of Cornwall. The north and south coasts of Devon and Cornwall are easily accessible, as are Dartmoor and Bodmin Moor. Heated indoor swimming pool with paddling pool (open all year); games room. Video recorders and DVD players in cottages.

• Contact •
Richard and Jackie Chapman
Tel: 01566 772141
Fax: 01566 775266
E-mail: Jackie@bamhamfarm.co.uk
www.cottages-cornwall.co.uk

CUTKIVE WOOD HOLIDAY LODGES

Nestling in the heart of a peaceful and lovely family-owned country estate, there are six well-equipped cedar-clad lodges. Set on the edge of bluebell woods with wonderful rural views, you can relax and enjoy yourself in this tranquil and idyllic setting. Ideally situated to enjoy year-round holidays. You can help to feed the animals, milk the goats, explore the woods and fields. Big play area. So much to see and do - including memorable beaches, wonderful coasts, walk the moors, theme attractions, historic gems and the Eden Project. Dogs welcome. Short breaks. Open all year.

St Ive, Liskeard, Cornwall PL14 3ND • Tel: 01579 362216
www.cutkivewood.co.uk • holidays@cutkivewood.co.uk

Step onto the Coastal Path ...

Escape the pressures of life. Relax! explore the Cornish Coast from Green Door Cottages in Port Gaverne.

8 comfortable, restored 18th Century cottages set around a sheltered courtyard, plus 2 prestigious apartments with panoramic sea views beside a picturesque cove, directly on the Coastal path, less than half a mile from Port Isaac.
An ideal location for your holiday and short breaks.
Well behaved dogs are very welcome.

Green Door Cottages
PORT GAVERNE
email: enquiries@greendoorcottages.co.uk
web: www.greendoorcottages.co.uk

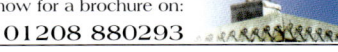

Call now for a brochure on:
01208 880293

RAINTREE HOUSE HOLIDAYS
Padstow, Cornwall

Comfortable, well equipped homes available all seasons. Near places of historic interest, wonderful walks, sandy beaches, surfing and extreme sports; famous and infamous restaurants all within easy reach.

e-mail: gill@raintreehouse.co.uk
www.raintreehouse.co.uk
Tel: 01841 520228

FHG

Visit the FHG website
www.holidayguides.com

for details of the wide choice of accommodation

featured in the full range of FHG titles

K·U·P·E·R·A·R·D

SOUTH DEVON

Best Beaches

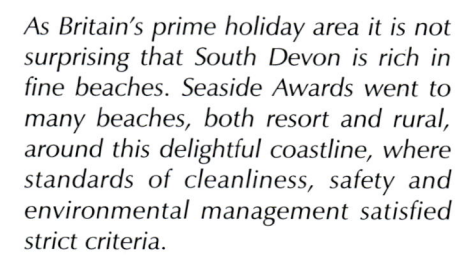

As Britain's prime holiday area it is not surprising that South Devon is rich in fine beaches. Seaside Awards went to many beaches, both resort and rural, around this delightful coastline, where standards of cleanliness, safety and environmental management satisfied strict criteria.

South West Tourism
(Bristol & Bath, Cornwall, Devon, Dorset, Gloucestershire & The Cotswolds, Somerset, Wiltshire).

- Tel: 0870 442 0880
- Fax: 0870 442 0881
- e-mail: post@swtourism.co.uk
- www.westcountrynow.com
- www.visitsouthwest.co.uk

BLUE FLAG BEACHES 2006
- *Dawlish Warren*
- *Blackpool Sands*
- *Challaborough*
- *Bigbury-on-Sea North*
- *Torbay*
  Breakwater Shoalstone
  Meadoot
  Oddicombe
  Broadsands
  Preston

Children Welcome!

See the *Family-Friendly Pubs & Inns* Supplement on pages 150-154 for establishments which really welcome children

South Devon 53

EXMOUTH

Family Fun Activities: Indoor swimming pool, children's playground, boating lake, indoor sports centre, amusement arcade, mini-railway • Bowls, tennis, indoor tennis centre, putting, cricket, approach golf • Boat trips, angling • Old tyme and modern dancing,

Special Events: End July: Carnival events. **October:** Winter Floodlit Carnival.

Tourist Information Centre,
Alexandra Terrace, Exmouth EX8 1NZ
01395 222299
e-mail: info@exmouthtourism.co.uk
www.exmouthguide.co.uk

Beaches

• **MAER, RODNEY BAY AND EXMOUTH BEACH.** Beaches two-and-a-half miles long. Rodney Bay naturally sheltered, others open; promenade and good parking. *Safety and maintenance:* warning flags, lifeguards peak summer season; cleaned daily. *Beach facilities:* deck chairs, swings; beach huts for hire from T.I.C.; ice-cream kiosks, snack bars, restaurants and pubs; toilets with & access. *Dog restrictions:* banned from main beach from 1st May to 30th September.

PLYMOUTH

Family Fun Activities: Plymouth Pavilions with leisure pool, ice-skating, bar, bistro and shops • Mayflower Visitor Centre • Plymouth Dome heritage centre • Crownhill Fort • National Marine Aquarium • Sports centre, indoor and outdoor swimming pools, parks with children's playgrounds • Tennis, putting, bowls, squash, dry-ski slope, bowling with quasar • Marina and water sports centre, sailing schools, sea angling • Theatre, multi-screen cinemas; museum and art gallery.

Special Events: May: Lord Mayor's Day Procession; Half Marathon, Vehicle and Bus Rally. **June:** Plymouth Playfair. **July:** Saltram Fair. **July:** World Championship Powerboat Race. **August:** National Fireworks Championships. **September:** Heritage Open Days. **November:** Christmas Lights.

Tourist Information Centre, Plymouth Mayflower, The Barbican, Plymouth (01752 306330)
e-mail: barbicantic@plymouth.gov.uk
www.visitplymouth.co.uk

Beaches

• **BEACHES.** The city itself has an attractive waterfront with sheltered promenades and rock pools, and a fully restored Art Deco Lido. There are good parking facilities, toilets, ice-cream kiosks, snack bars, and family restaurants/pubs.

SIDMOUTH

Family Fun Activities: Children's playgrounds • Cricket, golf, angling, sailing, putting, tennis, bowls.

Special Events: August: International Folk Festival. **September:** Sidmouth Carnival.

Tourist Information Centre,
Ham Lane, Sidmouth • 01395 516441
e-mail: enquiries@sidmouth.co.uk
www.visitsidmouth.co.uk

Beaches

• **MAIN BEACH.** Half-a-mile long, shingle and sand at low tide; promenade and ample parking. *Safety and maintenance:* lifeguards present only on Sundays; cleaned daily. *Beach facilities:* beach huts, deck chairs; ice-cream kiosk; toilets with & access. *Dog restrictions:* banned from 1st May to 30th September.

TEIGNMOUTH & SHALDON

Family Fun Activities: Victorian Pier • Children's play area • Outdoor heated pool • Crazy golf • Bowls • Angling • Golf course • Summer shows.

Special Events: June: Folk Festival. **July/August:** Summer Fun Fest. **July:** Carnival and Regatta. **August:** Water Carnival and Regatta. **November:** Jazz Festival, Winter Carnival.

i Tourist Information Centre, The Den, Teignmouth TQ14 8BE • 01626 215666. e-mail: teigntic@teignbridge.gov.uk www.southdevon.org.uk

Beaches

• **TEIGNMOUTH TOWN BEACH.** Long, sandy beach stretching from mouth of River Teign east towards Dawlish. *Safety and maintenance:* information signage, lifeguard patrol May-Sept; lifesaving equipment; daily beach cleaning. *Beach facilities:* deck chairs; beach wheelchair for hire; ice-cream kiosks and snack bars; toilets, showers; (♿ access to beach). *Dog restrictions:* not allowed on designated areas of the beach from 1st May to 30th Sept.

• **NESS BEACH, SHALDON.** Shingle beach sloping gently to the sea; safe bathing, rock pools at low tide No ♿ access. *Safety and maintenance:* lifesaving equipment, information signage; daily beach cleaning. *Beach facilities:* shops and toilets nearby. *Dog restrictions:* none.

FREE AND REDUCED RATE HOLIDAY VISITS!
Don't miss our
Readers' Offer Vouchers
on pages 9-38

DAWLISH

Family Fun Activities: Sports centre • Amusement arcades • Approach golf, putting, crazy golf, bowls • Angling • Theatre • Boat trips • Visitor Centre at Dawlish Warren Nature Reserve.

Special Events: June: Arts Festival. **July/August:** Summer Fun Fest. **August:** Carnival.

i Tourist Information Centre, The Lawn, Dawlish EX7 9PW • 01626 215665 e-mail: dawtic@teignbridge.gov.uk www.southdevon.org.uk

Beaches

• **DAWLISH TOWN BEACH.** Mixture of sand and shingle, gently sloping to sea; safe family beach a short walk from town centre; poor ♿ access. *Safety and maintenance:* information signage, lifesaving equipment; cleaned daily. *Beach facilities:* deck chairs, ice-cream kiosks and snack bars; toilets with ♿ access. *Dog restrictions:* not allowed on designated areas of the beach from 1st May to 30th September.

• **CORYTON COVE.** Secluded, sandy beach within easy walking distance of town centre; ♿ access. *Safety and maintenance:* information signage, lifesaving equipment; cleaned daily. *Beach facilities:* beach hut hire, snack bar; toilets with ♿ access, showers. *Dog restrictions:* not allowed on designated areas of the beach from 1st May to 30th September.

• **DAWLISH WARREN.** Golden sands backed by sand dunes; easy access from main roads, good public transport links; ♿ access. *Safety and maintenance:* information signage, lifeguards May to September, lifeasaving equipment; cleaned daily. *Beach facilities:* deck chairs; ice-cream kiosks and snack bars; toilets with ♿ access, showers. *Dog restrictions:* not allowed from slipway to groyne from 1st April to 30th September.

South Devon

TORQUAY

Family Fun Activities: Water ski-ing, windsurfing, sailing, angling • Indoor pools • Crazy golf, putting, tennis, squash, ten-pin bowling • Cinema, theatres, nightclubs, casino • Riviera Leisure Centre, museum, Babbacombe Model Village, cliff railway, Living Coasts.

☆ **Special Events: August:** Torbay Royal Regatta.

i **The Tourist Centre, Vaughan Parade, Torquay TQ2 5JG • 0906 6801268 – calls charged at 25p per minute www.englishriviera.co.uk**

Beaches

- **TORRE ABBEY SANDS.** 600 yards long, sandy and naturally sheltered; ♿ easy access, ample parking nearby. *Safety and maintenance:* warning flags, lifesaving equipment, first-aid post. *Beach facilities:* deck chairs/sunbeds for hire; cafe/ refreshments; toilets nearby. *Dog restrictions:* dogs banned.
- **ANSTEY'S COVE.** 220 yards long, rock and shingle. Access steep in places. Parking 10 minutes' walk. *Safety and maintenance:* warning flags, lifesaving equipment. *Beach facilities:* deck chair/ sunbed/chalet hire; refreshments, beach shop; toilets nearby. *Dog restrictions:* dogs allowed.
- **MEADFOOT BEACH.** 350 yards long, pebble and sand; easy access and ample parking. *Safety and maintenance:* lifesaving equipment. *Beach facilities:* deck chair/ sunbed/chalet hire; cafe/refreshments; toilets with baby changing facilities. *Dog restrictions:* allowed (Kilmorlie end).
- **ODDICOMBE BEACH.** 400 yards long, sand and shingle; access via clifflift. Parking 15 minutes' walk. *Safety and maintenance:* warning flags, lifesaving equipment, first aid post. *Beach facilities:* deck chair/sunbed hire; beach cafe/refreshments, beach shop; toilets with ♿ access and baby changing facilities. *Dog restrictions:* banned.

PAIGNTON

Family Fun Activities: Pier • Quay West water park and beach resort • Steam railway, amusement arcade, zoo, leisure centre with swimming pool • Boat trips, angling • Squash, badminton, tennis, putting, golf, go karting • Multiplex cinema, theatre.

☆ **Special Events: July:** It's A Knockout, Torbay Carnival. **August:** Paignton Regatta, Children's Festival.

i **Paignton TIC, Esplanade Road, Paignton TQ4 6ED • 0906 6801268 – calls charged at 25p per minute www.englishriviera.co.uk**

Beaches

- **BROADSANDS BEACH.** Sandy beach, one-and-a-half miles long; easy access and ample parking. *Safety and maintenance:* warning flags, life-saving equipment, first aid post. *Beach facilities:* deck chair/ sunbed/chalet hire; refreshments, beach shop; toilets with ♿ access. *Dog restrictions:* banned.
- **GOODRINGTON SANDS.** 1200 yards long, sandy; ample parking. *Safety and maintenance:* warning flags. *Beach facilities:* deck chair/sunbed hire; cafe/refreshments and restaurant, beach shop; toilets with ♿ access. *Dog restrictions:* banned on South Sands, allowed on North Sands.
- **PAIGNTON SANDS.** Sandy with rock pools, 1200 yards long; promenade and pier with arcades. *Safety and maintenance:* warning flags, life-saving equipment, first aid post. *Beach facilities:* deck chair/sunbed hire; cafe/refreshments, restaurant, beach shop; toilets with ♿ access. *Dog restrictions:* banned.
- **PRESTON SANDS.** 600 yards long, sandy and naturally sheltered. *Safety and maintenance:* warning flags, life-saving equipment. *Beach facilities:* deck chair/ sunbed/chalet hire; cafe/refreshments, beach shop; toilets (toilets with ♿ access nearby). *Dog restrictions:* banned.

BRIXHAM

Family Fun Activities: Indoor and outdoor swimming pools • Tennis, squash, mini-golf, putting, leisure centre • Fishing trips/cruises, sailing • Berry Head Country Park • Golden Hind replica, museums, aquarium.

Special Events: May: Heritage Festival. **June:** Brixham Trawler Race. **July:** Mardi Gras. **August:** Brixham Regatta.

Brixham T.I.C., Old Market House, The Quay, Brixham TQ5 8AW
0906 6801268 – calls charged at 25p per minute)
www.englishriviera.co.uk

Beaches

- **BREAKWATER BEACH.** Shingle beach, 100 yards long; easy access and ample parking; access difficult. *Safety and maintenance:* warning flags, life-saving equipment. *Beach facilities:* deck chairs; cafe/refreshments and restaurant, beach shop; toilets. *Dog restrictions:* banned.

- **SHOALSTONE BEACH.** Shingle, with rock pools and sea water swimming pool; access difficult. *Safety and maintenance:* warning flags, lifeguards, life-saving equipment. *Beach facilities:* deck chair/ sunbed hire; cafe; toilets with baby changing facilities. *Dog restrictions:* allowed.

- **ST MARY'S BAY.** Sand and shingle, parking 10 minutes' walk; access difficult. *Safety and maintenance:* swimming safe with care. *Dog restrictions:* allowed.

South Devon

☆ Fun for all the Family ☆

◆ **Babbacombe Model Village (01803 315315).** Masterpiece of miniature landscaping - hundreds of models and figures.
www.babbacombemodelvillage.co.uk

◆ **Bickleigh Castle, near Tiverton (01884 855363).** Medieval romantic home with armoury, thatched Jacobean wing, early Norman chapel, moat and gardens.

◆ **Buckfast Butterfly Farm and Dartmoor Otter Sanctuary, Buckfastleigh (01364 642916).** Free-flying butterflies and moths from all over the world, also birds, terrapins and insects.
www.ottersandbutterflies.co.uk

◆ **Dartmoor Wildlife Park, Sparkwell (01752 837645).** Over 100 animals ranging from tigers, bears and wolves to birds of prey and even guinea pigs.

◆ **Kent's Cavern Show Caves, Torquay (01803 215136).** Stalactite caves of great beauty. Guided tours to discover the magic of Britain's earliest known settlement.
www.kents-cavern.co.uk

◆ **National Marine Aquarium, Plymouth (01752 600301).** New attraction where memorable sights include a wall of ocean 15 metres wide and a shark theatre in over 700,000 litres of water.
www.nationalaquarium.co.uk

◆ **Paignton Zoo (01803 697500).** Over 300 species in spacious landscaped enclosures. Miniature railway, restaurant, activity centre.
www.paigntonzoo.org.uk

◆ **Paignton and Dartmouth Steam Railway (01803 555872).** Seven-mile trip along the spectacular Torbay coast; gift shop, buffet.
www.paignton-steamrailway.co.uk

◆ **River Dart Country Park, Ashburton (01364 652511).** Country fun for everyone - children's adventure playgrounds, nature trails, picnic meadow.
www.dartmoor.co.uk

◆ **South Devon Railway, Buckfastleigh (0845 345 1420).** Excursion trips on steam trains; museum, picnic area and play area.
www.southdevonrailway.org

◆ **Woodlands Leisure Park, Dartmouth (01803 712598).** Lots of family fun activities, indoor and outdoor, plus hundreds of animals and birds.
www.woodlands-leisure-park.co.uk

Looking for holiday accommodation?
for details of hundreds of properties throughout the UK try:
www.holidayguides.com

South Devon

The Glenorleigh
26 Cleveland Road
Torquay
Devon TQ2 5BE
Tel: 01803 292135
Fax: 01803 213717

As featured on BBC Holiday programme

David & Pam Skelly
AA ★★★★

Situated in a quiet residential area, Glenorleigh is 10 minutes' walk from both the sea front and the town centre. • Delightful en suite rooms, with your comfort in mind. • Good home cooking, both English and Continental, plenty of choice, with vegetarian options available daily. • Bar leading onto terrace overlooking Mediterranean-style garden with feature palms and heated swimming pool. • Discounts for children and Senior Citizens. • Brochures and menus available on request. • B&B £30–£40; Dinner £14. B&B £195-£265 per week.
e-mail: glenorleighhotel@btinternet.com • website: www.glenorleigh.co.uk

Farm & Cottage HOLIDAYS
holidaycottages.co.uk
01237 479698

freedom of choice

Enjoy the freedom and the beauty of this delightful corner of South West England with over 750 of the finest holiday cottages throughout Cornwall, Devon, Somerset and Dorset. All situated in superb coastal & rural locations. The perfect holiday is yours to choose!

• Log Cabins • Fisherman's Cottages • Luxury Riverside Apartments • Barn Conversions

---

Cofton Country HOLIDAYS
A glorious corner of Devon

– Fantastic four star facilities
– Outdoor swimming pools, children's play areas, Swan pub, take-away, games room, mini-market
– Five well-stocked coarse fishing lakes in the grounds
– Outstanding touring and camping pitches
– Holiday homes, cottages and apartments
– Five minutes by car from Dawlish Warren's famous Blue Flag beach
– Six David Bellamy Gold Awards for Conservation

0800 085 8649 www.coftonholidays.co.uk

Toad Hall Cottages

From Babes in arms to Teenagers and Grandparents. Our regular guests return year in year out to our fabulous selection of 250 holiday properties situated in locations to die for in Devon and Cornwall.
Prices from £180 per week per property, sleep 2-16.

For catalogue tel:
0845 612 7974 *24 hrs local rate*
www.toadhallcottages.com

The South Devon Hotel with a Different Outlook...

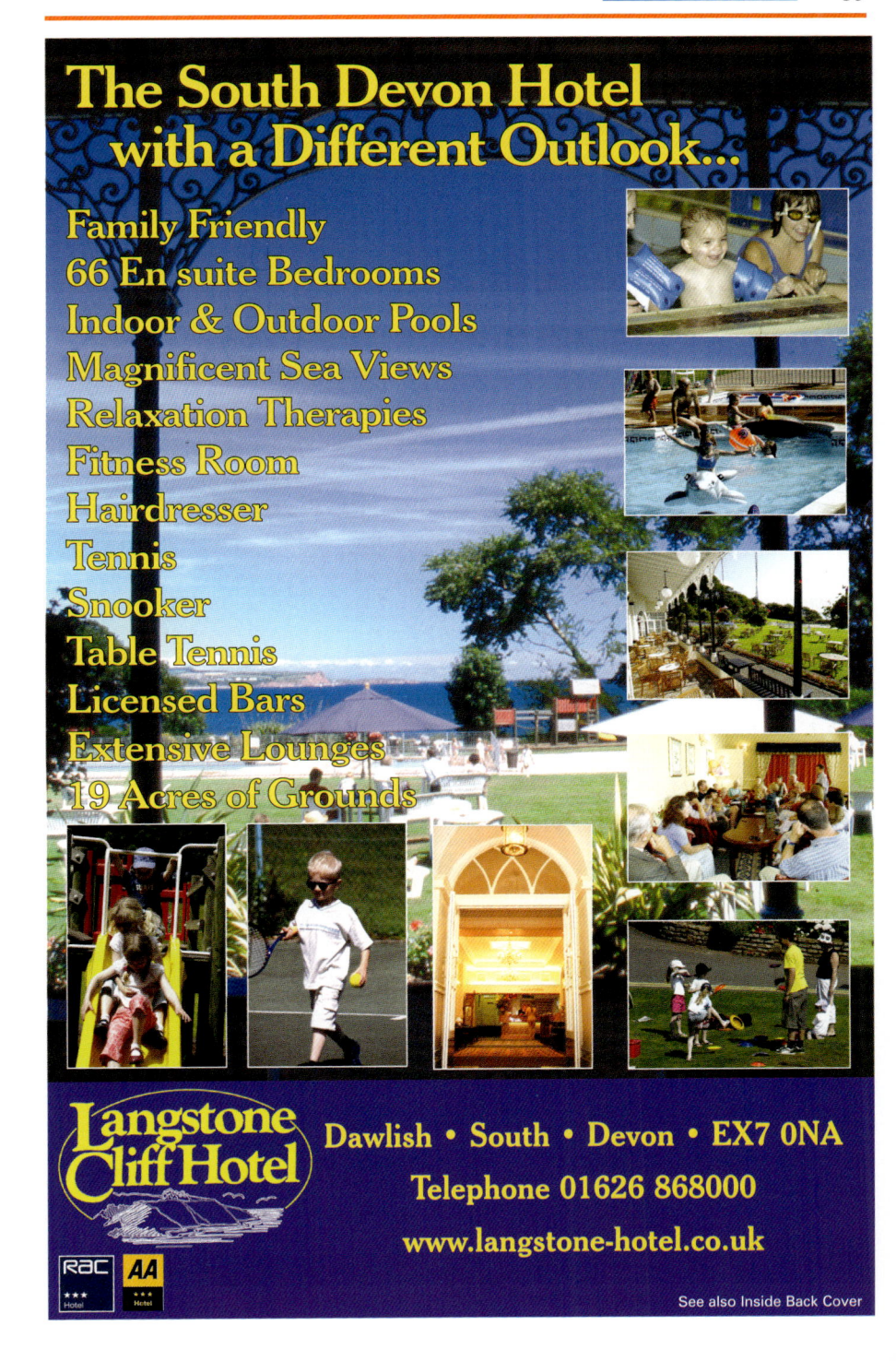

- Family Friendly
- 66 En suite Bedrooms
- Indoor & Outdoor Pools
- Magnificent Sea Views
- Relaxation Therapies
- Fitness Room
- Hairdresser
- Tennis
- Snooker
- Table Tennis
- Licensed Bars
- Extensive Lounges
- 19 Acres of Grounds

Langstone Cliff Hotel

Dawlish • South • Devon • EX7 0NA
Telephone 01626 868000
www.langstone-hotel.co.uk

RAC ★★★ Hotel   AA ★★★ Hotel

See also Inside Back Cover

SOUTH DEVON

Parkers Farm Cottages & Caravans
FARM COTTAGES • STATIC CARAVANS
Friendly, family-run self-catering complex with cottages and static caravans surrounded by beautiful countryside. 12 miles from the sea and close to Dartmoor National Park. Perfect for children and pets, with farm animals and plenty of space to roam. Large area to walk your dogs. Good discounts for couples. Bar and restaurant. A warm welcome awaits you.
British Farm Tourist Award, AA Four Pennants, 2006 Gold Award for Quality and Service, Silver David Bellamy Conservation Award, Practical Caravan 2004 Top 100 Parks, Rose Award 2005. ETC ★★★★

THE ROCKERY, CATON, ASHBURTON, DEVON TQ13 7LH • Tel: 01364 653008 • Fax: 01364 652915
e-mail: parkerscottages@btconnect.com
www.parkersfarm.co.uk

Parkers Farm Holiday Park
STATIC CARAVANS • TOURING SITE
Friendly, family-run touring site and static caravans for hire. Set in beautiful open countryside with views to Dartmoor. Children's paradise with all farm animals to see and touch on our regular farm walks. Family bar/restaurant, games room, outdoor play areas with trampolines. 12 miles from sea. Dogs very welcome.
British Farm Tourist Award, AA Four Pennants, 2006 Gold Award for Quality and Service, Silver David Bellamy Conservation Award, Practical Caravan 2004 Top 100 Parks, Rose Award 2005. ETC ★★★★

HIGHER MEAD FARM, ASHBURTON, DEVON TQ13 7IJ
Tel: 01364 654869 • Fax: 01364 654004
e-mail: parkersfarm@btconnect.com
www.parkersfarm.co.uk

DEVONCOURT HOLIDAY FLATS
BERRYHEAD ROAD, BRIXHAM, DEVON TQ5 9AB

Devoncourt is a development of 24 self-contained flats, occupying one of the finest positions in Torbay, with unsurpassed views. At night the lights of Torbay are like a fairyland to be enjoyed from your very own balcony.

MasterCard VISA

EACH FLAT HAS:
- Heating
- Sea Views over Torbay
- Private balcony
- Own front door
- Separate bathroom and toilet
- Separate bedroom
- Bed-settee in lounge
- Lounge sea views over Marina
- Kitchenette - all electric
- Private car park
- Opposite beach
- Colour television
- Overlooks lifeboat
- Short walk to town centre
- Double glazing
- Open all year
- Mini Breaks October to April

Tel: 01803 853748
(or 07050 853748 after office hours)
website: www.devoncourt.info

"SANDERLINGS"
Hope Cove, Near Kingsbridge, South Devon TQ7 3HD

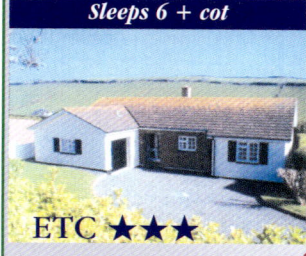

Sleeps 6 + cot

Three-bedroom bungalow - situated in a quiet location on the outskirts of Hope Cove. Six miles from the market town of Kingsbridge and seaside town of Salcombe. Close to safe, sandy beaches, ideal for children of all ages. Good location for all outdoor pursuits, with the attractions of Plymouth and Dartmoor within one hour's drive.

Fully equipped. Duvets on all beds; sheets, duvet covers and other linen are not provided but can be hired. Heating by night storage heaters, included in the price. Open fire and electric heaters are available if necessary. Electricity meter and pay telephone. Sun terrace overlooking a secluded lawned garden. More photos on request.

ETC ★★★

PRICES FROM £195 PER WEEK.

Contact Mrs D. Middleton on 0118 9690958
Mobile: +44 7766 496366 • e-mail: diana_middleton@yahoo.com

NORTH DEVON

Best Beaches

Along with three other fine beaches from the area, Woolacombe Beach is once again a proud winner of a European Blue Flag, indicating strict beach management and the highest standard of bathing water under EC legislation.

South West Tourism
(Bristol & Bath, Cornwall, Devon, Dorset, Gloucestershire & The Cotswolds, Somerset, Wiltshire).
- Tel: 0870 442 0880
- Fax: 0870 442 0881
- e-mail: post@swtourism.co.uk
- www.westcountrynow.com
- www.visitsouthwest.co.uk

BLUE FLAG BEACHES 2006
- Ilfracombe (Tunnels)
- Westward Ho!
- Woolacombe
- Croyde Bay

FREE AND REDUCED RATE HOLIDAY VISITS!
Don't miss our
READERS' OFFER VOUCHERS
on pages 9-38

Looking for holiday accommodation?
for details of hundreds of properties throughout the UK try:
www.holidayguides.com

LYNTON & LYNMOUTH

Family Fun Activities: Children's playgrounds • Putting, tennis, bowls, cricket, horse riding • Boat trips, river and sea fishing • Cinema • Brass rubbing, museum • Local crafts centre • Unique water-operated cliff railway linking twin resorts.

Tourist Information Centre,
Town Hall, Lynton
0845 660 3232 • Fax: 01598 752755
e-mail: info@lyntourism.co.uk
www.lyntourism.co.uk

Beaches

• **LEE BAY BEACH.** Half-a-mile long, sand and shingle, with access through Valley of Rocks and on to Lee Abbey bottom lodge (toll charge); parking in field overlooking sea. *Safety and maintenance:* safe within the bay, cleaned whenever necessary. *Beach facilities:* refreshments five minutes' walk (restricted opening), toilets two minutes' walk. *Dog restrictions:* banned.

• **LYNMOUTH BEACH.** Large rocky beach, long slipway, Rhenish tower guarding harbour. *Safety and maintenance:* safe within the bay, cleaned whenever necessary. *Dog restrictions:* none.

• **WRINGCLIFF BEACH.** 100 yards long with access from traffic island in Valley of Rocks. Naturally sheltered with fine cliff scenery; parking 10 minutes' walk. *Safety and maintenance:* safe at the sandy level, cleaned whenever necessary. *Dog restrictions:* none.

For information about Britain's Best Beaches see pages 39-44

ILFRACOMBE

Family Fun Activities: Heated indoor pool, children's playground, boating lake, go karting, sports canoes • Pier, angling • Tennis, putting, pitch and putt, crazy golf, golf course • Theatre with shows all year round, cinema, discos.

Tourist Information Centre, The Promenade, Ilfracombe • 01271 863001
e-mail: info@ilfracombe-tourism.co.uk
www.ilfracombe-tourism.co.uk

☆ **Special Events: June:** Victorian Celebration. **July:** North Devon Arts Youth Festival. **August:** Emergency Rescue Service Display. **August/September:** Flower Shows.

Beaches

• **HARBOUR BEACH.** 200 yards long, sandy and naturally sheltered; good parking. Promenade, pier with arcade and cafe; toilets and parking. *Beach facilities:* ice-cream kiosks, snack bars, restaurants and pubs; toilets with ♿ access.

• **HELE BAY BEACH.** Half-a-mile long, shingle (some sand) with rock pools; promenade, good parking. *Safety and maintenance:* cleaned regularly during season. *Beach facilities:* deck chairs, sports canoes; ice-cream kiosk, snack bars, restaurants and pubs; toilets with ♿ access

• **LARKSTONE BEACH.** 100 yards long, shingle and rock pools, naturally sheltered; good parking. *Safety and maintenance:* cleaned regularly in season. *Beach facilities:* ice-cream kiosk; toilets with ♿ access.

• **RAPPAREE BEACH.** 220 yards long, shingle with rock pools and cliffs, naturally sheltered; promenade, good parking. *Safety and maintenance:* warning signs; certain parts cut off at high tide; cleaned regularly during season.

North Devon

- **TUNNELS BEACHES.** 600 yards long, shingle with rock pools and cliffs; naturally sheltered, good parking. *Safety and maintenance:* warning signs, certain parts cut off at high tide; beach privately owned and cleaned daily during season. *Beach facilities:* deck chairs, sports canoes, rowing boats; ice-cream kiosk and snack bar; toilets.

- **WHITE PEBBLE BEACH.** 220 yards long, shingle and pebbles. Cliffs, naturally sheltered; parking. *Safety and maintenance:* warning signs, certain parts cut off at high tide.

- **WILDERSMOUTH BEACH.** 220 yards long, shingle with rock pools; naturally sheltered; promenade, good parking. *Safety and maintenance:* cleaned by Local Authority. *Beach facilities:* deck chairs; ice-cream kiosks, snack bars, restaurants and pubs; ramps with ♿ access.

WOOLACOMBE

Family Fun Activities: Repertory theatre and other entertainment in season.

Special Events: July: Grand Sandcastle Competition. **September:** National Surf Life Saving Championships (every 3rd year). Other surf and water competitions during year.

i Tourist Information Centre, The Esplanade, Woolacombe EX34 7DL • 01271 870553
e-mail: woolacombetic@visit.org.uk
www.woolacombetourism.co.uk

Beaches

WOOLACOMBE SANDS BEACH. 3 miles long, sandy and naturally sheltered; good parking. *Safety and maintenance:* flagged, warning signs, lifeguards (May to September); cleaned daily. *Beach facilities* (May to September): deck chairs, beach huts, children's amusements, ice-cream kiosks, snack bars, restaurants and pubs; toilets with ♿ access. *Dog restrictions:* some restricted areas in operation May to September. Blue Flag and Seaside Award since 1991. England for Excellence Award for Best Family Holiday 1999.

visit the **FHG** KUPERARD website
www.holidayguides.com
for details of the wide choice of accommodation featured in the full range of FHG titles

Fun for all the Family

◆ **Arlington Court (NT), Barnstaple (01271 850296).** A fascinating collection including shells and model ships. Surrounding park has Shetland ponies and a flock of Jacob's sheep. Teas and snacks.

◆ **The Big Sheep, Abbotsham (01237 472366).** All you ever wanted to know about sheep – lots of lambs, plus sheep dairy, shearing, sheepdog trials. Ewetopia indoor playground. Shop and restaurant.
www.thebigsheep.co.uk

◆ **Combe Martin Wildlife and Dinosaur Park (01271 882486).** Otters, falcons, nature walks, children's playground and zoo, large indoor model railway.
www.dinosaur-park.com

◆ **Dartington Crystal, Torrington (01805 626244).** Marvel at the glass-blower's skill and trace the development of manufacturing techniques over the centuries. Factory shop and restaurant.
www.dartington.co.uk

◆ **Exmoor Zoological Park, Bratton Fleming (01598 763352).** Formal and natural gardens with a large collection of tropical birds. Tarzanland for children; tearoom and gift shop.
www.exmoorzoo.co.uk

◆ **Jungleland, Barnstaple (01271 343884).** Collection of plants from all over the world in near as possible natural settings.

◆ **The Milky Way, Clovelly (01237 431255).** Hand milk a cow, bottle feed lambs, goats and calves. Adventure playground and old farm machinery.
www.themilkyway.co.uk

◆ **Once Upon A Time, Woolacombe (01271 870900).** Children's park with train rides, adventure trails, soft play area.

◆ **Quince Honey Farm, South Molton (01769 572401).** Unique exhibition of honey bees; shop and cafeteria.
www.quincehoney.co.uk

◆ **Rosemoor Garden, Great Torrington (01805 624067).** Garden (now RHS) started in 1959: rhododendrons, ornamental trees and shrubs, primulas, young arboretum.
www.rhs.org.uk/gardens/rosemoor

The Classified Listing Section on pages 141-149 is a quick, easy to use summary of the facilities offered by the accommodation featured in this guide.

North Devon

Close your eyes and dream...

Perfect for families...perfect for children.

Seemingly endless golden sands of Woolacombe's Blue Flag beach, Lundy Island on the horizon, this hotel set in an unspoilt village between rolling National Trust hills exudes a relaxed air of friendliness, good living, comfort and splendour in the traditional style, with wonderful cuisine and first class leisure facilities. Superb position for enjoying the National Trusts walks, miles of golden sandy beaches or just relaxing in the lounges or gardens with a book.

Hotel Guests enjoy FREE unlimited use of heated pools, sauna, steam room, spa, gym, aerobics, snooker, approach golf, tennis, squash, crèche, children's club, baby listening, entertainment. Golf, riding, 10-pin bowling within minutes, surfing and fishing seconds from the hotel. After all that...the bliss of relaxing in the Haven Beauty Salon has to be experienced to be believed!

Woolacombe Bay Apartments.....

combine the flexibility of self-catering with the use of hotel bars, entertainment, bistro, grounds and with sports facilities at preferential rates. All well equipped, sleep between 4 - 8 people, ideal for those wanting freedom and flexibility.

Woolacombe Bay Hotel

01271 870388
www.woolacombe-bay-hotel.co.uk

North Devon

"Valley View"
Guineaford, Marwood, Barnstaple EX31 4EA

"Valley View" is a bungalow set in 320 acres of farmland which visitors are free to enjoy. The farm, situated 3½ miles from Barnstaple, near Marwood Hill Gardens and Arlington Court, produces lamb and is home to Helenbrie Miniature Shetland ponies. Accommodation comprises two bedrooms each containing a double and single bed. Bed and Breakfast from £20. Children are welcomed, half-price for those under 12 years. Babysitting free of charge. Pets by arrangement. Car essential – parking. Open all year.

Tel: 01271 343458
www.helenbriestud.co.uk

Join us on the farm, help feed the animals!

A different, very child-friendly, highly recommended holiday, Torridge House Farm Cottages is where young families can join in helping to feed the animals: lambs, hens, ducks, pigs and rabbits, as well as chicks and ducklings. The nine cottages are welcoming, comfortable and well appointed. The small, friendly, family-run farm has panoramic views of glorious Devon countryside. There is plenty of room to play in the gardens, a heated outdoor summer swimming pool, BBQs, pool, table tennis and play room. We have over 19 years' experience in offering relaxed, hands-on farm holidays. To find out more, please phone for a brochure or visit our website.or visit our website.

TORRIDGE HOUSE FARM COTTAGES
LITTLE TORRINGTON, NORTH DEVON EX38 8PS
Tel: 01805 622542 • e-mail: holidays@torridgehouse.co.uk • www.torridgehouse.co.uk

---

Welcome to North Hill – deep in the rolling hills of Devon, a truly pastoral retreat.

17th century farm buildings, sympathetically converted into cottages sleeping 2-6, with exposed beams, wood stoves and central heating. Set in 9 acres of pastures and gardens with a children's play area. Facilities include: indoor heated swimming pool, sauna, all weather tennis court and games room.

This area of North Devon offers some of the finest beaches in the country and the National Park of Exmoor offers thousands of acres of moorland to explore.

Terms from £210 to £585.

Carol Ann and Adrian Black, North Hill, Shirwell, Barnstaple EX31 4LG

Tel: 01271 850611 or 07005 850413 • Fax: 07005 850423 • Mobile: 07834 806434 • www.north-hill.co.uk

COLLACOTT FARM
Quality Country Cottages

Eight delightful country cottages sleeping 2-12 set around a large cobbled courtyard, amidst twenty acres of tranquil Devon countryside. All are well equipped with wood-burning stove, dishwashers, heating, bed linen, and their own individual patio and garden. A tennis court, heated outdoor swimming pool (summer only), games room, children's play area, trampoline room and BHS approved riding centre makes Collacott an ideal holiday for the whole family.

Collacott Farm, King's Nympton, Umberleigh, North Devon EX37 9TP
Telephone: S.Molton 01769 572491
www.collacott.co.uk
e-mail: info@collacott.co.uk

North Devon 67

PLEASE NOTE

All the information in this book is given in good faith in the belief that it is correct. However, the publishers cannot guarantee the facts given in these pages, neither are they responsible for changes in policy, ownership or terms that may take place after the date of going to press. Readers should always satisfy themselves that the facilities they require are available and that the terms, if quoted, still apply.

fun filled holidays

Best beach in Britain and awarded family resort of the year

See our advert on the back page for further details

01271 870 343
www.woolacombe.com/fcw

WOOLACOMBE BAY
HOLIDAY PARCS

Cottages with a Difference

High quality conversion of 18th century watermill and barns into cosy, centrally heated, well equipped accommodation with great rustic charm, surrounded by 11 acres of tranquil award-winning grounds, views of Exmoor, near North Devon's superb beaches. Indoor heated pool, sauna, fitness room, tennis court, playground, four-posters, log fires, dishwashers, TV and video, bed linen, cots and high chairs, midweek maid service, fresh flowers, laundry room, provision service, babysitting. Nearby: riding, cycling, walking, golf, sea and lake fishing, surfing, family attractions, historic houses and gardens. 8 cottages and 2 apartments (sleep 2 to 6 +cot). Open February to October, Low Season short breaks available. Sorry, no pets.

Wheel Farm Country Cottages, Berry Down, Combe Martin, Devon EX34 0NT
Tel: 01271 882100 • Fax: 01271 883120
e-mail: holidays@wheelfarmcottages.co.uk • website: www.wheelfarmcottages.co.uk

West Millbrook

ADJOINING EXMOOR. Two fully-equipped bungalows and one farmhouse annexe (properties sleep 2/8) in lovely surroundings bordering Exmoor National Park. Ideal for touring North Devon and West Somerset including moor and coast with beautiful walks, lovely scenery and many other attractions. North Molton village is only one mile away. All units have electric cooker, fridge/freezer, microwave and digital TV; two bungalows also have washing machines/dryers. Children's play area; cots and high chairs available free. Linen hire available. Games room. Car parking. Central heating if required. Electricity metered. Out of season short breaks. Weekly prices from £90 to £420. Colour brochure available.

Mike and Rose Courtney, West Millbrook, Twitchen, South Molton EX36 3LP
Tel: 01598 740382 • e-mail: wmbselfcatering@aol.com
www.westcountrynow.com • www.westmillbrook.co.uk

SOMERSET & WILTSHIRE

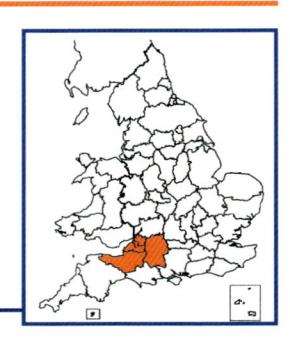

Best Beaches

There are some fine beaches in this delightful part of the country, including some of the West Country's most popular family holiday resorts. A Seaside Award (Resort) has been gained in 2006 by Weston-Super-Mare and Burnham-on-Sea, as well as several rural beaches.

South West Tourism
(Bristol & Bath, Cornwall, Devon, Dorset, Gloucestershire & The Cotswolds, Somerset, Wiltshire).

- Tel: 0870 442 0880
- Fax: 0870 442 0881
- e-mail: post@swtourism.co.uk
- www.westcountrynow.com
- www.visitsouthwest.co.ukv

Other specialised holiday guides from FHG

Recommended **INNS & PUBS** OF BRITAIN
Recommended **COUNTRY HOTELS** OF BRITAIN
Recommended **SHORT BREAK HOLIDAYS** IN BRITAIN
The bestselling and original **PETS WELCOME!**
The **GOLF GUIDE,** Where to Play, Where to Stay IN BRITAIN & IRELAND
COAST & COUNTRY HOLIDAYS
SELF-CATERING HOLIDAYS IN BRITAIN
BED & BREAKFAST STOPS
CARAVAN & CAMPING HOLIDAYS
BRITAIN'S BEST **LEISURE & RELAXATION GUIDE**

Published annually: available in all good bookshops or direct from the publisher:
FHG Guides, Abbey Mill Business Centre, Seedhill, Paisley PA1 1TJ
Tel: 0141 887 0428 • Fax: 0141 889 7204
• e-mail: admin@fhguides.co.uk • www.holidayguides.com

Somerset & Wiltshire

MINEHEAD

Family Fun Activities: New look seafront with extensive sandy beach • Aquasplash Leisure Pool with wave machine • cruises and steam train rides • Horse riding and walking on nearby Exmoor • Theatre • Classic Car Collection • Butlins Family Entertainment Resort with a host of attractions including funfair, go karts, cinema, leisure pool and live shows.

☆ **Special Events: Late April/early May:** Hobby Horse festivities. **July:** Minehead and Exmoor Festival; Friends of Thomas the Tank Engine Weekend.

ⓘ Tourist Information Centre,
17 Friday Street, Minehead TA24 5UB
01643 702624 • Fax: 01643 707166
e-mail: mineheadtic@visit.org.uk
www.minehead.co.uk

Beaches

• **MINEHEAD STRAND BEACH.** Wide sandy beach with access down ramps from new sea wall. Ample parking. *Safety and maintenance:* cleaned daily. *Beach facilities:* cafe and takeaway food outlets; toilets with ♿ access. *Dog restrictions:* not allowed on beach from 1st May to 30th September; must be kept on lead on promenade.

• **MINEHEAD TERMINUS BEACH.** A mixture of sand and pebbles (continuation of the Strand in a westwards direction). *Facilities and Dog Restrictions:* as for Strand beach.

WESTON-SUPER-MARE

Family Fun Activities: The SeaQuarium • Grand Pier with amusements, land train, miniature railway, kids' play area • Marine lake • Donkey rides, amusements • Leisure centre • Tennis, putting, bowls, pitch and putt, ten-pin bowling, riding, rugby, football, cricket, fishing, golf • Cinema, museum, shows, night clubs, live music.

☆ **Special Events:** for a full up-to-date listing of events visit
www.somersetcoast.com
or call the Tourist Information Centre. Events include national waterski races, Helidays, children's activities, Playhouse shows, motorcycle beach race and carnival.

ⓘ Tourist Information Centre,
Beach Lawns, Weston-super-Mare BS23
1AT 01934 888800
Minicom: 01934 643172
westontouristinfo@n-somerset.gov.uk
www.somersetcoast.com

Beaches

• **BEACH.** Two miles long, sandy with rock pools and shingle at Anchor Head. Promenade and piers; good parking. *Safety and maintenance:* beach cleaned daily all year. *Beach facilities:* deck chairs, donkeys and pony carts, marine lake and fun castle; ice-cream kiosks, snack bars, restaurants and pubs; toilets, some with ♿ access. *Dog restrictions:* dog ban on section of main beach between May and September.

The Classified Listing Section
on pages 141-149 is a quick, easy to use summary of the facilities offered by the accommodation featured in this guide.

Somerset & Wiltshire

☆ Fun for all the Family ☆

◆ **Avon Valley Railway, near Bristol (0117 932 5538).** Working railway museum with locos and coaches. Enjoy a 5-mile trip along the lovely River Avon valley.
www.avonvalleyrailway.co.uk

◆ **Bee World and Animal Centre, Stogumber (01984 656545).** Unravel the mysteries of bee-keeping and meet lots of friendly animals at this unique "hands-on" centre. Children's play area.

◆ **Bristol Zoo (0117 974 7300).** Extensive and fascinating collection including pygmy hippos and gorillas. Over 300 species from lions to dung beetles.
www.bristolzoo.org.uk

◆ **Cheddar Caves & Gorge (01934 742343).** Famous for its caves and underground pools, in a deep winding fissure in the Mendip Hills. Exhibitions.
www.chedddarcaves.co.uk

◆ **Cricket St Thomas Wildlife Park, near Chard (01460 30111).** Large collection of wild animals and birds in 1000 acres of woodland and lakes.
www.cstwp.co.uk

◆ **Haynes Motor Museum, Sparkford, Near Yeovil (01963 440804).** Magnificent collection of over 250 vintage, veteran and classic cars, and 50 motorcycles. Experience 100 smiles per hour!
www.haynesmotormuseum.co.uk

◆ **Longleat Safari Park, Warminster (01985 844400).** 100-acre reserve for lions, giraffes, monkeys, zebras and tigers roaming free. World's longest hedge maze, Postman Pat village.
www.longleat.co.uk

◆ **Rode Bird Gardens, near Bath (01373 830326).** 17 acres of beautifully laid out grounds with hundreds of exquisitely coloured birds. Children's play area.

◆ **SS Great Britain, Bristol (0117 926 0680).** Splendid six-masted ocean going vessel dating from 1843 and associated with engineering genius Isambard Kingdom Brunel.
www.ss-great-britain.com

◆ **STEAM - Museum of Great Western Railway, Swindon (01793 466646).** Fun hands-on exhibits and rare archive footage tell the story of this famous railway company.
www.steam-museum.org.uk

◆ **West Somerset Railway, Bishops Lydeard (01643 704996).** A nostalgic journey through the unspoilt beauty of the Quantock Hills and along the coast; Visitor Centre and model railway.
www.west-somerset-railway.co.uk

◆ **Wookey Hole, Wells (01749 672243).** Britain's most spectacular caves, with dramatic lighting effects. Also paper making demonstrations, Magical Mirror Maze.
www.wookey.co.uk

Readers are requested to mention this FHG guidebook when seeking accommodation

Somerset & Wiltshire 71

Spinney Farmhouse ~ Thoulstone, Chapmanslade, Westbury BA13 4AQ

Off A36, three miles west of Warminster; 16 miles from historic city of Bath. Close to Longleat, Cheddar and Stourhead. Reasonable driving distance to Bristol, Stonehenge, Glastonbury and the cathedral cities of Wells and Salisbury. Pony trekking and fishing available locally.

- Washbasins, tea/coffee-making facilities and shaver points in all rooms.
- Family room available. • Guests' lounge with colour TV.
- Central heating. • Children and pets welcome.
- Ample parking. • Open all year. • No smoking.

Enjoy farm fresh food in a warm, friendly family atmosphere.
Bed and Breakfast from £23 per night. Reduction after 2 nights.
Evening Meal £12.

Telephone 01373 832412 • Madeline Hoskins & Family

BATCH COUNTRY HOTEL
LYMPSHAM, NEAR WESTON-SUPER-MARE
SOMERSET BS24 0EX
Tel: 01934 750371 • Fax: 01934 750501

★ Family-run Hotel with friendly atmosphere and excellent food ★ Fully licensed Lounge Bar ★ Own grounds with unlimited parking, spacious lawns ★ All bedrooms en suite with colour TV, tea/coffee making facilities ★ Golfers most welcome ★ Reduced terms for children ★ Credit cards accepted ★ Easy access from M5 motorway

Weston, Burnham, Brean and Worlebury Golf Courses all within 10 minutes' drive

Weston-Super-Mare Hotels and Restaurants Merit Award

www.batchcountryhotel.co.uk

RAC ★★ Hotel | AA ★★

A Taste of Somerset...

Come and enjoy the beauty of Somerset for that relaxing break. Wick House is a charming old family house in the picturesque West Somerset village of Stogumber, in an area of outstanding beauty, where many country pursuits are available. We offer a friendly, informal atmosphere and high standard of accommodation. All bedrooms are en suite, with television and tea/coffee making facilities. A full English breakfast is served, evening meals by prior arrangement.
Disabled accommodation available • Children of all ages welcome

Tel: 01984 656422   Credit cards accepted
e-mail: sheila@wickhouse.fsbusiness.co.uk
www.wickhouse.fsbusiness.co.uk

Wick House
Brook Street, Stogumber, Somerset TA4 3SZ
Bed & Breakfast Accommodation

ST AUDRIES BAY Holiday Club
West Quantoxhead, Near Minehead, Somerset TA4 4DY
Tel: 01984 632515

- Family-owned and run award-winning Park near Exmoor and The Quantocks
- 15 miles from the M5 • Fantastic views across the sea and beach access
- Sport & leisure facilities • Entertainment • Licensed bars and restaurant
- Coffee Shop • On-site shop • Children's play area
- Peaceful relaxing Park with family time in school holidays

Self-Catering & Half-Board Holidays • Touring Caravans & Camping • Luxury Holiday Homes for sale

e-mail: info@staudriesbay.co.uk • www.staudriesbay.co.uk

HAMPSHIRE & DORSET

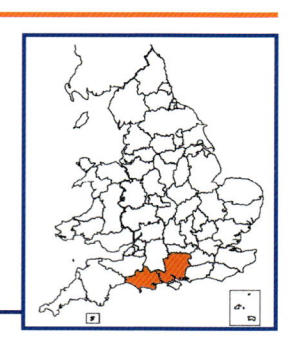

Best Beaches

No less than nine beaches in the area have won European Blue Flag Awards for 2006, and Seaside Awards have been gained by Weymouth Central, and two beaches at Bournemouth: Bournemouth Pier and Boscombe Pier

BLUE FLAG BEACHES 2006
- **Bournemouth**
   - Fisherman's Walk
   - Alum Chine
   - Durley Chine
   - Southbourne
- **Poole**
   - Canford Cliffs Chine
   - Sandbanks
   - Shore Road
   - Branksome Chine
- **Swanage Central**

South East England Tourist Board
- Tel: 023 8062 5400
- Fax: 023 8062 0010
- e-mail: enquiries@tourismse.com
- www.visitsoutheastengland.com

South West Tourism
(Bristol & Bath, Cornwall, Devon, Dorset, Gloucestershire & The Cotswolds, Somerset, Wiltshire).

- Tel: 0870 442 0880
- Fax: 0870 442 0881
- e-mail: post@swtourism.co.uk
- www.westcountrynow.com
- www.visitsouthwest.co.uk

For information about Britain's Best Beaches
see pages 39-44

Readers are requested to mention this FHG guidebook when seeking accommodation

BOURNEMOUTH

Family Fun Activities: Seven miles of golden sand, first-class attractions, beautiful gardens and summer festivals offer something for everyone from the Oceanarium to the Bournemouth International Centre and the Russell-Cotes Museum. There is plenty to do whatever the weather. Try the Bournemouth Eye tethered balloon ride.
Free 'Family Fun' brochure available on request from Visitor Information Bureau.

Special Events: School Summer Holidays: Kids Fun Festival with more than 100 free shows and activities. Sporting events, competitions and festivals take place throughout the year.

Visitor Information Bureau, Westover Road, Bournemouth BH1 2BU
Information line and accommodation enquiries: 0845 0511700
e-mail: info@bournemouth.gov.uk
www.bournemouth.co.uk

Beaches

- **BEACH.** 7 miles long, sandy with traffic-free promenade, reached by zig-zag paths or cliff lifts. *Safety and maintenance:* lifeguard patrols, close-circuit TV surveillance, first-aid posts; cleaned twice daily. *Beach facilities:* children's beach GameZone in summer; rowing boats, pedalos, speed boats, kayaks, surfing; beach hut hire. "No Smoking" zones. Special 'Kidzone' safety areas. Excellent catering facilities. *Dog restrictions:* Dog-friendly sections of beach at Fisherman's Walk and Alum Chine between May and September inclusive; allowed on the promenade on lead.

POOLE

Family Fun Activities: Poole Quay with shops, crafts, museums, Poole pottery, restaurants • Crab lining, fishing trips, harbour boat trips, wind-surfing and sailing in Europe's largest natural harbour • Brownsea Island and road train • Poole Park with Gus Gorilla's indoor playground, crazy golf, Poole Park train • Sports centres with swimming, badminton, squash, etc • Tower Park Entertainment Centre with cinema, Megabowl, Splashdown, restaurants etc • Monkey World.
Free 'Family Fun' brochure available on request from Poole Tourist Office.

Special Events: May/September: programme of spectacular weekday events featuring motorcycles, car nostalgia, fireworks, speedway, live entertainment, children's activities. **September:** Animal Windfest.

Poole Welcome Centre, Enefco House, Poole Quay, Poole BH15 1HJ
01202 253253
e-mail: tourism@pooletourism.com
www.pooletourism.com

Beaches

- **BEACH.** Three miles of sands stretching from Sandbanks to Branksome Dene Chine. 7 car parks. *Safety and maintenance:* cleaned daily; lifeguard coverage in main season, beach station at Sandbanks manned throughout year. *Beach facilities:* beach huts, deckchairs and windbreaks for hire; watersports; ice-cream kiosks, snacks and cafe; toilets with ♿ facilities. *Dog restrictions:* banned from main beaches from May to September, must be kept on lead on promenade at all times.

Visit the FHG website   www.holidayguides.com

Hampshire & Dorset

SWANAGE

Family Fun Activities: Bowling green, tennis, putting, crazy golf, 18-hole pitch and putt course, trampolines • Swanage Bay View Restaurant • Holiday park with swimming pool, skittle alley, indoor bowls and trimnasium • Water ski-ing, windsurfing, sailing, motor boats, sea angling • Castle, lighthouse, country park • Theatre/cinema.

☆ **Special Events: July:** Swanage Jazz Festival. **August:** Regatta and Carnival Week. **September:** Swanage Folk Festival

i Tourist Information Centre, Shore Road, Swanage BH19 1LB • 0870 4420680
e-mail: mail@swanage.gov.uk
www.swanage.gov.uk

Beaches

• **SWANAGE BAY BEACH.** Three miles long, sandy and naturally sheltered; promenade and good parking. *Safety and maintenance:* cleaned daily. *Beach facilities:* deck chairs, Punch and Judy; pedalcraft; toilets with ♿ facilities. *Dog restrictions:* banned from main beach from 1st May to 30th September; must be kept on lead on promenade.

WEYMOUTH

Family Fun Activities: Country Park with Model World, Sea Life Park, Miniature Railway, Mini-Golf, Leisure Ranch and RSPB Nature Reserve • Weymouth Old Harbour including Brewers Quay Complex and Weymouth Timewalk, Deep Sea Adventure, Nothe Fort and Gardens, Tudor House. • Pleasure cruises, float and boat hire, sailing, sub-aqua sports • Tennis, bowls • Swimming pool • Theatre with family shows, cinemas, night clubs • Superbowl

☆ **Special Events: May:** Beach Kite Festival, Trawler Race and Water Carnival. **July/August:** Beach Volleyball Championships. **August:** weekly Firework Festival, Weymouth Carnival. **October:** Beach Motocross.

i Tourist Information, King's Statue, Weymouth • 01305 785747
e-mail: tourism@weymouth.gov.uk
www.weymouth.gov.uk

Beaches

• **WEYMOUTH BAY BEACH.** Two and a half miles long, sand running into shingle; promenade and piers. *Safety and maintenance:* Beach Control Centre, lifeguards; first aid and lost children post; beach cleaned daily. *Beach facilities:* deck chairs, Punch and Judy, trampolines, amusement arcades; floats, canoes; ice-cream kiosks, restaurants and pubs; toilets with ♿ facilities. *Dog restrictions:* dogs restricted to special areas May-September.

FREE AND REDUCED RATE HOLIDAY VISITS!
Don't miss our
Readers' Offer Vouchers
on pages 9-38

Hampshire & Dorset

☆ Fun for all the Family ☆

◆ **Beaulieu (01590 612345).** National Motor Museum – motoring heritage brought back to life. Includes James Bond Experience. Also 13th century Abbey and Monastic Life exhibition.
www.beaulieu.co.uk

◆ **Brownsea Island (NT), Poole Harbour.** 200-acre nature reserve with marsh, salt water lagoon and two lakes. Safe, sandy beaches, nature trail; restaurant.
www.nationaltrust.org.uk

◆ **Dinosaur Museum, Dorchester (01305 269741).** Children of all ages love these scaly creatures, so make for this superb "hands on" exhibition dedicated entirely to dinosaurs.
www.thedinosaurmuseum.com

◆ **Marwell Zoological Park, near Winchester (01962 777407).** 200-acre park with rare wild animals including tigers, zebras, cheetahs, leopards, etc. Children's zoo, picnic area, cafe.
www.marwell.org.uk

◆ **New Forest Museum and Visitor Centre, Lyndhurst (023 8028 3444).** Learn the story of the Forest in an audio-visual show; gift shop specialising in local crafts.
www.newforestmuseum.org.uk

◆ **Paultons Park, near Romsey (023 8081 4442).** A fun-filled day out at this family leisure park with rides and thrills galore. Over 40 attractions/rides.
www.paultonspark.co.uk

◆ **Blue Reef Aquarium, Portsmouth (02392 875222).** Innovative displays provide an insight into the mysterious world of the deep. Restaurant and children's attractions.
www.bluereefaquarium.co.uk

◆ **Tank Museum, Bovington, near Wareham (01929 405096).** Tanks and armoured cars from all over the world; "drive a tank" simulator; gift shop and restaurant.
www.tankmuseum.co.uk

Hampshire & Dorset

Lulworth Cove, Dorset
Cromwell House Hotel

Catriona and Alistair Miller welcome guests to their comfortable family-run hotel, set in secluded gardens with spectacular sea views. Situated 200 yards from Lulworth Cove, with direct access to the Jurassic Coast. A heated swimming pool is available for guests' use from May to October.

Accommodation is in 17 en suite bedrooms, with TV, direct-dial telephone, and tea/coffee making facilities; most have spectacular sea views. Restaurant, bar wine list. Two nights dinner, bed and breakfast (fully en suite) from £114 per person. Off-peak midweek breaks all year except Christmas.

Cromwell House Hotel, Lulworth Cove, Dorset BH20 5RJ
Tel: 01929 400253/400332 • Fax: 01929 400566
ETC/AA/RAC ★★

website: www.lulworthcove.co.uk

Laurel Lodge
Tel: 01425 618309

Ideally situated for the delights of the New Forest, scenic cliff top walks, local beaches, pleasure cruises to the Isle of Wight, the Needles and historic Hurst Castle, horse riding, cycling, golf and a whole host of indoor and outdoor pursuits. Laurel Lodge is a comfortable, centrally heated, converted bungalow, offering twin, double & family rooms, all fully en suite with tea and coffee making facilities, comfortable chairs, colour TV and alarm clock radio. Ground floor rooms available. Breakfast is served in our conservatory/diningroom with views over the garden. Bed and Breakfast from £25 per person. Special deals for longer breaks. Children welcome, cot and high chair supplied by prior arrangement. Off-road parking for all rooms. Strictly no smoking. Open all year. *Please phone Lee & Melanie Snook for further details.*
48 Western Avenue, Barton-on-Sea, Hampshire BH25 7PZ

FREE AND REDUCED RATE HOLIDAY VISITS!
Don't miss our **READERS' OFFER VOUCHERS** on pages 9-38

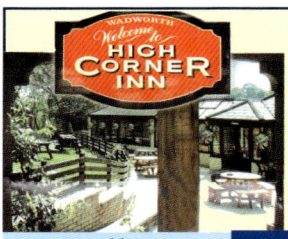

The High Corner Inn

Nestled deep in the heart of the New Forest, the High Corner Inn is set in 7 beautiful acres of woodland. Both oak-beamed bars have open fireplaces and views across the patio and gardens. Children are welcome, and will delight in playing in the outdoor adventure playground.

A full range of Wadworth cask-conditioned ales is available, as well as an excellent selection of wines and spirits. We serve a wide range of quality home-cooked meals, bar snacks, plus a Sunday carvery.

Accommodation is available in 7 en suite double bedrooms, all with colour TV and tea/coffee facilities.

Dogs and horses are welcome – stables and paddocks are available for DIY livery.

The High Corner Inn
Near Linwood, Ringwood, Hampshire BH24 3QY
Tel: 01425 473973 • www.highcornerinn.com

DENEWOOD HOTEL
40 Sea Road,
Bournemouth BH5 1BQ
Tel: 01202 309913
Fax: 01202 391155
www.denewood.co.uk

Warm, friendly hotel in excellent central location, just 500 yards from the beach and close to the shops. Good parking. Single, twin, double and family rooms available, all en suite. Residential and restaurant licence. TV, tea/coffee and biscuits in rooms. Health salon and spa on site. Open all year. Children and pets welcome. Please check out our website.

Bed and Breakfast from £22.50-£25. Special weekly rates available and Short Break discounts.

THE KNOLL HOUSE
Studland Bay

A peaceful oasis and wonderful atmosphere
where families matter
~
Easy access to three miles of golden beach
Outdoor pool (level deck), golf and tennis for all ages
Health Spa with plunge pool and sauna
~
Connecting rooms for families with children
Separate younger children's restaurant
Playroom and fabulous Adventure Playground
~
Open Easter - end October. Dogs also welcome

Studland Bay
Dorset
BH19 3AF
01929 · 450450
info@knollhouse.co.uk
www.knollhouse.co.uk

ONLY 2 HOURS FROM HEATHROW

Hampshire & Dorset

Cardsmill Farm Holidays

**Whitchurch Canonicorum, Charmouth
Bridport, Dorset DT6 6RP
Tel & Fax: 01297 489375 • e-mail: cardsmill@aol.com
website: www.farmhousedorset.com**

Stay on a real working family farm in the Marshwood Vale, an Area of Outstanding Natural Beauty. Enjoy country walks to the village, coast and around farm and woods. Watch the daily milking, see baby calves and lambs, and seasonal activities here on this 590 acre farm. En suite family, double and twin rooms available, with CTV, tea/coffee trays.
Also available, three large, rural, quiet farmhouses. Each has private garden, double glazed conservatory and ample parking. TAPHOUSE has 6 bedrooms, 3 bathrooms, lounge, 22'x15' kitchen/diner. COURTHOUSE FARMHOUSE and DAIRY each have 4 bedrooms and 2 or 3 bathrooms. Games room, parking, separate gardens. All have C/H, dishwasher, washing machine and very well equipped kitchen/diner/lounge.
All available all year for long or short stays. Brochure available, or check the website. **B&B £24–£30pppn**

Tamarisk Farm

**West Bexington, Dorchester DT2 9DF
Tel/Fax: 01308 897784   Mrs J. Pearse**

On slope overlooking Chesil beach between Abbotsbury and Burton Bradstock.
Four large (Mimosa is wheelchair disabled Cat. M3(i) and Granary Lodge M1 is disabled-friendly, awaiting inspection) and two small cottages. Each one stands in own fenced garden.
Glorious views along West Dorset and Devon coasts. Lovely walks by sea and inland. Part of mixed organic farm with arable, sheep, cattle, horses and market garden (organic vegetables, meat and wholemeal flour available). Sea fishing, riding in Portesham and Burton Bradstock, lots of tourist attractions and good markets. Good centre for touring Thomas Hardy's Wessex. Safe for children and excellent for dogs. Very quiet. Terms from £250 to £995.
e-mail: holidays@tamariskfarm.com • • www.holidays/tamariskfarm.com

Mimosa
Two Wings
Granary Lodge

Lancombes House ~ Holiday Cottages

ETC ★★★

Four superbly converted cottages, each with its own sitting-out area, barbecue and garden furniture. Some have fenced gardens. Spacious open plan living areas, most with wood burning stoves. Deep in the heart of Hardy country, this is a delightful area to explore whether on foot or horseback. There are many things to do and pets and children are very welcome. Prices start at £120 for mini-breaks; open all the year round.
**Lancombes House, West Milton, Bridport DT6 3TN
Tel: 01308 485375 • www.lancombeshouse.co.uk**

Dormer Cottage

"Dormer Cottage", Woodlands, Hyde, Near Wareham

This secluded cottage, cosy and modern, is a converted old barn of Woodlands House. Standing in its own grounds, it is fronted by a small wood with a walled paddock at the back. Pleasant walks in wooded forests nearby. In the midst of "Hardy Country" and ideal for a family holiday and for those who value seclusion. All linen included, beds ready made on guests' arrival and basic shopping arranged on request. Amusements at Bournemouth, Poole and Dorchester within easy reach. Five people and a baby can be accommodated in two double and one single bedrooms; cot and high chair available.
Bathroom, two toilets; lounge and diningroom, colour TV. Kitchen with cooker, fridge, washing machine, small deep freeze, etc. Pets welcome.
Open all year. Golf course half-mile; pony trekking, riding nearby. SAE, please, for terms.
Mrs M.J.M. Constantinides, "Woodlands", Hyde, Near Wareham BH20 7NT (01929 471239)

ISLE OF WIGHT

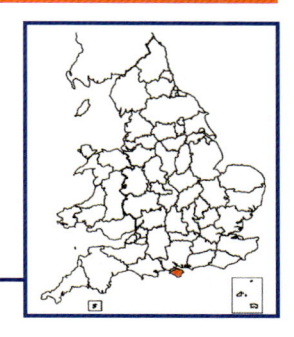

Best Beaches

The varied coastline of the Isle of Wight includes many safe, sandy beaches. Several have won a Seaside Award in the rural category, for beaches which are quieter, and are usually enjoyed for their simplicity rather than their facilities.

BLUE FLAG BEACHES 2006

- *Shanklin*
- *Sandown*

Isle of Wight Tourism
- Tel: 01983 813813
- Fax: 01983 823031
- e-mail: info@islandbreaks.co.uk
- www.islandbreaks.co.uk

Children Welcome!

Ryde, Sea View & St Helens

Family Fun Activities: Boating lake, bowling alley, swimming pool, ice skating rink, cinema • Dotto train along seafront and into town • Flamingo Park where children can hand-feed penguins, macaws and parrots • Travel back in time on the Isle of Wight steam railway.

Special Events: July: Ryde Regatta. August/September: Ryde Carnival.

Beaches

- **BEACH.** Coastline three-and-a-half miles long; sand at Ryde, rockpools at Seaview; ample parking. *Safety and maintenance:* inshore rescue; cleaned daily. *Beach facilities:* canoe lake on esplanade, swimming pools, playground, mini fun fair, trampolines; snack bars and restaurants (some licensed); toilets with & access. *Dog restrictions:* banned on main areas of beach from 1st May to 30th September; must be kept on lead on promenade; "poop scoop" regulations in force.

Sandown & Lake

Family Fun Activities: Fishing, tennis, basketball, putting, pitch and putt, crazy golf • Pier with bowling and other attractions • Street market • Zoo • Leisure centre • Dinosaur Isle • Dotto train • Go-karts.

Isle of Wight

⭐ **Special Events:** **July/August:** Carnival. **August:** Regatta. **October:** White Air Extreme Sports Festival.

Beaches

• **BEACH.** Approximately three miles long, sandy with cliffs at back; promenade, pier complex with bar, restaurant, amusements and boat trips. *Safety and maintenance:* warning flags, lifeguards; cleaned daily in season. Kidzone in selected parts. *Beach facilities:* deck chairs, windsurfing, pedalcraft, children's entertainment; snack bars on promenade open during summer season; toilets with ♿ access. *Dog restrictions:* banned from main areas of beach from 1st May to 30th September; "poop scoop" regulations in force.

Ventnor

Family Fun Activities: Botanic Gardens and Winter Gardens with regular entertainment • Golf • Paddling pool • Marina • Nearby Blackgang Chine has attractions and rides for the whole family.

⭐ **Special Events:** **April:** Jazz Divas. **August:** Carnival.

Beaches

• **BEACH.** Approximately quarter-of-a-mile long; mainly sand, some shingle; promenade. *Safety and maintenance:* cleaned daily. *Beach facilities:* deck chairs; snack bars and restaurants, amusements; public house; toilets with ♿ access. *Dog restrictions:* banned on main beach areas from 1st May to 30th September; "poop scoop" regulations in force.

Colwell & Totland

Small resort on Totland Bay, three miles south-west of Yarmouth.

Beaches

• **BEACH.** One-and-a-half miles long; sandy at Colwell, sand with some shingle at Totland; sea wall connects the two bays. *Safety and maintenance:* partly cleaned daily in season. *Beach facilities:* deck chairs and paddlecraft at Colwell; snacks and ice-cream at both locations. *Dog restrictions:* not allowed on Colwell beach between 1st May and 30th September.

Shanklin

Family Fun Activities: Water activities • Indoor play area, crazy golf, golf, putting • Dotto train • Cliff lift to town.

⭐ **Special Events:** Shanklin Theatre shows. **August:** Shanklin Town regatta and sea events.

Beaches

• **BEACH.** Sandy beach, access via cliff lift; two-mile long promenade connects town to Sandown. Shanklin Chine illuminated on summer evenings. *Beach facilities:* refreshments, toilets; deck chairs, beach huts. *Dog restrictions:* banned from main beach from 1st May to 30th September.

Yarmouth

One of the oldest towns on the Island with a busy harbour. Boat trips to Needles from pier. Nearby attractions include Fort Victoria, Dimbola Lodge and Dinosaur Farm Museum.

⭐ **Special Events:** **June:** Old Gaffers Festival.

Beaches

• **BEACH.** Shingle beach with pier; swimming at Sandhard area. *Beach facilities:* refreshments; toilets. *Dog restrictions:* must be kept on lead.

Isle of Wight

★ Fun for all the Family ★

◆ **Amazon World, Newchurch (01983 867122).** All-weather Amazon Rain Forest attraction with over 200 species of birds and animals. Falconry displays.
www.amazonworld.co.uk

◆ **Blackgang Chine, Chale (01983 730052).** 40 acres of cliff top gardens, exhibitions, fantasy attractions – Cowboy Town, Nurseryland, Giant Snakes 'n' Ladders, Water Force, a 100m high speed boat ride.
www.blackgangchine.com

◆ **Brickfields Horse Country, near Ryde (01983 566801).** From mighty Shires to miniature Shetland ponies. Unique collections of bygones, children's farm corner, restaurant and bar.
www.brickfields.net

◆ **Butterfly World and Fountain World, Wootton (01983 883430).** Hundreds of exotic butterflies and insects; displays of fountains and indoor gardens. Play area.

◆ **Dinosaur Isle, Sandown (01983 404344).** Exciting new exhibition centre in a spectacular pterosaur-shaped building, with life-size dinosaurs; guided fossil walks to sites of interest on the island.
www.dinosaurisle.com

◆ **Isle of Wight Steam Railway, Near Ryde (01983 882204).** 5½ mile round trip on genuine vintage train. Station at Havenstreet with museum, shop, cafe and bar.
www.iwsteamrailway.co.uk

◆ **Isle of Wight Zoo, Sandown (01983 405562).** Big cats, snakes and spiders. Cafe, play areas, animal contact area — be photographed with a snake!
www.isleofwightzoo.com

◆ **Natural History Centre, Godshill (01983 840333).** A fascinating display of tropical seashells, birds, butterflies and even a lizard embalmed in amber, all housed in a 17th century coach house.
www.shellmuseum.co.uk

◆ **Needles Park, Alum Bay (0870 458 0022).** A great family day out with attractions including chairlift, dare-devil rides, crazy golf, glass-making studio, sweet making; restaurant.
www.theneedles.co.uk

◆ **Osborne House, East Cowes (01983 200022).** Magnificent residence much loved by Queen Victoria. The 'Swiss Cottage' in the grounds was the playroom of the royal children; carriage rides through the grounds.

◆ **Robin Hill Country Park, near Newport (01983 527352).** Activities for all ages: Time Machine and Colossus rides; Countryside Centre, Play Village, Splash Attack and lots more.
www.robin-hill.com

◆ **Shipwreck Centre and Maritime Museum, Bembridge (01983 872223/ 873125).** Museum devoted to local maritime heritage. Shipwreck artefacts, ship models, diving equipment etc.

◆ **Isle of Wight Wax Works, Brading (01983 407286/0870 4584477).** World-famous museum set in 11th century rectory mansion. Visit the Chamber of Horrors and Animal World.

Isle of Wight

Orchardcroft Hotel

One of the best value quality hotels on the Isle of Wight

- Heated covered swimming pool • Jacuzzi • Sauna • Games room with snooker, table football & large screen TV • Reputation for good food and wines • Family rooms and child discounts • Ground floor rooms and Senior Citizen discounts • Smoking and non smoking public areas and rooms • Child-friendly with high chairs, cots and baby monitors • Ferry inclusive packages available • Well behaved pets accepted at our discretion

You will have trouble finding another hotel on the Island with these facilities at our prices

Orchardcroft Hotel, Victoria Avenue, Shanklin, Isle of Wight PO37 6LT • Tel: 01983 862133
www.orchardcroft.co.uk • admin@orchardcroft.co.uk

Frenchman's Cove
ALUM BAY OLD ROAD, TOTLAND, ISLE OF WIGHT PO39 0HZ

Our delightful family-run guesthouse is set amongst National Trust downland, not far from the Needles and safe sandy beaches. Ideal for ramblers, birdwatchers, cyclists and those who enjoy the countryside. We have almost an acre of grounds. Cots and high chairs are available. All rooms are en suite, with colour TV and tea/coffee making facilities. Guests can relax in the attractive lounges. Also available is the Coach House, a well appointed self-catering apartment (ETC 3 Stars) for two adults and two children. No smoking. No pets.

Please contact Sue or Chris Boatfield for details.
Tel: 01983 752227 • www.frenchmanscove.co.uk

FERNSIDE HOTEL

30 Station Avenue, Sandown, Isle of Wight PO36 9BW
Tel: 01983 402356 •• Fax: 01983 403647
e-mail: enquiries@fernsidehotel.co.uk •• www.fernsidehotel.co.uk

This family-run hotel is ideally situated within walking distance of sandy beaches, town centre and visitor attractions - the perfect location for a relaxing and enjoyable holiday or short break.

- Bed & Breakfast accommodation
- 11 comfortable en suite rooms (all non-smoking). Ground floor and family rooms (cots available).
- Remote-control colour TV and tea/coffee in all rooms, comfortable lounge with books, magazines and games
- Traditional full English breakfasts served in our dining room.

SANDHILL HOTEL

6 Hill Street, Sandown, Isle of Wight PO36 9DB
Tel: 01983 403635 • Fax: 01983 403695

Trevor Sawtell and family welcome you to a friendly family hotel five minutes' walk from the beach and train station. All rooms are en suite, with colour TV, tea/coffee and telephone with internet ports. We have a reputation for quality food served in our comfortable dining room, and after dinner, why not take a stroll in nearby Los Altos Park. Bed and Breakfast from £37. Bed, Breakfast and Evening Meal (five courses) from £42 per night. Special rates for children. Disabled friendly. Please call for brochure.

e-mail: sandhillhotel@btconnect.com • www.sandhill-hotel.com

Isle of Wight

83

ISLAND COTTAGE HOLIDAYS

ETC ★★★ to ★★★★★

Charming individual cottages in lovely rural surroundings and close to the sea. Over 65 cottages situated throughout the Isle of Wight. Beautiful views, attractive gardens, delightful country walks.

All equipped to a high standard and graded for quality by the Tourist Board.

For a brochure please **Tel: (01929) 480080** • **Fax: (01929) 481070**
e-mail: enq@islandcottageholidays.com • website: www.islandcottageholidays.com
Open all year (Sleep 1 - 12) £185 – £1595 per week. Short breaks available in low season (3 nights) from £155.

HILLGROVE PARK
Field Lane, St Helens, Ryde PO33 1UT

Rose award park

A small, secluded, family-run holiday caravan park. Only minutes from safe sandy beaches, beautiful countryside and places of interest. Try our centrally heated units for that early or late season break. *Heated swimming pool, large play areas for both older and younger children, games room. Car ferries arranged on any route.*

For details ring (01983) 872802 *or visit our website* **www.hillgrove.co.uk**

See the
Family-Friendly Pubs & Inns

Supplement on pages 150-154 for establishments which really welcome children

LYON COURT
Westhill Road, Shanklin PO37 6PZ
Tel: 01983 865861

An elegant country house, under the personal supervision of owners, Paul and Sandra Humphreys. Just a 10 minute walk from Shanklin Old Village with its thatched cottages and nearby sandy beaches. Tastefully converted to provide nine individual self-catering apartments, sleeping from 2 to 6.

Large landscaped garden • Enclosed heated pool and spa pool • Sauna • Children's play area with Wendy house, climbing frames and swings
• Separate toddlers' play area • Garden toys
• Video library • Cots & high chairs provided
• Pets Corner• Open all year
Prices from £275 to £760
Short breaks available in low season
info@lyoncourtshanklin.co.uk
www.lyoncourtshanklin.co.uk

SUSSEX

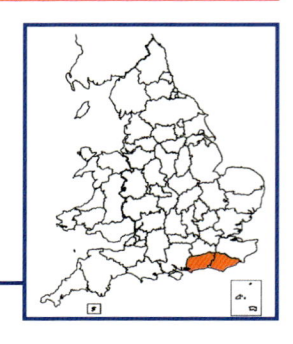

Best Beaches

Beaches at Bexhill and Worthing are among the winners of the 2006 Seaside Award (Resort Category) after meeting a variety of strict criteria.

South East England Tourist Board
- Tel: 023 8062 5400
- Fax: 023 8062 0010
- e-mail: enquiries@tourismse.com
- www.visitsoutheastengland.com

BLUE FLAG BEACHES 2006
- *West Wittering*
- *Littlehampton*
- *Eastbourne*
- *Bognor Regis*

Sussex

BRIGHTON

⚓ Family Fun Activities: Brighton Pier, Sea Life Centre, Royal Pavilion, Brighton Museum, British Engineerium, Preston Manor, Foredown Tower, West Blatchington Windmill, Fishing Museum, National Museum of Penny Slot Machines; Marina Village • Fishing, boat trips, windsurfing, sailing • Horse racing, greyhound racing • 10-pin bowling, putting, crazy golf, pitch and putt, golf courses, skate boarding, roller blading, ice skating, tennis, squash, bowls, badminton, cycle hire, indoor swimming pools • Cinemas, theatres, nightclubs, discos • Churchill Square, North Laine and Lanes shopping districts with family-friendly restaurants and cafes.

☆ **Special Events:** **May:** Brighton Festival. **June:** London-Brighton Bike Ride. **July:** Kite Festival. **August:** Circus. **November:** Veteran Car Run.

ℹ️ Visitor Information Centre,
10 Bartholomew Square, Brighton BN1 1JS
0906 7112255 – premium rate
brighton-tourism@brighton-hove.gov.uk
www.visitbrighton.com

🏖 Beaches

• **BEACH.** 7 miles long, shingle and rockpools; cliff walk, promenade with Volks Railway, pier with funfair and arcades. Artists' and fishing quarters. Naturist area at eastern end of promenade, near marina; warning flags, lifeguards (some undertow at extreme eastern end); cleaned daily in season. *Beach facilities:* deck chairs; ramp and lift to lower promenade; paddling pool, new children's play area; volleyball, basketball; showers; ice-cream kiosks, snack bars, restaurants and pubs; toilets with ♿ access, baby changing facilities. *Dog restrictions:* dogs allowed from West Pier to Hove boundary and from Volks Railway to Banjo Groyne. Not allowed on any other part of the beach.

BOGNOR REGIS

⚓ Family Fun Activities: Free summer Sunday afternoon bandstand concerts on Promenade and in Hotham Park • Playgrounds, amusement arcades, tennis, putting, crazy golf, golf course, sailing • Cinema • Day visitors welcome at Butlins Family Entertainment Centre • Miniature railway in Hotham Park.

☆ **Special Events:** Various events throughout the summer including: carnival and fair, Bognor Birdman (the original), Bognor Live!, Sands of Time Seaside Festival, Illumination Gala and Procession.

ℹ️ Visitor Information Centre, Belmont Street, Bognor Regis • 01243 823140
e-mail: bognorregis.vic@arun.gov.uk
www.sussexbythesea.com

🏖 Beaches

• **BEACH.** 8 miles long, sand and shingle, naturally sheltered; promenade and pier with arcades; ample voucher parking. *Safety and maintenance:* warning signs, rocks at low tide; cleaned regularly. *Beach facilities:* deck chairs, showers, children's play area; Kidcare Scheme along 50-metre stretch of seafront; seafront landtrain; ice-cream kiosks, snack bars, restaurants, pubs; toilets (toilets with ♿ access on sea front). *Dog restrictions:* not allowed on main beach from May to September.

FREE AND REDUCED RATE HOLIDAY VISITS!
Don't miss our
READERS' OFFER VOUCHERS
on pages 9-38

EASTBOURNE

**Tourist Information Centre, Cornfield Road, Eastbourne BN21 4QL
0906 711 2212 (calls cost 50p per minute)
e-mail: tic@eastbourne.gov.uk
www.visiteastbourne.com**

Family Fun Activities: Fort Fun and Treasure Island theme parks, Miniature Steam Railway, Sovereign Centre, Knockhatch Adventure Park, Drusillas Zoo, Seven Sisters Sheep Centre, Museum of Shops, Redoubt Fortress, Lifeboat Museum, historic Pevensey Castle and Michelham Priory, Victorian Pier with arcades, family pub and Camera Obscura • Multiplex cinema, four theatres, seafront bandstand, indoor karting, 10-pin bowling, tennis, mini-golf, Dotto Train, speedway stadium.

Special Events: May: Magnificent Motors. **June:** Classic Motorcycle Run, International Tennis Championships **July:** Emergency Services Display, Dragon Boat Racing Festival. **August:** International Air Show, Family Festival of Tennis, Tennis championships; It's a Knockout, South of England Tennis championships. **September:** MG South Downs Run. **October:** Victorian Festival, Beer Festival.

Beaches

- **BEACH.** Five miles of beaches; shingle, sand and rockpools; promenade and pier with arcades, seafront cycleway; Dotto Train service; ample parking. *Safety and maintenance:* warning flags, lifeguards; Kidzone wristband scheme, first aid, rookie lifeguard classes. *Beach facilities:* deck chairs, sun loungers, parasols, beach huts, paddlecraft, water sports, boat trips, seafront bandstand, Punch & Judy; ice-cream kiosks, snack bars, restaurants and pubs; showers, toilets with access and baby changing facilities.

Sussex

★ Fun for all the Family ★

◆ **1066 Battle Abbey and Battlefield, Battle (01424 773792).** Founded by William the Conqueror to commemorate the Battle of Hastings in 1066. The battle site, Abbey ruins and grounds are open to the public.

◆ **Bentley Wildfowl and Motor Museum, near Lewes (01825 840573).** Hundreds of waterfowl and wildlife, including flamingos, cranes and peacocks, in 23 acres.
www.bentley.org.uk

◆ **Bluebell Railway, near Uckfield (01825 720800).** Collection of veteran locos from 1865 to 1958. Trains steam through miles of Sussex countryside.
www.bluebellrailway.co.uk

◆ **Buckley's Yesterday's World, Battle (01424 775378).** Experience a day in a bygone age and explore the re-created shop and room displays. Children's activity areas, gift shop, teas.
www.yesterdaysworld.co.uk

◆ **Drusillas Park, Alfriston (01323 874100).** Collection of rare cattle, exotic flamingos, waterfowl, monkeys and parrots. Farm playground, miniature railway, shops.
www.drusillas.co.uk

◆ **Paradise Park, Newhaven (01273 512123).** Journey through time and see how plants and animals lived 200 million years ago. Miniature railway, gnome settlement.
www.paradisepark.co.uk

◆ **Royal Pavilion, Brighton (01273 290900).** The former seaside palace of George IV, with lavish Chinese-style interiors. Shop and tearoom.
www.royalpavilion.org.uk

◆ **Sea Life Centre Brighton (01273 604234).** Come face to face with thousands of fascinating sea creatures. Restaurants and shops.
www.sealife.co.uk

◆ **A Smuggler's Adventure, Hastings (01424 444412).** Relive the dangers and excitement that faced smugglers and customs men in times past. Displays and tableaux with life-sized figures.
www.smugglersadventure.co.uk

◆ **Weald and Downland Open Air Museum, near Chichester (01243 811363).** A collection of historic buildings, 16th century treadwheel etc saved from destruction. Heavy horses, shop, cafe.
www.wealddown.co.uk

See the *Family-Friendly Pubs & Inns* Supplement on pages 150-154 for establishments which really welcome children

Sussex

Situated in quiet private country lane one mile north of the market town of Hailsham with its excellent amenities including modern sports centre and leisure pool, surrounded by footpaths across open farmland. Ideal for country lovers. Dogs and children welcome. The coast at Eastbourne, South Downs, Ashdown Forest and 1066 country are all within easy access.

The non-smoking accommodation comprises one twin room, double room en suite; family room en suite and tea/coffee making facilities. Bed and Breakfast from £22. Reductions for children.

Tel & Fax: 01323 841227
www.longleysfarmcottage.co.uk

David and Jill Hook, Longleys Farm Cottage, Harebeating Lane, Hailsham BN27 1ER

Mrs G. Burgess
Polhills
Arlington, Polegate
East Sussex BN26 6SB
01323 870004

Idyllically situated on shore of reservoir and edge of Sussex Downs within easy reach of the sea. Fully furnished period cottage (approached by own drive along the water's edge) available for self-catering holidays from April to October (inclusive). Fly fishing for trout can be arranged during season. Accommodation consists of two double bedrooms; tiled bathroom. Lounge with colour TV; large well-fitted kitchen with fridge freezer, electric cooker, microwave, washing machine; dining room with put-u-up settee; sun lounge. Central heating. Linen supplied. Most rooms contain a wealth of oak beams. Car essential. Ample parking. Shops two miles. Golf, hill climbing locally. Sea eight miles.

Weekly terms from £295 to £340 (electricity included).

Chiddingly, East Sussex

Adorable, small, well-equipped cottage in grounds of Tudor Manor

- Two bedrooms • Full kitchen and laundry facilities
- Telephone • Use of indoor heated swimming pool, sauna/jacuzzi, tennis and badminton court • Large safe garden

From £385 – £730 per week inclusive • Pets and children welcome • Short Breaks £240-£340

Apply: Eva Morris, "Pekes", 124 Elm Park Mansions, Park Walk, London SW10 0AR
Tel: 020-7352 8088 Fax: 020-7352 8125 e-mail: pekes.afa@virgin.net web:www.pekesmanor.com

CROWHURST PARK

Telham Lane, Battle, East Sussex TN33 0SL
Telephone 01424 773344

Award-winning holiday park featuring luxury log cabin accommodation. Magnificent heated pool complex with children's paddling area, Jacuzzi, steam room, sauna, gym with cardiovascular and resistance training equipment, solarium, beauty therapies, aquafit classes, tennis court, children's adventure play area, restaurant, bars and clubhouse.
All this plus beautiful, historic 1066 Country on your doorstep and the Sussex coast just five miles away. Call for a brochure today.
Clubhouse, bars and restaurant all non-smoking from 1st March 2007
virtual tour: www.crowhurstpark.co.uk

KENT

Best Beaches

A record number of beaches on the Kent coast have gained the prestigious Blue Flag Award for the highest standards of beach management and cleanliness.

BLUE FLAG BEACHES 2006

- *Beach Street, Sheerness*
- *Leysdown Beach*
- *Birchington Minnis Bay*
- *Margate Main Sands*
- *Margate Westbrook Bay*
- *Margate Walpole Bay*
- *St Mildreds Bay, Westgate*
- *West Bay Westgate*
- *Viking Bay, Broadstairs*

South East England Tourist Board
- Tel: 023 8062 5400
- Fax: 023 8062 0010
- e-mail: enquiries@tourismse.com
- www.visitsoutheastengland.com

For information about
Britain's Best Beaches
see pages 39-44

Visit the FHG website
www.holidayguides.com
for details of the wide choice of accommodation featured in the full range of FHG titles

BROADSTAIRS

Family Fun Activities: Ice-cream parlours, amusement arcade, Pavilion with all-year entertainment, bandstand • Tennis, putting, golf course, crazy golf, bowls, angling • Award-winning St Peter's Village Tour • Skate park and climbing centre • North Foreland Lighthouse, Dickens House, Bleak House, Crampton Tower Museum.

Special Events: June: Dickens Festival Week, Carnival Parade. **July:** Steam and Transport Fair. Sea Sunday. **August:** Water Gala Day. Folk Week **September:** Open Bowls Tournament.

Visitor Information Centre, (in Dickens House Museum), 2 Victoria Parade, Broadstairs CT10 1QS
0870 2646111
e-mail: tourism@thanet.gov.uk
www.tourism.thanet.gov.uk

Beaches

- **VIKING BAY.** Sandy beach, 150 metres long; promenade and pier, parking; access. *Safety and maintenance:* first-aid station, warning flags, animal logo signposts; lifeguards, bay inspector/information; cleaned daily. *Beach facilities:* deck chairs/sun loungers for hire, children's rides, donkey rides, Punch and Judy (August only), chalets for hire; pubs, shops and restaurants nearby, amusements, surfski/belly boards; lift to beach; toilets (toilets with RADAR key access Albion Road car park, Broadstairs Harbour, and Victoria Gardens). *Dog restrictions:* not permitted on beach 1 May to 30 September incl.

- **STONE BAY.** 200 metres long, sandy with chalk cliffs and rockpools; promenade; access via Broadstairs Harbour. *Safety and maintenance:* cleaned daily. *Dog restrictions:* banned 15 May to 15 September between 10am and 6pm.

- **LOUISA BAY.** 150 metres long, quiet sandy bay; promenade. *Safety and maintenance:* warning signs; beach cleaned daily. *Beach facilities:* chalets for hire; cafe, tidal pool. *Dog restrictions:* "poop scoop" beach.

- **JOSS BAY.** 200 metres long, sandy beach, parking, access. *Safety and maintenance:* warning flags, lifeguards; cleaned daily; animal logo signposts to help children find their way back to parents. *Beach facilities:* deck chairs for hire, surf skis/belly boards; cafe; toilets with RADAR key access. *Dog restrictions:* "poop scoop" beach.

- **KINGSGATE BAY.** 150 metres long; quiet and secluded sandy beach. *Safety and maintenance:* cleaned daily. *Beach facilities:* chalets for hire; clifftop pub. *Dog restrictions:* "poop scoop" beach.

- **BOTANY BAY.** 200 metres long, sandy beach; access. *Safety and maintenance:* warning signs, cleaned daily. *Beach facilities:* cafe, clifftop pub; toilets. *Dog restrictions:* "poop scoop" beach.

MARGATE

Family Fun Activities: Heated indoor leisure pool, indoor sports/leisure centre, amusement arcades • Shell Grotto, The Droit House, museums • Windmill, lifeboat station • Ten-pin bowling, bowls, indoor bowls, tennis, putting, pitch and putt, golf course, mini-golf, crazy golf, angling • Casino, theatres, cinemas, nightclubs, disco, bandstand.

Visitor Information Centre, 12-13 The Parade, Margate CT9 1EY
0870 2646111
e-mail: tourism@thanet.gov.uk
www.tourism.thanet.gov.uk

Kent

⭐ **Special Events: June:** Great Bucket & Spade Run. **June/July:** Open Bowls Tournament, Kent Air Show. **August:** Margate Fiesta Weekend and Carnival Parade.

🏖 Beaches

- **MARGATE MAIN SANDS.** 200 metres long, sandy beach, promenade and boardwalk, parking, ♿ access. *Safety and maintenance:* warning flags, animal logo signposts to help children find their way back to parents, first-aid station, lifeguards and lifeboat; bay inspector/ information, beach cleaned daily. *Beach facilities:* sun loungers, deckchairs for hire; tidal boating pool, paddlecraft, donkey rides; kiddies' corner; cafes, restaurants, pubs; toilets with ♿ access. *Dog restrictions:* not permitted on beach 1 May to 30 September incl.

- **PALM BAY/HODGES GAP & FORENESS POINT.** 200 metres long; sandy, sheltered beach, parking. *Safety and maintenance:* cleaned daily. *Beach facilities:* designated water-ski area; toilets. *Dog restrictions:* "poop scoop" beach.

- **WALPOLE BAY.** Sandy beach 400 metres long, popular watersports bay, tidal pool, lift, promenade, parking, ♿ access. *Safety and maintenance:* warning flags, lifeguards; cleaned daily. *Beach facilities:* chalets and jet skis for hire; cafe, toilets. *Dog restrictions:* dog ban 1 May to 30 September incl.

- **WESTBROOK BAY.** 200 metres long, sandy; promenade and parking. *Safety and maintenance:* warning flags, lifeguards, bay inspector/information; first-aid station; cleaned daily. *Beach facilities:* deck chairs, chalets for hire; designated water ski area; children's fun park; cafe; toilets with ♿ access. *Dog restrictions:* banned from 15 May to 15 September 10am to 6pm.

Children Welcome!

RAMSGATE

🏊 **Family Fun Activities:** Heated indoor leisure pool, sports and leisure centre • Maritime museum • Royal harbour and yacht marina • Amusement arcades, leisure park and boating pool, tennis, bowls, angling • Theatre, cinema, discos, casino.

⭐ **Special Events: July:** Powerboat Grand Prix, Carnival Parade, sailing regatta, Costumed Walks. **August:** Open Bowls Tournament, International Sailing Week. **September:** Model Ships Rally.

ℹ **Visitor Information Centre,
17 Albert Court, York Street, Ramsgate
CT11 9DN
0870 2646111
e-mail: tourism@thanet.gov.uk
www.tourism.thanet.gov.uk**

🏖 Beaches

- **MAIN SANDS.** Popular sandy beach, 250 metres long; promenade and parking, ♿ access. *Safety and maintenance:* animal logo signposts to help children find their way back to their parents, warning flags, lifeguards, bay inspector/information; first-aid station; beach cleaned daily. *Beach facilities:* donkey rides; deck chairs, sun loungers for hire; amusements, children's play area; cafes, restaurants, pubs, shops; toilets with ♿ access; Edwardian lift to beach. *Dog restrictions:* not permitted on beach 1 May to 30 September incl.

- **DUMPTON GAP.** Quiet sandy bay with some rocks, 150 metres long; promenade and parking. *Safety and maintenance:* warning signs; cleaned daily. *Beach facilities:* chalets for hire; cafe; toilets. *Dog restrictions:* "poop scoop" beach.

- **PEGWELL BAY.** A stretch of unprotected sea cliffs with great geological interest. Part of Kent's largest national Nature Reserve. Toilets, cafe, picnic area, parking.

Kent

★ Fun for all the Family ★

◆ **A Day at the Wells, Royal Tunbridge Wells (01892 546545).** Experience the sights and sounds of 18th century Tunbridge Wells. Special commentary for children.

◆ **Canterbury Tales, Canterbury (01227 479227).** Chaucer's 14th century tales brought vividly to life by the latest audio-visual technology.
www.canterburytales.org.uk

◆ **Finchcocks, Goudhurst (01580 211702).** Living museum of early keyboard instruments, played whenever the house is open.
www.finchcocks.co.uk

◆ **Howletts Wild Animal Park, near Canterbury (01303 264647).** Caged and free-roaming animals including tigers and gorillas. Teas, picnics.
www.howletts.net

◆ **Kent and East Sussex Steam Railway** operates 80-minute steam train rides from Tenterden Town Station to Northiam **(01580 765155).**
www.kesr.org.uk

◆ **Museum of Kent Life, Cobtree (01622 763936).** History of the county in displays and live exhibits. Rare breeds and farm animals; play area.
www.museum-kentlife.co.uk

◆ **Romney, Hythe and Dymchurch Railway (01797 362353).** Runs from Hythe to Dungeness – 80 minute journey through beautiful landscape.
www.rhdr.org.uk

◆ **Wildwood, Herne Bay (01227 712111).** Kent's unique woodland discovery park. Wildlife and early man in a classic Kent setting. Special events.
www.wildwoodtrust.org

◆ **Wingham Bird Park, near Canterbury (01227 720836).** Set in 25 acres of beautiful countryside, with large walk-through aviaries, reptile house, adventure playground.

◆ **Historic Dockyard, Chatham (01634 823800).** Step back 200 years at the world's most complete Georgian dockyard, now a living museum. New permanent lifeboat exhibition.
www.chdt.org.uk

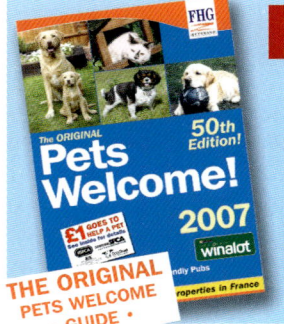

Pets Welcome!

"THE PET WORLD'S VERSION OF THE ULTIMATE HOTEL GUIDE!" (The Times)

Now better than ever and with full colour throughout, **Pets Welcome!** is used every year by thousands of discriminating owners who simply refuse to leave their pets "home alone".
Published twice a year in Autumn and Spring.

**Only £8.99 from booksellers or direct from the publishers:
FHG Guides, Abbey Mill Business Centre, Seedhill,
Paisley PA1 1TJ** (postage charged outside UK)

Kent

THE BULL HOTEL

Bull Lane, Wrotham, Near Sevenoaks TN15 7RF
Tel: 01732 789800 • Fax: 01732 886288
www.bullinnhotel.co.uk
e-mail: bookings@bullhotel.freeserve.co.uk

Once a stopping-off point for pilgrims on their way to Canterbury, the Bull Hotel is a family-run 14th century Coaching Inn of great charm and character in the historic village of Wrotham.

It specialises in comfortable accommodation and superb cooking at reasonable prices, with an à la carte restaurant, set menus and home-made bar snacks. All rooms have colour television, telephone and tea-making facilities. Ideal as a base for visiting London and places of local interest, it lies just off the M20/M26, 40 minutes by train from London and near the Channel ports and Gatwick.

The Croft Hotel & La Dolce Vita
Ashford, Kent

Set in two acres of well-maintained gardens, the Croft Hotel is conveniently located on the A28 between Ashford and Canterbury. The M20, Ashford International Station, the gateway to Europe, are only minutes away, Junction 9 the closest.

The Croft is family owned and operated, and warmly welcomes children in our large family rooms. The large gardens are at your disposal and we will be happy to recommend activities in the local area. Cots and baby accessories are readily available for infants.

AA ♦♦♦

The Croft Hotel, Canterbury Road, Ashford TN25 4DU
Tel: 01233 622140 • Fax: 01233 635271
e-mail: info@crofthotel.com
www.crofthotel.com

Bolden's Wood
Fiddling Lane, Stowting, Near Ashford, Kent TN25 6AP

Between Ashford/Folkestone. Friendly atmosphere – modern accommodation (one double/twin, two singles) on our Smallholding, set in unspoilt countryside. No smoking throughout. Log-burning stove in TV lounge. Full English breakfast. Country pubs (meals) nearby. Children love the old-fashioned farmyard, free range chickens, friendly sheep and... Llamas, Alpacas and Rheas. Treat yourself to a Llama-led Picnic Trek to our private secluded woodland and downland and enjoy watching the bird life, rabbits, foxes, badgers and occasionally deer. Easy access to Channel Tunnel and Ferry Ports.

Bed and Breakfast £25.00 per person.
Contact: Jim and Alison Taylor

Tel & Fax: 01303 812011
e-mail: StayoverNight@aol.com
www.countrypicnics.com

Great Field Farm

Stelling Minnis, Canterbury, Kent CT4 6DE
Tel: 01227 709223

Situated in beautiful countryside, our spacious farmhouse provides friendly, comfortable accommodation.
• Full central heating and double glazing.
• Traditional breakfasts cooked on the Aga.
• Courtesy tray and colour TV in each suite/bedroom.
• Cottage suite with its own entrance.
• Annexe suite ideal for B&B and self-catering.
• New detached ground floor "Sunset Lodge".
• Ample off-road parking.
• Good pub food nearby. • Non-smoking establishment.
**Bed and Breakfast from £25 per person;
reductions for children.**

Bed & Breakfast • Self Catering • www.great-field-farm.co.uk

LONDON & HOME COUNTIES

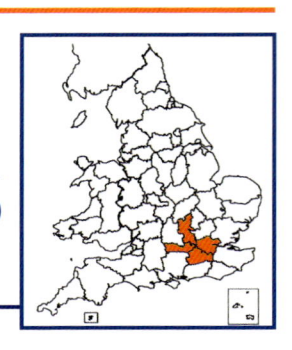

ℹ **Visit London**
1 Warwick Row, London SW1E 5ER
- Tel: 020 7932 2000
- Fax: 020 7932 0222
- e-mail: enquiries@visitlondon.com
- www.visitlondon.com
  www.kidslovelondon.com

HISTORIC BUILDINGS

◆ **Hampton Court, East Molesey, Surrey (020 8781 9500).** Built over 400 years ago, this became one of Henry VIII's royal palaces. Tudor tennis court, Great Vine and Maze. Nearest BR station: Hampton Court.

◆ **Houses of Parliament and Strangers' Gallery**: if you wish to listen to a debate apply in advance to your MP or join the queue at St Stephen's Entrance on the day.

◆ **Kensington Palace (0870 751 5170).** State Apartments of the late Stuart and Hanoverian periods containing 17th century furniture and pictures. Nearest Tube: Queensway.

◆ **St Paul's Cathedral (020 7246 8348).** Sir Christopher Wren's masterpiece built between 1675 and 1710. Nearest Tube: St Paul's, Mansion House.

◆ **Tower of London (020 7709 0765).** Built by William the Conqueror as a fortress, this magnificent building today houses the Crown Jewels. Nearest Tube: Tower Hill.

◆ **Westminster Abbey (020 7222 7110).** Founded by Edward the Confessor in 1065, the Abbey has become the burial place of many famous people. Nearest Tube: Westminster.

MUSEUMS & GALLERIES

British Museum (020 7323 8000).
Imperial War Museum (020 7416 5000).
Museum of London (020 7600 3699).
National Gallery (020 7839 3321).
National Maritime Museum (020 8858 4422).
National Portrait Gallery (020 7312 2463).
Natural History Museum (020 7942 5000).
Royal Academy of Arts (020 7300 8000).
Science Museum (020 7938 8000).
Tate Britain (020 7887 8008).
Tate Modern (020 7887 8734).
Victoria & Albert Museum (020 7942 2197).

◆ **Bethnal Green Museum of Childhood (020 8983 5200).** A child's world of toys, dolls, dolls' houses, children's costumes.
www.museumofchildhood.org.uk

London & Home Counties

◆ **London Dungeon (020 7403 7221).** The world's first medieval horror exhibition featuring gruesome scenes of torture, murder and depravation. Perfect for the kids! Nearest Tube: London Bridge.
www.dungeons.co.uk

◆ **London Transport Museum (020 7379 6344).** A collection of historic vehicles illustrating the development of London's transport system. Nearest Tube: Covent Garden.
www.ltmuseum.co.uk

VISITOR ATTRACTIONS

◆ **British Airways London Eye, South Bank, London (0870 5000 600).** Stunning views over Central London and beyond during a half-hour ride on the gently moving 135m high observational wheel.
www.londoneye.com

◆ **Chessington World of Adventures (0870 444 7777).** Exciting theme areas, rides, circus and zoo – a world of adventure for all the family. BR: Chessington South.
www.chessington.com

◆ **Cutty Sark, Greenwich Pier (020 8858 3445).** This famous clipper ship built for the tea trade contains a fine collection of figureheads and seafaring relics.
www.cuttysark.org.uk

◆ **HMS Belfast (020 7940 6328).** The last survivor of the Royal Navy's big ships, now a permanent floating museum. Nearest Tube: London Bridge.
www.iwm.org.uk/belfast

◆ **Kew Gardens, near Richmond (020 8332 5655).** 300 acres, once belonging to the Royal family, now contains 25000 different plant species; greenhouses, herbarium and museums. Tube: Kew Gardens.
www.rbgkew.org.uk

◆ **Legoland, Windsor (08705 040404).** A theme park with a difference, all set in 150 acres of wooded parkland.
www.lego.com

◆ **London Zoo (020 7722 3333).** One of the largest zoos in the world containing a varied collection of animals, birds, reptiles and insects. New Children's Zoo tells how people and animals live side by side. Nearest Tube: Camden Town.
www.londonzoo.co.uk

◆ **Madame Tussaud's (0870 400 3000).** The world famous waxworks of contemporary and historic figures complete with the inevitable Chamber of Horrors. Nearest Tube: Baker Street.
www.madame-tussauds.com

◆ **Royal Observatory, Greenwich (020 8858 4422).** Includes Wren's Flamsteed House, Meridian Building and Planetarium. New high precision pendulum clock donated by Moscow Research Centre.
www.nmm.ac.uk

◆ **London Planetarium (0870 400 3000).** The story of the stars and planets told by means of an elaborate and intriguing projection system. Nearest Tube: Baker Street.
www.london-planetarium.com

◆ **Thames Barrier (020 8305 4188).** Multi-media exhibition tells the story of the city's defence against floods. Can also be visited by boat.

FREE AND REDUCED RATE HOLIDAY VISITS!
Don't miss our
Readers' Offer Vouchers
on pages 9-38

London & Home Counties

Chase Lodge Hotel
An Award Winning Hotel
with style & elegance, set in tranquil surroundings at affordable prices.
10 Park Road Hampton Wick Kingston-Upon-Thames KT1 4AS
Children Welcome
Tel: 020 8943 1862 . Fax: 020 8943 9363
E-mail: info@chaselodgehotel.com Web: www.chaselodgehotel.com & www.surreyhotels.com

Quality en suite bedrooms
Close to Bushy Park
Buffet-style Full Continental Breakfast
A la carte menu
Licensed bar
Wedding Receptions
Honeymoon suite
available with jacuzzi & steam area
20 minutes from Heathrow Airport
Close to Kingston town centre & all major transport links.

AA♦♦♦♦ Les Routiers RAC ★★★

All Major Credit Cards Accepted

Barry House
12 Sussex Place, Hyde Park, London W2 2TP
- Comfortable, family-friendly B&B
- Most rooms with en suite facilities
- Rates include English Breakfast
- Near Hyde Park and Oxford Street
- Paddington Station 4 minutes' walk

www.barryhouse.co.uk
hotel@barryhouse.co.uk
fax: 020 7723 9775

Call us now on: 0207 723 7340

We believe in family-like care

WHITE LODGE HOTEL
White Lodge Hotel is situated in a pleasant North London suburb, with easy access via tube and bus to all parts of London. Alexandra Palace is the closest landmark and buses pass the front door. Prices are kept as low as possible for people on low budget holidays, whilst maintaining a high standard of service and cleanliness. Many guests return year after year which is a good recommendation. Six single, ten double bedrooms, four family bedrooms (eight rooms en suite), all with washbasins; three showers, six toilets; sittingroom; diningroom

Cot, high chair, babysitting and reduced rates for children.
No pets, please.
Open all year for Bed and Breakfast from £32 single, £42 double.

White Lodge Hotel, No. 1 Church Lane, Hornsey, London N8 7BU
e-mail: info@whitelodgehornsey.co.uk • website: www.whitelodgehornsey.co.uk
Tel: 020 8348 9765 / 4259 • Fax: 020 8340 7851

See the *Family-Friendly Pubs & Inns*
Supplement on pages 150-154 for establishments
which really welcome children

London & Home Counties

ATHENA HOTEL

110-114 SUSSEX GARDENS, HYDE PARK, LONDON W2 1UA
Tel: 0207 706 3866; Fax: 0207 262 6143
E-Mail: athena@stavrouhotels.co.uk   Website: http//:www.stavrouhotels.co.uk

TREAT YOURSELVES TO A QUALITY HOTEL AT AFFORDABLE PRICES

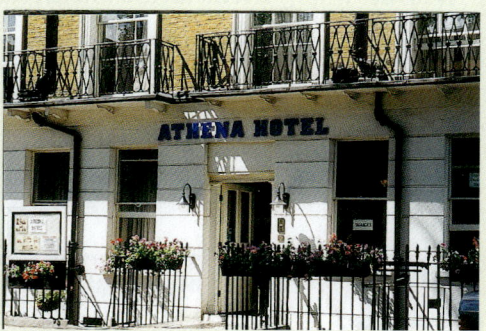

The Athena is a newly completed family run hotel in a restored Victorian building. Professionally designed, including a lift to all floors and exquisitely decorated, we offer our clientele the ambience and warm hospitality necessary for a relaxing and enjoyable stay. Ideally located in a beautiful tree-lined avenue, extremely well-positioned for sightseeing London's famous sights and shops; Hyde Park, Madame Tussaud's, Oxford Street, Marble Arch, Knightsbridge, Buckingham Palace and many more are all within walking distance.

Travel connections to all over London are excellent, with Paddington and Lancaster Gate Stations, Heathrow Express, A2 Airbus and buses minutes away.
Our tastefully decorated bedrooms have en suite bath/shower rooms, satellite colour TV, bedside telephones, tea/coffee making facilities. Hairdryers, trouser press, laundry and ironing facilities available on request. Ample car parking.

All prices include a full traditional English Breakfast and VAT
CREDIT CARDS WELCOME

Single Rooms from £50-£65
Double/Twin Rooms from £64-£95
Triple & Family Rooms from £28 per person

WE LOOK FORWARD TO SEEING YOU

LONDON HOTELS

Gower Hotel

**129 SUSSEX GARDENS, HYDE PARK
LONDON W2 2RX**
Tel:020 7262 2262; Fax:020 7262 2006
E-mail: gower@stavrouhotels.co.uk
Website: http://www.stavrouhotels.co.uk

The Gower Hotel is a small family-run Hotel, centrally located within two minutes' walk from Paddington Station, which benefits from the Heathrow express train, "15 minutes to and from Heathrow Airport". Excellently located for sightseeing London's famous sights and shops, Hyde Park, Madame Tussaud's, Harrods, Oxford Street, Marble Arch, Buckingham Palace and many more close by. All rooms have private shower and WC, radio, TV (includes satellite and video channels), direct dial telephone and tea and coffee facilities. All recently refurbished and fully centrally heated. 24 hour reception. Private car park.   ETC ♦♦

**Single Rooms from £30–£54
Double/Twin Rooms from £26–£36
Triple & Family Rooms from £20–£30
Prices are per person**

Discount available on 3 nights or more if you mention this advert!

QUEENS HOTEL

33 Anson Road, Tufnell Park, London N7
Tel: 020 7607 4725 Fax: 020 7697 9725
E-mail: queens@stavrouhotels.co.uk
Web Address: http://www.stavrouhotels.co.uk

The Queens Hotel is a large double-fronted Victorian building standing in its own grounds five minutes walk from Tufnell Park Station. Quietly situated with ample car parking spaces; 15 minutes to West End and close to London Zoo, Hampstead and Highgate. Two miles from Kings Cross and St. Pancras stations. Many rooms en suite, TV and tea/coffee making facilities.

All prices include full English Breakfast plus VAT   ETC ♦♦

**CHILDREN HALF PRICE
DISCOUNTS ON LONGER STAYS.**
*Singles from £25-£34
Double/Twins from £30-£54*
Triples and Family Rooms from £18 per person

CREDIT CARDS WELCOME
We look forward to seeing you

EAST ANGLIA

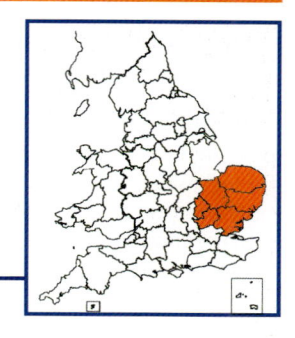

Best Beaches

A very impressive total of 17 beaches in this area were proud winners in 2006 of the European Blue Flag for beaches meeting the strictest of standards.

East of England Tourist Board
Bedfordshire, Cambridgeshire, Essex, Hertfordshire, Norfolk, Suffolk).

- Tel: 0870 225 4800
- Fax: 0870 225 4890
- e-mail: information@eetb.ork.uk
www.visiteastofengland.com

BLUE FLAG BEACHES 2006
- *Dovercourt Bay*
- *Southend*
  - *Shoebury Common*
  - *Shoeburyness*
  - *Three Shells Beach*
  - *Jubilee*
- *Cromer*
- *Great Yarmouth Gorleston*
- *Great Yarmouth Central*
- *Hunstanton*
- *Mundesley*
- *Sea Palling*
- *Sheringham*
- *Lowestoft*
  - *North*
  - *South of Pier*
- *Southwold Pier*
- *Felixstowe South*
- *Brightlingsea*

FHG
K·U·P·E·R·A·R·D

FHG Guides
publish a large range of well-known accommodation guides. We will be happy to send you details or you can use the order form at the back of this book.

For information about Britain's Best Beaches
see pages 39-44

CLACTON-ON-SEA

Family Fun Activities: Fun-packed pier with rides, amusements, cafes and fishing (wheelchair accessible) • Leisure centre with swimming pool • Two theatres, cinema, bingo, night clubs • Clacton Factory Shopping Village.

Tourist Information Centre,
Town Hall, Station Road, Clacton-on-Sea
CO15 1SE • 01255 686633
e-mail: emorgan@tendringdc.gov.uk
www.essex-sunshine-coast.org.uk

Beaches

• **BEACH.** Long sandy beach, gently sloping. *Beach facilities:* deck chairs, beach cafes; toilets. *Dog restrictions:* dogs banned on some beaches during main holiday season.

SOUTHEND

Family Fun Activities: Pier (longest pleasure pier in the world), Sea Life Adventure, Cliffs Pavilion, Adventure Island • Sailing, water ski-ing, windsurfing, motor boats, marine activity centre • Indoor swimming pools, skateboard park, tennis, bowls, golf, miniature golf, putting, children's playgrounds • Museums, planetarium, art gallery; theatres, nightclubs, discos • The Kursaal indoor entertainments centre

Visitor Information Centre,
Southend Pier, Western Esplanade,
Southend-on-Sea SS1 1EE
01702 215120 • Fax: 01702 431449
www.visitsouthend.co.uk

Beaches

• **BEACHES.** 7 miles of sea and foreshore with sand and shingle beach, stretching from Shoeburyness to Chalkwell and Leigh; ample parking. *Safety and maintenance:* cleaned daily boards with information on bathing water quality. *Beach facilities:* paddling pool, activity frame, beach shower; cafes, restaurants; toilets. *Dog restrictions:* from 1st May to 30th September must be kept on a lead on promenade.

GREAT YARMOUTH

Family Fun Activities: Marina Leisure Centre, Hollywood Indoor Golf, Pleasure Beach, Sea Life Centre, House of Wax, Model Village, Joyland Fun Park, "Amazonia" • Stock car racing, greyhound racing, horse racing, golf; putting, pitch and putt, outdoor bowls, ten-pin bowling, petanque, indoor karting • Marina, boating, fishing, sea cruises, Broads cruises, horse riding, indoor swimming pools, squash, tennis amusement arcades, children's playgrounds, Pirates' Cove (novelty golf), piers, road train • Museums, theatres, circus, cinema, nightclubs.

Special Events: Fireworks Displays, Herring Festival, Festival of Bowls, Maritime Festival. Carnivals and fêtes, band concerts.

Tourism Information Centre, 25
Marine Parade, Great Yarmouth NR30
2EN • 01493 836345
tourism@great-yarmouth.gov.uk
www.great-yarmouth.co.uk

Please mention CHILDREN WELCOME! when enquiring about accommodation featured in this guide

🏖 Beaches.

- **GREAT YARMOUTH BEACH.** Sandy beach, five miles long; two piers with entertainment. *Safety and maintenance:* warning flags, lifeguards; cleaned regularly. *Beach facilities:* deck chairs, windbreaks, beach huts; trampolines, donkey rides, inflatables, horse drawn landaus, pleasure boat trips; ice-cream kiosks, snack bars, restaurants and pubs; toilets on sea front with ♿ access. *Dog restrictions:* banned from beach during main season.

- **GORLESTON BEACH.** One and a half miles long, sandy; promenade and pier with good parking adjacent. *Safety and maintenance:* warning flags, lifeguards; beach cleaned during summer season. *Beach facilities:* deck chairs, trampolines, beach huts and chalets; ice-cream kiosks, snack bars, restaurants and pubs; toilets with ♿ access. *Dog restrictions:* banned from Blue Flag section during main summer months.

LOWESTOFT

Family Fun Activities: Mayhem soft play area, museums, pier; swimming pool, indoor football centre, adventure golf, golf, putting, pitch and putt, tennis, bowling, horse riding, water sports, parks with children's playgrounds • Theatres, cinemas, discos, nightclubs. Nearby: New Pleasurewood Hills, Suffolk Wildlife Park, Transport Museum, Lowestoft Ness (Britain's most easterly point).

ℹ️ **Tourist Information Centre,
East Point Pavilion, Royal Plain,
Lowestoft NR33 0AP • 01502 533600
e-mail: touristinfo@waveney.gov.uk
www.visit-lowestoft.co.uk
Brochure info line: 0870 6061303**

🏖 Beaches

- **KESSINGLAND BEACH.** Pebble and shingle with some sand; low cliffs, easy access. *Safety and maintenance:* cleaned by Local Authority. *Dog restrictions:* banned from 1st May to 30th September; must be kept on lead on promenade.

- **PAKEFIELD BEACH.** Sandy beach with some shingle below low grassy cliffs; parking. *Safety and maintenance:* cleaned by Local Authority; dangerous to clamber or swim near groynes. *Beach facilities:* pubs; toilets with ♿ access.

- **LOWESTOFT RESORT BEACHES.** Sandy pleasure beaches with two piers; esplanade and ample parking. *Safety and maintenance:* warning flags, lifeguards; dangerous to clamber or swim near groynes; cleaned daily. *Beach facilities:* children's corner, chalets, ice-cream kiosks, restaurants, snack bars, pubs; toilets with ♿ access. *Dog restrictions:* banned from 1st May to 30th September; must be kept on lead on promenade.

- **SOUTHWOLD RESORT BEACH.** Part sand, part shingle with sand dunes; refurbished pier including amusements and refreshments. Parking. *Safety and maintenance:* warning flags, lifeguards; cleaned by Local Authority. *Beach facilities:* beach huts; cafes, pubs; toilets. *Dog restrictions:* banned from 1st May to 30th September; must be kept on lead on promenade.

- **SOUTHWOLD DENES.** Part sand, part shingle with sand dunes. This rural beach is secluded and peaceful, an ideal place for walkers and nature enthusiasts. Parking. *Safety and maintenance:* cleaned by Local Authority.

Children Welcome!

East Anglia

★ Fun for all the Family ★

BEDFORDSHIRE
◆ **Whipsnade Wild Animal Park, Dunstable (01582 872171).** Britain's largest conservation centre specialising in breeding certain endangered species. Children's zoo, steam railway.
www.whipsnade.co.uk

◆ **Woburn Safari Park (01525 290407).** Britain's largest drive-through safari park. Roundabouts and rides.
www.woburnsafari.co.uk

CAMBRIDGESHIRE
◆ **Nene Valley Railway, Peterborough (01780 784444).** A preserved steam railway with 7½ miles of track. Cafe shop, museum and engine shed.
www.nvr.org.uk

◆ **Sacrewell Farm and Country Centre, Thornaugh (01780 782254).** 500-acre farm with working watermill, nature trails, displays of farming bygones.
www.sacrewell.org.uk

ESSEX
◆ **Colchester Zoo, Colchester (01206 331292).** World-wide collection of animals and birds, with daily displays of parrots, sealions and falcons. Penguin parade, snake handling, meet the elephants.
www.colchester-zoo.co.uk

HERTFORDSHIRE
◆ **Paradise Wildlife Park, Broxbourne (01992 470490).** 17 acres with lots of animals; woodland railway, pony rides, aviary, education centre.
www.pwpark.com

NORFOLK
◆ **Banham Zoo, Banham (01953 887771).** Over 25 acres of wildlife in parkland setting with extensive collection of rare and endangered species. Road train, adventure playground and World of Penguins.
www.banhamzoo.co.uk

◆ **Dinosaur Adventure Park, Weston Longville (01603 876310).** Walk through woodland to view dinosaurs in natural settings. Adventure rides, play area, wooded maze; bygones museum.
www.dinosaurpark.co.uk

◆ **Sea Life Centre, Great Yarmouth (01493 330631).** A spectacular way to experience the underwater world, with themed tanks on local marine life.
www.sealife.co.uk

SUFFOLK
◆ **Easton Farm Park, Wickham Market (01728 746475).** Victorian farm setting for many species of farm animals including rare breeds. Nature trail, pets paddock and adventure playground.

◆ **Pleasurewood Hills Family Theme Park, Lowestoft (01502 586000).** Live shows and all the rides your family can handle! Off A12 between Great Yarmouth and Lowestoft.
www.pleasurewoodhills.co.uk

◆ **Suffolk Wildlife Park, Kessingland (01502 740291).** Suffolk's "walking safari" set in 100 acres of dramatic coastal parkland. Daily feeding sessions, safari road train, adventure playground.
www.suffolkwildlifepark.co.uk

East Anglia 103

THE MEADOW HOUSE
2a High Street, Burwell, Cambridge CB5 0HB
Tel: 01638 741926 • Fax: 01638 741861

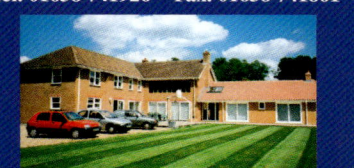

e-mail: hilary@themeadowhouse.co.uk

The Meadow House is a magnificent modern house set in two acres of wooded grounds offering superior Bed and Breakfast accommodation in spacious rooms, some with king-size beds. The variety of en suite accommodation endeavours to cater for all requirements; a suite of rooms sleeping six complete with south-facing balcony; a triple room on the ground floor with three single beds and the Coach House, a spacious annexe with one double and one single bed; also one double and two twins sharing a well equipped bathroom. All rooms have TV, central heating and tea/coffee facilities.
Car parking. No smoking
Family rate available on request.
www.themeadowhouse.co.uk

High House Farm ETC ♦♦♦
Cransford, Framlingham, Woodbridge, Suffolk IP13 9PD
Tel: 01728 663461 * Fax: 01728 663409
e-mail: b&b@highhousefarm.co.uk
website: www.highhousefarm.co.uk

Exposed oak beams ♦ inglenook fireplaces ♦ one double room, en suite and one large family room with double and twin beds and private adjacent bathroom ♦ children's cots ♦ high chairs ♦ books ♦ toys ♦ outside play equipment ♦ attractive semi-moated gardens ♦ farm and woodland walks
Explore the heart of rural Suffolk, local vineyards, Easton Farm Park, Framlingham and Orford Castles, Parham Air Museum, Saxtead Windmill, Minsmere, Snape Maltings, Woodland Trust and the Heritage Coast.
Bed and Breakfast from £25. Reductions for children and stays of three nights or more.

Experience the great joy of Norfolk... **Idyllic Cottages @ Vere Lodge**

We offer a choice of 14 cottages, sleeping 2 to 7, all extensively equipped, set in 8 acres of beautiful grounds.
• A modern Leisure Centre with large heated indoor pool, games room, sauna, solarium and lounge. • Grass tennis court, croquet lawn and enchanted wood. • Paddocks with miniature goats, rabbits, ducks, geese, peacocks, a donkey and Shetland pony. • Children's playground with swings, seesaw, slide etc.
We cater particularly for families with young children, for whom Vere Lodge is a paradise of unrestricted freedom. We welcome canine visitors. From September to June we offer Short Breaks. Open all year.
**1991 Norfolk Tourism Partnership Award
ALL COTTAGES INSPECTED & GRADED BY E.E.T.B.**
Free colour brochure from:
Vere Lodge, South Raynham, Fakenham, Norfolk NR21 7HE
Tel: (01328) 838261 (anytime) • Fax: (01328) 838300
e-mail: major@verelodge.co.uk • www.idylliccottages.co.uk

WHITEHOUSE BARNS
**Blythburgh, near Southwold
Contact: Mrs P. Roskell-Griffiths
Tel: 020 8802 6258
www.whitehousebarns.co.uk
peneleperoskell@blueyonder.co.uk**

Two beautiful architect-converted barns in spectacular peaceful location overlooking the Blyth estuary. In two acres of land with stunning views all around, they are ideal for families, walkers and birdwatchers. Southwold and Walberswick sandy beaches 4 miles. Reductions for couples midweek.
• Wood-burning stoves and underfloor heating.
• Sleep 5/6 and 8/9.
• Spacious playbarn and babysitting service available.
• Terms from £300 to £745.

East Anglia

Southwold • Walberswick

Furnished Holiday Cottages, Houses and Flats, available in this charming unspoilt seaside town. Convenient for beaches, sailing, fishing, golf and tennis. Near to 300 acres of open Common. Attractive country walks and historic churches are to be found in this area, also the fine City of Norwich, the Festival Town of Aldeburgh and the Bird Sanctuary at Minsmere, all within easy driving distance. SAE, please, for brochure with full particulars.

**H.A. Adnams, Estate Agents, 98 High Street,
Southwold IP18 6DP
01502 723292 • Fax: 01502 724794
www.haadnams.com**

KESSINGLAND COTTAGE
SUPERB LOCATION, KESSINGLAND

A three-bedroomed semi-detached, self-catering cottage situated on the beach, three miles south of sandy beach at Lowestoft. Fully furnished with colour TV. Accommodation for up to 6 people. Well-equipped kitchen with electric cooker, fridge, electric immersion heater. Bathroom with coloured suite, bath and shower. No linen or towels provided. Few yards to beach; one mile to wildlife country park. Buses quarter-of-a-mile and shopping centre half-a-mile. Parking, car not essential. Children and disabled persons welcome. Available 1st March to 7th January. Weekly terms from £95 in early March and late December to £375 in peak season.

SAE to Mr S. Mahmood, 156 Bromley Road,
Beckenham, Kent BR3 6PG (020 8650 0539)
E-mail: jeeptrek@kjti.freeserve.co.uk
Website: www.k-cottage.co.uk

FREE AND REDUCED RATE HOLIDAY VISITS!

Don't miss our

READERS' OFFER VOUCHERS

on pages 9-38

CASTAWAYS HOLIDAY PARK

BH & HPA approved

Set in the quiet, peaceful village of Bacton, with direct access to fine sandy beach, and ideal for beach fishing and discovering Norfolk and The Broads. Modern Caravans, Pine Lodges and Flats with all amenities. Licensed Club. Entertainment. Amusement Arcade. Children's Play Area.

PETS WELCOME

Enquiries and Bookings to:
**Castaways Holiday Park, Paston Road, Bacton-on-Sea,
Norfolk NR12 0JB • Tel: (01692) 650436 and 650418
www.castawaysholidaypark.co.uk**

MIDLANDS

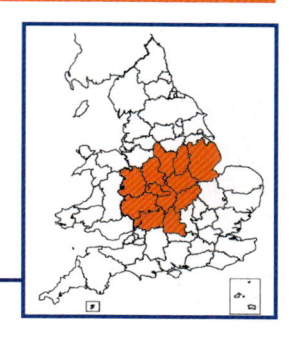

Best Beaches

Three beaches in the East Midlands area have attained the standards necessary to have won a Seaside Award for 2006 - Mablethorpe, Sutton on Sea and Skegness (Tower Esplanade)

Heart of England Tourist Board
(Gloucestershire, Herefordshire, Shropshire, Staffordshire, Warwickshire, West Midlands, Worcestershire).

- Tel: 01905 761100
- info@visitheartofengland.com
- www.visitheartofengland.com

East Midlands Tourist Board
(Leicestershire & Rutland, Lincolnshire, Northamptonshire, Nottinghamshire, Peak District & Derbyshire).

www.enjoyenglandseastmidlands.com

Midlands

☆ Fun for all the Family ☆

DERBYSHIRE

◆ **Gulliver's Kingdom, Matlock Bath. (01925 444888).** Theme park set in 15 acres of wooded hillside, designed especially for younger children.
www.gulliversfun.co.uk

◆ **Heights of Abraham, Matlock Bath. (01629 582365).** Spectacular cable car ride to hilltop country park. Show caverns, visitor centre, restaurant.
www.heights-of-abraham.co.uk

◆ **National Tramway Museum, Crich. (01773 854321).** Tramcars from all over the world; scenic displays, restaurant, children's playground.
www.tramway.co.uk

GLOUCESTERSHIRE

◆ **National Waterways Museum, Gloucester. (01452 318200).** Recreates the story of Britain's inland waterways. Working machinery, demonstrations.
www.nwm.org.uk

◆ **Slimbridge Wildfowl and Wetlands Centre, Slimbridge (01453 891900).** Over 2300 birds of 180 different species, including in winter wild swans, geese and ducks. Activities throughout the year.
www.wwt.org.uk

◆ **Sudeley Castle, Winchcombe. (01242 602308).** Toys, treasures, peacock gardens, children's play area. Katherine Parr (Henry VIII's Queen) buried here.
www.sudeleycastle.co.uk

LEICESTERSHIRE

◆ **Moira Furnace & Craft Workshops, Near Ashby de la Zouch. (01283 224667).** Impressive 19th century blast furnace museum. Woodland walks, nature trail, children's play area.

◆ **Snibston Discovery Park, Coalville. (01530 278444).** Exhibition hall with 5 galleries exploring the county's industrial heritage, plus outdoor science play area, colliery tours.

LINCOLNSHIRE

◆ **Natureland Seal Sanctuary, Skegness (01754 764345).** Entertainment, education and conservation: baby seals, penguins, free-flight tropical birds, plus lots of other fascinating creatures.
www.skegnessnatureland.co.uk

◆ **National Fishing Heritage Centre, Grimsby (01472 323345).** Tells the story of fishermen, their boats and the waters they fished in; the dangers and hardships of life at sea are explained.
www.nelincs.gov.uk

NORTHAMPTONSHIRE

◆ **Turner's Musical Merry-go-round, Queen Eleanor Vale, Newport Pagnell Road, Wootton (01604 763314).** Indoor fairground with historic and functioning fairground organs, rides on giant roundabout.

NOTTINGHAMSHIRE

◆ **Sherwood Forest Country Park and Visitor Centre, Near Mansfield (01623 823202).** Includes visitor centre with Robin Hood Exhibition, guided walks, picnic sites, and refreshments.
www.robinhood.co.uk

◆ **Tales of Robin Hood, Nottingham. (0115 9483284).** The latest audio-visual technology transports you through 700 years of history as you ride through Medieval Nottingham.
www.robinhood.uk.com

Fun for all the Family

OXFORDSHIRE

◆ **Blenheim Palace, Woodstock (08700 602080).** Home of the Duke of Marlborough, with magnificent collection of tapestries and porcelain. Landscaped grounds with butterfly house, adventure playground and railway. World Heritage Site.
www.blenheimpalace.com

◆ **Cotswold Wild Life Park, Burford (01993 823006).** A large and varied collection of animals from all over the world in natural surroundings.
www.cotswoldwildlifepark.co.uk

SHROPSHIRE

◆ **Ironbridge Gorge Museum, Telford (01952 432166).** Award-winning museum complex which brings industrial history to life. Working museums and real history - the images and objects of the industrial revolution.
www.ironbridge.org.uk

◆ **Hoo Farm Animal Kingdom, near Telford (01952 677917).** Friendly llamas, inquisitive ostriches, plus lots more. Undercover and outdoor attractions.
www.hoofarm.com

STAFFORDSHIRE

◆ **Alton Towers, Alton (0870 444 4455).** Europe's premier leisure park – rides, gardens, monorail, shops, adventure play areas etc. New interactive adventure ride – Duel.
www.alton-towers.co.uk

◆ **Drayton Manor Theme Park and Zoo, Near Tamworth. (01827 287979).** Over 100 heart stopping range of rides, including Apocalypse, Shockwave and Stormforce 10; nature trail, zoo, parkland and lakes.
www.draytonmanor.co.uk

WARWICKSHIRE

◆ **Heritage Motor Centre, Gaydon (01926 641188).** Purpose-built transport museum containing collection of historic British cars. Site includes four-wheel drive circuit.
www.heritage.org.uk

◆ **The Shakespearian Properties, Stratford-upon-Avon (01789 204016).** Five distinctive homes including Shakespeare's Birthplace and Anne Hathaway's Cottage, all administered by the Shakespeare Birthplace Trust.
www.stratford-upon-avon.co.uk

◆ **Warwick Castle, Warwick (0870 442 2000).** Britain's greatest medieval experience – castle with dungeon, armoury and torture chamber, all set in 60 acres of grounds.
www.warwick-castle.co.uk

WEST MIDLANDS

◆ **National Sea Life Centre, Birmingham (0121-633 4700).** Bringing the magic of the marine world to the heart of Birmingham with over 55 displays of marine and freshwater creatures. Features the world's first 360° fully transparent viewing tunnel.
www.sealife.co.uk

WORCESTERSHIRE

◆ **West Midland Safari & Leisure Park, Spring Grove (01299 402114).** From reptiles to roller coasters – it's all here!
www.wmsp.co.uk

Midlands

Cotswold Wildlife Park and Gardens

from ANTS to WHITE RHINOS and BATS to BIG CATS in 160 acres of Landscaped Parkland

Enjoy a Fantastic Day Out at **COTSWOLD Wildlife Park and Gardens**

- ADVENTURE PLAYGROUND
- CHILDRENS FARMYARD
- CAFETERIA • PICNIC AREAS
- NARROW GAUGE RAILWAY (RUNS FROM APR-OCT)

INFORMATION HOTLINE: **01993 823006**
OPEN DAILY FROM 10AM

BURFORD • OXON OX18 4JP - MID-WAY BETWEEN OXFORD & CHELTENHAM

www.cotswoldwildlifepark.co.uk

White Post Farm Centre

See lots of friendly animals, including chicks, piglets, cattle, deer, llamas and lambs – all year! Large indoor and outdoor play areas including pedal go-karts and indoor sledge run. Tea rooms, gift shop and pet and reptile shops. Ample parking. Open all year round. Located 12 miles north of Nottingham on the A614.

Farnsfield, Notts NG22 8HL
Tel: 01623 882977
www.whitepostfarmcentre.co.uk

NEW! PET HOTEL

East Midlands Visitor Attraction of the Year 2005

Please see our website or telephone 01623 882977 for current prices and opening times.

OLD KILNS
Tel & Fax 01989 562051
Howle Hill, Ross-on-Wye HR9 5SP

A high quality bed and breakfast establishment in picturesque, quiet village location. Central for touring Cotswolds, Malvern, Stratford-upon-Avon, Wye Valley and Royal Forest of Dean.

Centrally heated, private parking. Some rooms with super king-size bed plus en suite shower, toilet; also brass king-size four-poster bed with private bathroom and jacuzzi. Colour TV and tea/coffee making facilities in bedrooms. Lounge with log fire. Full English breakfast. Open all year. Children and pets welcome (high chair, cots and babysitting service provided). RAC Sparkling Diamond Award. Bed and Breakfast from £20 per person. Please telephone for free brochure.

Self-catering cottages also available, sleeping 2–14, with four-poster beds and jacuzzi.

Midlands

THE HOLIDAY INN TELFORD/IRONBRIDGE
Telford, Shropshire TF3 4EH
Tel: 01952 527000

150-bedroom hotel ideally positioned in the centre of Telford. Single and double occupancy; interconnecting rooms available for families. En suite bathrooms with power showers and tea/coffee facilities. Full air-conditioning. Modern, inviting bar and lounge area. Pets welcome. Within walking distance of Ice Rink, Bowling Alley, Town Park and Shopping Centre. The Wonderland Theme Park is within two minutes of the hotel; admission is free to hotel guests. Rates from £65 B&B.

THE INTERNATIONAL HOTEL

101-bedroom hotel ideally positioned in the centre of Telford. Single and double occupancy; interconnecting rooms enabling families to have comfort and space. All bedrooms have en suite bathrooms with power showers and tea/coffee facilities. Continental breakfast. Modern, inviting bar and lounge area. Pets welcome. Within walking distance of Ice Rink, Bowling Alley, Town Park and Shopping Centre. The Wonderland Theme Park is within five minutes of the hotel; admission free to hotel guests. Rates are from £35 pppn.

St Quentin Gate,
Telford, Shropshire TF3 4EA • Tel: 01952 521600

Croft Guest House, Bransford, Worcester WR6 5JD

AA ◆◆◆ Guest Accommodation

16th-18th century part black-and-white cottage-style country house situated in the Teme Valley, four miles from Worcester and Malvern. Croft House is central for visiting numerous attractions in Worcester, Hereford, the Severn Valley and surrounding countryside. River and lake fishing are close by, and an 18-hole golf course is opposite. Three en suite guest rooms (two double, one family) and two with washbasins are available. All bedrooms are non-smoking. Rooms are double glazed and have colour TV, radio alarm and courtesy tray. TV lounge, residential licence. Dogs welcome by arrangement.

B&B from £26 to £35 single
£44 to £60 double

Full English breakfast and evening meals are prepared from home-grown/made or locally sourced produce.

Ann & Brian Porter • Tel: 01886 832227 • Fax: 01886 830037
e-mail: hols@crofthousewr6.fsnet.co.uk • www.croftguesthouse.com

---

Alison Park Hotel

"EMTB Best of Tourism"
"Tourism for all Award 1990"

Situated close to the Pavilion Gardens and within a few minutes' walk of the Opera House, **Alison Park Hotel** is licensed and has 17 bedrooms, all with either en suite or private bathroom. We offer full English or Continental breakfast, a full dinner menu and an extensive wine list.

- Lunches, bar meals & dinner available to non-residents
- Vegetarian and special diets catered for
- Lounge with colour TV
- All bedrooms have tea & coffee makers, also direct-dial telephones, central heating, shaver sockets & colour TVs.
- Wheelchair ramp access • Ground floor bedrooms • Lift to all floors
- Conference facilities • Off-road parking

For brochure, phone David Noon or Geoff Ward on 01298 22473, Fax: 01298 72709 or write to us:
Alison Park Hotel, 3 Temple Road, Buxton, Derbyshire SK17 9BA
e-mail: reservations@alison-park-hotel.co.uk   website: www.alison-park-hotel.co.uk

---

FREE AND REDUCED RATE HOLIDAY VISITS!

Don't miss our

READERS' OFFER VOUCHERS

on pages 9-38

DOG AND PARTRIDGE
Swinscoe, Ashbourne,
Derbyshire DE6 2HS

Mary and Martin Stelfox welcome you to a family-run 17th century inn and motel set in five acres, 5 miles from Alton Towers, close to Dovedale and Ashbourne. We specialise in family breaks, and special diets and vegetarians are catered for. All rooms have private bathroom, colour TV, direct-dial telephone, tea making facilities and baby listening. Ideal for touring Potteries, Derbyshire Dales, Staffordshire moorlands. Restaurant open all day, non-residents welcome. Bargain Breaks:– 2 nights DBB £115; 3 nights DBB £155. Open Christmas & New Year. Why not visit our pets corner of rabbits and rare hens.

Tel: 01335 343183   Fax: 01335 342742
E-mail: info@dogandpartridge.co.uk • www.dogandpartridge.co.uk

NORTH-EAST ENGLAND

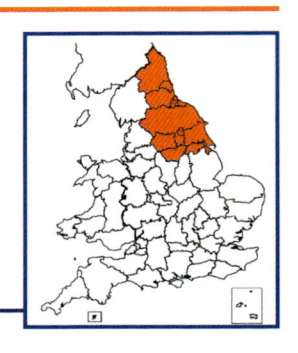

Best Beaches

This year no less than 11 beaches on this impressive stretch of coastline have won a European Blue Flag. Several beaches have gained the Tidy Britain Group's Seaside Award in 2006 (Resort Category).

Blue Flag Beaches 2006
- Tynemouth
    King Edward's Bay
    Longsands South
- Roker
- Seaburn
- Whitby West Cliff
- Filey
- Scarborough North Bay
- Hornsea
- Whitley Bay South
- Withernsea
- Cleethorpes Central

North East England Tourist Board
- Tel: 01904 707961
- Fax: 01904 707070
- www.northeastengland.co.uk

Northumbria Tourist Board
(Durham, Northumberland, Tyne & Wear, Tees Valley)
- Tel: 0191-375 3010
- Fax: 0191-386 0899
- www.visitnorthumbria.com

Yorkshire Tourist Board,
- Tel: 01904 707961
- Fax: 01904 707070
- www.yorkshirevisitor.com

Readers are requested to mention this FHG guide when seeking accommodation

BRIDLINGTON

Family Fun Activities: Summer shows • Children's attractions • Sports and games, golf, boating, fishing, wind-surfing • Indoor Leisure World (4 pools).

Special Events: May: Week-long festival of street and theatre shows. **August:** Lions Carnival. September: Sea angling week. **October:** Carnival Championships.

Information Centre, 25 Prince Street, Bridlington YO15 2NP • 01262 673474
www.discoveryorkshirecoast.com
www.visitbrid.co.uk
www.visiteastyorkshire.com

Beaches

• **NORTH BEACH.** Two miles long, sandy and naturally sheltered, with cliffs and rock pools towards northern end. Promenade; good parking. *Safety and maintenance:* cleaned daily. *Beach facilities:* deck chairs; various entertainments on beach; ice cream kiosks, snack bars, restaurants and pubs; toilets with access. *Dog restrictions:* banned May to end September, must be kept on lead on Promenade.

• **SOUTH BEACH.** Two miles long, sandy and naturally sheltered with some dunes at southern end. Promenade and good parking. *Safety and maintenance:* cleaned daily. *Beach facilities:* deck chairs; beach chalets for hire; beach activities; donkey rides; ice cream kiosks, snack bars, restaurants and pubs; toilets with access (open 24 hours in summer). *Dog restrictions:* banned May to end September, must be kept on lead on Promenade.

CLEETHORPES

Family Fun Activities: Leisure Centre, Pleasure Island Theme Park, Cleethorpes Coast Light Railway, Discovery Centre, The Jungle; 10-Pin Bowling Centre, Promenade Gardens, Lakeside Sand Pit and Paddling Pool, Fantasy World; Laser Adventure • Crazy golf, amusement arcades, children's entertainment, night clubs, discos.

Special Events: May: Kite Festival. **July/August:** Carnival Week and Parade. Markets: Wednesday and Sunday.

**Tourist Information Centre, 42/43 Alexandra Road, Cleethorpes DN35 8LE
01472 323111 • Fax: 01472 323112
e-mail: cleetic@nelincs.gov.uk
www.nelincs.gov.uk/tourism**

Beaches

• **NORTH PROMENADE.** Sandy and naturally sheltered; promenade; good parking. *Safety and maintenance:* Beach Safety Officers; sandbanks; beach cleaned daily. *Beach facilities:* deck chairs; donkeys, swings, Big Wheel, fairground; ice cream kiosks, snack bars, restaurants, pubs; toilets with ramps. *Dog restrictions:* from 1st April to 30th September dogs are restricted on various clearly marked areas of the beach.

• **CENTRAL PROMENADE.** Three-quarters of a mile long, sandy; naturally sheltered Promenade and good parking. *Safety and maintenance:* cleaned daily; Beach Safety Officers, warning signs. *Beach facilities:* deck chairs; donkeys, horses and carts, land train; ice cream kiosks, snack bars, pubs; toilets with ramps. *Dog restrictions:* from April 1st to 30th September dogs are restricted on various clearly marked areas of the beach.

FREE AND REDUCED RATE HOLIDAY VISITS!
Don't miss our Readers' Offer Vouchers on pages 9-38

FILEY

Family Fun Activities: Boating lake, putting, crazy golf, trampolines, children's play area, miniature golf • Folk Museum, Filey Dams Nature Reserve, Filey Brigg Nature Trail, Filey Sculpture Trail.

Special Events: **June/July:** Edwardian Festival. **July:** Filey Regatta. **August:** Life Boat Day. **August/September:** Fishing Festival.

Tourist Information Centre, John Street, Filey YO14 9DW
01723 383637 • Fax: 01723 518001
www.discoveryorkshirecoast.com

Beaches
• **BEACH.** Miles of open sand, naturally sheltered; parking. *Safety and maintenance:* cleaned daily, flagged, warning signs; lifeguards. *Beach facilities:* deckchairs, beach chalets; donkey rides; cafe and ice-cream kiosk; toilets with access. *Dog restrictions:* banned between Coble Landing and Royal Parade (seasonal).

SCARBOROUGH

Family Fun Activities: Heated indoor pool, spa, sports centre, crown green bowls, 10-pin bowling, tennis, putting, two golf courses • Mini railway, boating lake, angling in harbour • Amusement arcades, bingo, cinemas, theatre, nightclubs • Museums and 12th century castle • Bird of Prey Centre, Shire Horse Farm, mini "naval warfare", Sea Life Centre, Honey Farm, Terror Tower, pleasure boat trips, Dino Days (Dinosaur Coast events).

Special Events: **May/June:** Scarborough Fayre; festivals, International Music Festival. **July:** Seafest. **September:** Jazz Festival.

Tourist Information Centre, Sandside, Scarborough YO11 1PP
01723 383637 • Fax: 01723 383604
tourismbureau@scarborough.gov.uk
www.discoveryorkshirecoast.com

Beaches
• **NORTH BAY BEACH.** Three-quarters of a mile long, sandy with rockpools and cliffs. Promenade, good parking. *Safety and maintenance:* cleaned daily; flagged, warning signs, lifeguards. *Beach facilities:* deck chairs and beach chalets; donkey rides; putting and boating lake. *Dog restrictions:* 1st May to 30th September - no dogs permitted between Scalby Mills and mini roundabout; must be kept on lead on Promenade.

• **SOUTH BAY BEACH.** Half a mile long, sandy and naturally sheltered. Promenade, bay includes Scarborough harbour with three piers. Good parking. *Safety and maintenance:* cleaned daily; flagged, warning signs, lifeguards. *Beach facilities:* deck chairs and beach chalets; donkey rides; swings and roundabouts; toilets with access. *Dog restrictions:* 1st May to 30th September - no dogs permitted from West Pier to Spa Footbridge.

For information about Britain's Best Beaches see pages 39-44

WHITBY

Family Fun Activities: Heated indoor pool, boating, yachting, trout and salmon fishing, putting, crazy golf, golf,; bowls • Leisure Centre • Theatres, pavilion, museum, art gallery • Remains of 11th century abbey, Dracula Experience Trail, Captain Cook Heritage Trail, Funtastic indoor play area.

Special Events: March: Eskdale Festival of Arts. **August:** Whitby Regatta.

Tourist Information Centre,
Langborne Road, Whitby YO21 1YN
01723 383637 • Fax: 01947 606137
tourismbureau@scarborough.gov.uk
www.discoveryorkshirecoast.com

Beaches

• BEACH. Three miles long, sandy and naturally sheltered. Good parking. *Safety and maintenance:* cleaned daily; warning signs, lifeguards. *Beach facilities:* deck chairs and beach chalets; donkey rides; ice cream kiosk and snack bar; toilets with access. *Dog restrictions:* May to September – banned between Battery Parade and former Beach Cafe; must be kept on lead on Battery Parade and Promenade.

Children Welcome!

Fun for all the Family

COUNTY DURHAM

♦ **The Josephine and John Bowes Museum, Barnard Castle (01833 690606).** Outstanding art collection, plus ceramics, porcelain, tapestries, and objects d'art (including Silver Swan automaton).
www.bowesmuseum.org.uk

♦ **Beamish, The North of England Open Air Museum, Beamish (0191 370 4000).** A vivid re-creation of how people lived and worked at the turn of the century. Town Street, Home Farm, Colliery, Railway Station; tram rides, tea rooms.
www.beamish.org.uk

EAST YORKSHIRE

♦ **Elsham Hall Country and Wildlife Park, Near Brigg (01652 688698).** See working craftsmen demonstrate their traditional skills in the craft centre set in beautiful grounds and lakeside gardens. Children's farm, lake, adventure playground, falconry centre.
www.elshamhall.co.uk

♦ **The Deep, Hull (01482 381000).** Discover the story of the world's oceans on a dramatic journey back in time and into the future! The world's only underwater lift and Europe's deepest viewing tunnel!
www.thedeep.co.uk

NORTHUMBERLAND

♦ **Alnwick Castle (01665 510777).** A mighty fortress, seat of the Duke of Northumberland since 1309. Location for the 'Harry Potter' films.
www.alnwickcastle.com

♦ **Grace Darling Museum, Bamburgh (01668 214465).** Many original relics re-create the rescue by Grace and her father of the survivors of the wrecked Forfarshire.

♦ **Leaplish Waterside Park, Kielder Water (01434 220643).** Ideal base for exploring the largest man-made lake in Britain; all sorts of sports, forest playground, restaurant.
www.kielder.org

☆ Fun for all the Family ☆

TEES VALLEY

◆ **Captain Cook Birthplace Museum, Middlesbrough (01642 311211).** Special effects add realism to the museum displays which tell the story of the famous explorer.

◆ **Hartlepool Historic Quay, Hartlepool (01429 860006).** Travel back in time to the sights, sounds and smells of 18th century seaport life. New attractions include children's adventure playship.
www.thisishartlepool.co.uk

◆ **Saltburn Smugglers Heritage Centre, Saltburn-by-the-Sea (01287 625252).** Experience the sights, sounds and smells of Saltburn's dark past in authentic settings.

TYNE & WEAR

◆ **Life Science Centre, Newcastle-upon-Tyne (0191 243 8223).** Discover just how truly amazing life is. Explore where life comes from and how it works. Meet your 4 billion year old family, find out what makes you unique, test your brainpower and enjoy the thrill of the Motion Simulator Ride.
www.lifesciencecentre.org.uk

◆ **Wildfowl and Wetlands Trust, Washington (0191-416 5454).** Have a great day out supporting conservation on a nose-to-beak voyage of discovery – many birds feed from the hand. Exhibition area, tea room, play area.
www.wwt.org.uk

NORTH & WEST YORKSHIRE

◆ **Colour Museum, Bradford (01274 390955).** Examines colour, light and the history of dyeing and textile printing. Interactive galleries and workshops.
www.sdc.org.uk/museum

◆ **Eden Camp Modern History Theme Museum, Malton (01653 697777).** Civilian life in Britain during WWII – experience the sights, sounds and even smells of 1939-1945 at this award-winning museum.
www.edencamp.co.uk

◆ **Flamingo Land Theme Park, Zoo and Holiday Village, off Malton-Pickering Road (0870 7528000).** Rides and slides, zoo, indoor playcentre, cable car ride etc.
www.flamingoland.co.uk

◆ **Lightwater Valley Theme Park, Ripon (0870 458 0040).** The world's longest roller coaster, thrill rides, theatre, crazy golf, boating lake and much more. Restaurant and cafes.
www.lightwatervalley.co.uk

◆ **National Museum of Photography, Film and Television, Bradford (0870 701 0200).** Packed with things to do and find out, this bright, modern museum is a fun day out for all the family, telling the fascinating story of still and moving pictures.
www.nmpft.org.uk

◆ **National Railway Museum, York (01904 621261).** See how Britain's railways shaped the world at the largest railway museum in the world. BR's up to-the-minute exhibit gives a glimpse into the future. Restaurant and gift shop.
www.nrm.org.uk

◆ **Royal Armouries Museum, Leeds (0113-220 1916).** New attraction with thousands of items from a collection previously housed in the Tower of London. Jousting displays, Wild West gun fights, Oriental swordsmanship, plus lots more.
www.armouries.org.uk

North East 115

The Mizen Head Hotel
Lucker Road, Bamburgh, Northumberland NE69 7BS

En suite bedrooms, a residents' conservatory lounge and non-smoking à la carte restaurant using local produce. Public bar offers good food and real ales, live music, with an open log fire in winter. Children welcome – family rooms are available with cots if required. Car park. Pets welcome in bedrooms and bar. Local attractions include Bamburgh Castle and Holy Isle. Three-and-a-half mile sandy beach five minutes away. Pets welcome. For golfers discounts can be arranged. Short break details on request.

Tel: 01668 214254 • Fax: 01668 214104
www.themizenheadhotel.co.uk
e-mail: reception@themizenheadhotel.co.uk

Saughy Rigg Farm
info@saughyrigg.co.uk
www.saughyrigg.co.uk

- High quality en suite rooms
- Delicious home-cooked food
- Open to non-residents
- Pets and families welcome

Saughy Rigg Farm, Twice Brewed, Haltwhistle, Northumberland NE49 9PT • Tel: 01434 344120

Ash Vale Holiday Homes Park
Easington Road, Hartlepool TS24 9RF
01429 862111

Quiet and pretty country park. Situated only one mile from Crimdon's long and sandy beach, three miles from centre of Hartlepool with its historic quay; Durham 15 miles, Newcastle 20 miles. A walker's paradise: The Cleveland Way, North Yorkshire Moors, the North Pennines, the Northumberland Coast, Hadrian's Wall and the Border Counties. Beautiful "Catherine Cookson" country.
Holiday homes for sale and hire. Modern six-berth caravans and tourers with hook-ups. On site laundry, showers with hot water. Children and pets welcome. Terms from £10. Open Easter to end October, Short Breaks and last minute deals available. Golf, stables, fishing, bowling and recreation centre nearby.

e-mail: joy@ashvalepark.fsnet.co.uk
www.ashvalepark.demon.co.uk

Isaac's Cottage

Situated in the hills between Northumberland and Durham, Isaac's Cottage overlooks the River Allen. Surrounded by open fields and with the benefit of fishing in the little river only a field away, this cottage is a paradise for families wanting a 'get away from it all' holiday in lovely countryside.

There are three bedrooms (sleeps 7) - one double, one twin, one double + one single. Upstairs - bathroom; downstairs - shower, toilet, washbasin. Facilities include electric cooker, microwave, fridge, separate freezer, kettle, toaster, coffee maker, slow cooker. Automatic washing machine. Colour TV, DVD/video player. Oil-fired central heating, logs for the open fire, electricity included in the rent. Bed linen and a selection of hand towels. Cot and high chair. Garden with furniture. Ample parking. Prices from £180–£450 per week.

Mrs Heather Robson, Allenheads Farm, Allenheads, Hexham NE47 9HJ • 01434 685312

North East

Set in the tiny hamlet of Greenhouses and enjoying splendid views over open countryside, three cottages offering a very quiet and peaceful setting for a holiday. The cottages have been converted from the traditional farm buildings and the olde world character has been retained in the thick stone walls, exposed beams and red pantile roofs. All are well equipped, and linen, fuel and lighting are included in the price. There are ample safe areas for children to play. Sorry, no pets. Prices from £220 to £585 per week. Winter Breaks from £170.

Nick Eddleston, Greenhouses Farm Cottages, Greenhouses Farm, Lealholm, Near Whitby YO21 2AD • 01947 897486

Low Lands Farm
Low Lands, Cockfield, Bishop Auckland, Co. Durham DL13 5AW
Tel 01388 718251 • Mobile: 07745 067754
e-mail: info@farmholidaysuk.com • website: www.farmholidaysuk.com

Two award-winning, beautifully renovated self-catering cottages on a working family farm. If you want peace and quiet in an area full of beautiful unspoilt countryside packed with things to see and do, then come and stay with us. Each cottage sleeps up to four people, plus cot. Beams, log fires, gas BBQ, own gardens and parking. Close to Durham City, the Lake District and Hadrian's Wall. Pets and children most welcome; childminding and equipment available. Terms from £150 to £340, inclusive of linen, towels, electricity and heating.

Please contact Alison or Keith Tallentire for a brochure.

Category 3 (one cottage)

Situated in the heart of Nidderdale, this well-maintained group of holiday cottages is set in beautiful surroundings, with converted stables, the Granary and outbuildings adjoining the Georgian farmhouse which is occupied by the owners. The cottages sleep from two to six persons and all have linen, fully equipped kitchens and colour TV; all heating is included. Laundry facilities and payphone on site; barbecue and woodland garden. Pets and children welcome; cots and high chairs available. Two properties are suitable for disabled guests. Riding stables on site and excellent walking close by. York 45 minutes, coast 1½ hours, Fountains Abbey and Studley Royal 2½ miles.

THE COURTYARD AT DUKE'S PLACE
Bishop Thornton, Near Harrogate HG3 3YJ
Tel: 01765 620229 • Fax: 01765 620454
e-mail: jakimoorhouse@aol.com
www.dukesplace-courtyard.co.uk

£135 for 3 nights (2 persons)
£160 for 3 nights (4 persons)
4th night free
(subject to availability)

Moorgair Cottage

This charming cottage for 4/5 people is attached to the owner's home on a small working farm in rural Northumberland, home of Moorgair Alpacas. The cottage is furnished to a high standard and has every convenience to make your holiday stress free and enjoyable. Cot and high-chair available. Private garden and parking.

From the doorstep there are miles of forest tracks and country lanes for walkers and cyclists, and the cottage is ideally situated to explore Northumberland, Durham and the Scottish Borders. A small shop, post office and two pubs serving food (one with an excellent adventure playground) are within 1½ miles of the cottage.

Vicki Ridley, Moorgair Cottage, Slaley, Hexham NE47 0AN • Tel: 01434 673873
e-mail: g_ridley@lineone.net • www.moorgair.co.uk

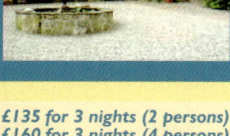

NORTH WEST ENGLAND

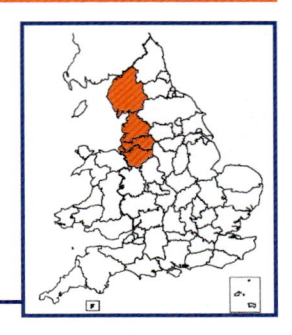

🏖 Best Beaches 🏖

There are lovely stretches of coastline and clean sands, and lively resorts whose efforts to maintain their high place in British holiday planning are showing successful results, with Ainsdale Beach earning the right to fly a Blue Flag. Seaside Awards (Resort Category) have gone to beaches at Blackpool (Central), Southport, and St Annes Pier as well as several in the Rural Beach Category.

BLUE FLAG BEACHES 2006
- *Ainsdale*

Cumbria Tourist Board
- Tel: 015394 44444
- Fax: 015394 44041
- Brochure Line: 08705 133059
- Booking hotline: 0808 100 8848
- www.cumbria-the-lake-district.co.uk

North West Tourist Board
(Cheshire, Greater Manchester, High Peak, Lancashire, Merseyside).

- Tel: 01942 821222
- Fax: 01942 820002
- e-mail: venw@nwda.cco.uk
- www.englandsnorthwest.com

North West

BLACKPOOL

Family Fun Activities: Pleasure Beach with over 145 rides and attractions including Europe's tallest, fastest rollercoaster and Valhalla, the world's biggest dark ride • Blackpool Tower with 7 levels of fun including a circus, ballroom, adventure playground and aquarium • Zoo, Sealife Centre, Sandcastle Waterworld indoor water paradise, Louis Tussaud's Waxworks • Stanley Park with lake, Italian Gardens, bowling, children's playgrounds, putting and Sports Centre • Three piers with arcades, shows and amusements, Winter Gardens with ballroom and Opera House, Grand Theatre • 10-pin bowling, golf, putting, go-karts, fishing, swimming pools • Multiplex cinemas, shows, pubs.

Special Events: July/August: Kids MegaFest Children's Festival. **1st September to 5th November:** Blackpool Illuminations.

*Blackpool Tourism, 1 Clifton Street, Blackpool FYl ILY • 01253 478222
e-mail: tourism@blackpool.gov.uk
www.visitblackpool.com*

Beaches

• **BEACH.** Approximately 7 miles long, sandy. Promenade, tramcars; good parking. *Safety and maintenance:* foreshore flagged, warning signs; lifeguards; beach cleaned daily. *Beach facilities:* deck chairs, donkey rides; ice cream kiosks, snack bars, restaurants, pubs; toilets with special needs access and mother/baby changing facilities. *Dog restrictions:* banned from the beach between North Pier and South Pier from May to September; must be kept on a lead on every street in Blackpool.

LYTHAM ST ANNES

Family Fun Activities: Heated indoor pool; pier, donkey rides on beach; children's playground, boating lake, floral gardens; tennis, putting, bowls, trampolines; miniature railway; golf courses (4); sailing; pubs, cafes and restaurants; theatre at Lytham; RSPB Discovery Centre at Fairhaven Lake.

Special Events: May/August: Carnivals and Fete days, miscellaneous local shows and competitions throughout the year.

*Visitor and Travel Information, Lytham St Annes FY8 ILH
01253 725610 • Fax: 01253 640708*

Beaches

• **BEACH.** Sandy, three miles long, and backed by dunes and promenade. Pier with arcade and refreshments. Good parking. *Safety and maintenance:* patches of soft sand and mud; river estuary; warning signs. Cleaned daily in season. *Beach facilities:* deck chairs, donkey rides; ice cream kiosks, snack bars, restaurants; toilets with access. *Dog restrictions:* can be exercised north of St. Annes pier, past the high water mark.

FREE AND REDUCED RATE HOLIDAY VISITS!
Don't miss our
READERS' OFFER VOUCHERS
on pages 9-38

North West

MORECAMBE

Family Fun Activities: Superbowl, cinema, Megazone, Happy Mount Park • Promenade and play areas, Stone Jetty with seabird-themed pavement games, the Eric Morecambe Stage and Statue.

Special Events: September: Golf Festival, Heritage Open Days, Heritage Gala.

i Morecambe Tourist Information Centre, Old Station Buildings, Marine Road Central, Morecambe LA4 4DB
01524 582808 • Fax: 01524 832549
e-mail: morecambetic@lancaster.gov.uk
www.citycoastcountry.gov.uk

Beaches

• **BEACH.** Several stretches of sand, backed by 5 mile long flat promenade with beautiful views across the wide expanse of Morecambe Bay towards the Lake District. Ample parking. *Safety and maintenance:* safety signs and lifebelts; Promenade Supervisor. *Beach facilities:* ice cream kiosks; toilets incl. some with ♿ access; miniature train. *Dog restrictions:* dogs not allowed on amenity beaches.

The **CLASSIFIED LISTINGS SECTION** on pages 141-149 is a quick, easy to use summary of the facilities offered by the accommodation featured in this guide.

★ Fun for all the Family ★

CHESHIRE

◆ **Blue Planet Aquarium, Ellesmere Port (0151 357 8804).** The UK's largest aquarium with moving walkway through tropical fish and a large collection of sharks.
www.blueplanetaquarium.com

◆ **Boat Museum, Ellesmere Port (0151-355 5017).** World's largest floating collection of canal craft on a 7-acre site. Steam engines, blacksmith's forge etc. Cafe.
www.boatmuseum.org.uk

◆ **Brookside Miniature Railway, Poynton (01625 872919).** Cheshire's greatest little railway. Super train rides, authentic detail in half-mile circuit of gardens. Restaurant.
www.brookside-miniature.railway.co.uk

◆ **Catalyst, Widnes (0151-420 1121).** Science and technology comes alive with hands-on exhibits, observatory. The only science centre solely devoted to chemistry, with over 30 interactive exhibits.
www.catalyst.org.uk

◆ **Chester Zoo, Chester (01244 380280).** Britain's largest zoo outside London. Spacious enclosures. Restaurants and cafeteria.
www.chesterzoo.org.uk

◆ **Jodrell Bank Science Centre, Planetarium and Arboretum, Near Macclesfield (01477 571339).** 'Hands on' gallery and space exhibition; planetarium. Lovell Radio Telescope.
www.jb.man.ac.uk

North West

☆ Fun for all the Family ☆

CUMBRIA

◆ **Cars of the Stars Motor Museum, Keswick (017687 73757).** Celebrity TV and film vehicles including Chitty Chitty Bang Bang and the Batmobile plus film set displays.
www.carsofthestars.com

◆ **The Cumberland Pencil Museum, Southey Works, Keswick (017687 73626).** The first-ever pencils were produced in Keswick and the museum traces the history of this everyday writing instrument. See the longest pencil in the world.
www.pencils.co.uk

◆ **Eden Ostrich World, Penrith (01768 881771).** See these magnificent birds in the setting of a real farm on the banks of the River Eden. Play areas, farm animals.
www.ostrich-world.com

◆ **Lake District National Park Visitor Centre, Brockhole, Windermere (01539 724555).** Exciting Lake District exhibitions, including the 'Living Lakeland' display. Restaurant and tearooms.
www.lake-district.gov.uk

◆ **Rheged, The Upland Kingdom Discovery Centre. Penrith (01768 868000).** Journey through 2000 years of Cumbria's magic in this new attraction set under a grass-covered roof. Discover the village in the hill.
www.rheged.com

◆ **Windermere Steamboat Museum, Windermere (015394 45565).** A unique collection of Victorian steam launches and other historic craft. Steam launch trips subject to weather and availability.
www.steamboat.co.uk

GREATER MANCHESTER

◆ **The Lowry, Salford (0870 787 5780).** A world-class venue for performing and visual arts. Theatres and galleries.
www.thelowry.com

◆ **Museum of Science and Industry, Manchester (0161-832 2244).** Like no other museum you've ever been in. Xperiment! – interactive science centre; Power Hall; Victorian Sewers – and lots more.
www.msim.org.uk

LANCASHIRE

◆ **Blackpool Tower (01253 292029).** 520 ft high, houses a circus, aquarium, dance hall and other shows. The famous Illuminations start early in September.
www.theblackpooltower.co.uk

◆ **Wildfowl Trust, Martin Mere (01704 895181).** Exotic and native breeds plus thousands of migrant visitors observed from spacious hides.
www.wwt.org.uk

MERSEYSIDE

◆ **The Beatles Story, Liverpool (0151-709 1963).** Re-live the sights and sounds of the Swinging Sixties a magical mystery tour!
www.beatlesstory.com

◆ **World of Glass, St Helens (08707 114466).** The fascinating history of glass-making. Enter the magical mirror maze and explore the cone building tunnels.
www.worldofglass.com

"Ultimately Unique"

'Where the children bring their parents'

60 years

Celebrating 60 years of being owned and managed by the Webb family, the hotel is situated on the seafront in Lytham St Annes, overlooking soft, sandy, child friendly beaches. We offer accommodation from standard to premier, comprising doubles, family rooms and apartments. The facilities include:

• 3 restaurants • Large indoor swimming pool • Children's splash pool • Gym
• Steam room • Sauna • Aerobic Centre • Beauty Salon • Family and children's entertainment provided every weekend and holiday periods • Ofsted approved crèche

Only a short journey's ride from the Northwest's biggest attractions in Blackpool.
Special family offers available, children from as little as £5 Dinner, Bed & Breakfast.

The Dalmeny Hotel, 19-33 South Promenade, St Annes, Lancashire FY8 1LX
Tel: 01253 712236 • Fax: 01253 724447
e-mail: reservations@dalmenyhotel.co.uk
www.dalmenyhotel.co.uk

dalmeny
hotel

NORTH WEST

The Chadwick Hotel
South Promenade, Lytham St Annes FY8 1NP

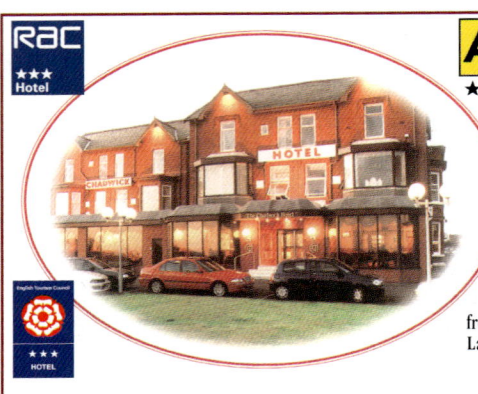

RAC ★★★ Hotel

AA ★★★

Owned and run by the Corbett family since 1947, the Chadwick Hotel commands a delightful seafront position overlooking the Ribble Estuary, just five miles from Blackpool and conveniently situated for touring the Lake District, Manchester, the Yorkshire Dales and North Wales. The friendly atmosphere and modern facilities encourage guests to return again and again.

The Bugatti Bar is cosy and relaxed, while the Four Seasons Restaurant offers a classically elegant atmosphere in which to enjoy quality food and service. All 75 bedrooms are en suite, some with spa baths, others with four-poster beds. Open throughout the year, the hotel also boasts a luxurious health and leisure complex.

Facilities include family rooms, a soft play adventure area, games room, baby listening and launderette. Children can have high tea or dinner with their parents. A special Children's Menu features a selection of children's favourites. Children sharing family rooms - less than half adult rate. Babies in cots FREE of charge.

- 24 hour food and drinks service
- Night porter • Ample parking.

Tel: 01253 720061
Fax: 01253 714455
www.thechadwickhotel.com
sales@thechadwickhotel.com

GREEN GABLES
37 Broad Street, Windermere LA23 2AB

AA ♦♦♦

A family-owned and run licensed guesthouse in Windermere centrally situated one-minute's walk from village centre with shops, banks and pubs and only five minutes from the station or bus stop. Accommodation comprises two doubles, one family triple/twin and one single room, all en suite; one family (four) and two family triple/twin rooms with private facilities; all with central heating, colour TV, hairdryers, kettles, tea & coffee. Comfortable lounge bar on the ground floor. No smoking in bedrooms. We can book tours and trips for guests and can advise on activities and special interests. B&B from £23 to £30 pppn. Special Winter offers available. Open just about all year round. Contact **Carole Vernon and Alex Tchumak**.

Tel: 015394 43266 • e-mail: greengables@FSBdial.co.uk • e-mail: info@greengablesguesthouse.co.uk

LEA FARM

Charming farmhouse set in landscaped gardens, where peacocks roam, on 150-acre working family farm. Spacious bedrooms, colour TVs, electric blankets, radio alarm and tea/coffee making facilities. Centrally heated throughout. Family, double and twin bedrooms, en suite facilities. Luxury lounge, dining room overlooking gardens. Pool/snooker; fishing in well stocked pool in beautiful surroundings. Bird watching. Children welcome, also dogs if kept under control. Help feed the birds and animals and see the cows being milked. Near to Stapeley Water Gardens, Bridgemere Garden World. Also Nantwich, Crewe, Chester, the Potteries and Alton Towers.
B&B from £24pp children half price.

Wrinehill Road, Wybunbury, Nantwich CW5 7NS
Tel: 01270 841429
Fax: 01270 841030

AA/ETC ★★★ Farmhouse

e-mail: jean@leafarm.freeserve.co.uk • www.leafarm.co.uk

North West

ROTHAY MANOR HOTEL & RESTAURANT

Families are welcome at this Regency Country House in the heart of the Lake District, just a quarter of a mile from Lake Windermere and a short walk from the centre of Ambleside.

Personally managed by the Nixon family for 40 years, it still retains the comfortable, relaxed atmosphere of a private house and is well known for the excellent cuisine.

The hotel has 19 bedrooms (including 6 family rooms) and 3 suites, two of which are in the grounds.

Guests have free use of a nearby leisure club with children's pool, sauna, steam room and jacuzzi.

Family rooms have TV and video

Children's High Tea

Cots, high chairs

Baby listening

Non-smoking

All major credit cards accepted

Good Food Guide • Cumbria for Excellence Awards: Small Hotel of the year 2006

Rothay Bridge, Ambleside LA22 0EH
Tel: (015394) 33605 • Fax: (015394) 33607
e-mail: hotel@rothaymanor.co.uk • www.rothaymanor.co.uk/family

---

Greenhowe Caravan Park
Great Langdale, English Lakeland.

Greenhowe Caravan Park
Great Langdale, Ambleside,
Cumbria LA22 9JU

Greenhowe is a permanent Caravan Park with Self Contained Holiday Accommodation. Subject to availability Holiday Homes may be rented for short or long periods from 1st March until mid-November. The Park is situated in the Lake District half-a-mile from Dungeon Ghyll at the foot of the Langdale Pikes. It is an ideal centre for Climbing, Fell Walking, Riding, Swimming, Water-Skiing. **Please ask about Short Breaks.**

For free colour brochure
**Telephone: (015394) 37371 • Fax: (015394) 37464
• Freephone: 0800 0717371 • www.greenhowe.com**

Quality Holiday Homes
in the beautiful Lake District

VisitBritain ★★★ – ★★★★★

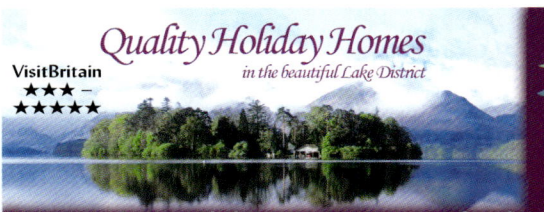

Lakelovers
lakeland's self catering specialists

Quality Holiday Homes in England's Beautiful Lake District
Hundreds of VisitBritain inspected and graded properties throughout the southern and central Lake District.
Lakelovers are sure to have a property to meet your needs. Free Leisure Club membership with every booking
Tel: 015394 88855 • Fax: 015394 88857 • e-mail: bookings@lakelovers.co.uk • www.lakelovers.co.uk
Lakelovers, Belmont House, Lake Road, Bowness-on-Windermere, Cumbria LA23 3BJ

SCOTLAND

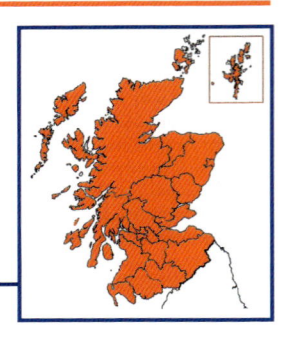

🏖 Best Beaches 🏖

Scotland has a huge coastline, one of the longest in Europe, with great stretches of sand along the Solway, on the Ayrshire coast, East Lothian and Fife, around Aberdeen, along the Moray Firth and in the North West. Good beach management practices in the Fife region have been rewarded with five European Blue Flags; Montrose and Broughty Ferry in Dundee & Angus have also been successful, as has a beach in the Highland region. In addition Seaside Awards (Resort and Rural Categories) have gone to 33 other beaches which meet the high standards required.

BLUE FLAG BEACHES 2006
- *St Andrews West Sands*
- *St Andrews East Sands*
- *Elie Harbour*
- *Aberdour Silver Sands*
- *Burntisland*
- *Montrose*
- *Broughty Ferry*
- *Nairn Central*

Scottish Tourist Board
- Tel: 0845 2255 121
- Fax: 01506 832222
- e-mail: info@visitscotland.com
- www.visitscotland.com

ABERDEEN

Family Fun Activities: Winter Gardens, Art Gallery, museums, cinemas, theatres, Music Hall • Doonies Farm, Hazlehead Park, Aberdeen Fun Beach, Satrosphere Hands-on Science Centre, Storybook Glen • Windsurfing, bowling, squash, tennis, Linx Ice Arena, cricket, rugby, riding, walking, climbing, fishing, golf.

Aberdeen Visitor Information Centre,
23 Union Street, Aberdeen AB11 5BP
01224 288828
e-mail: Aberdeen@visitscotland.com
www.aberdeen-grampian.com

Beaches

• **BEACH.** Two and a half miles of sandy beach, promenade and harbour; ample parking. *Safety and maintenance:* cleaned daily; lifeboats, lifebelts; lifeguards in summer. **Aberdeen Fun Beach:** Scotland's largest family entertainment centre, open all year. Restaurants, multi-plex cinema, leisure centre with swimming pool and flumes, ice arena, indoor and outdoor funfair, ten-pin bowling, pool and Ramboland – children's adventure play area

ISLE OF ARRAN

Family Fun Activities: This peaceful island, "Scotland in Miniature", offers a wealth of leisure activities and places of interest including Brodick Castle, Gardens and Country Park, Isle of Arran Distillery, Balmichael Visitor Centre, Isle of Arran Heritage Museum, Arran Aromatics.

Tourist Information Centre,
The Pier, Brodick KA27 8AU
0845 2255 121
e-mail: Brodick@visitscotland.com
www.ayrshire-arran.com

Special Events: **July:** Arran Fleadh. **August:** Highland Games. **October:** Ladies Golf Competition. **November:** Gents Golf Competition.

Beaches

• **BEACHES.** Varied coastline with shingle and pebble shores and sandy beaches suitable for all the family.

AYR

Family Fun Activities: Citadel Leisure Complex • Swimming pool, 10-pin bowling, golf, putting, pitch and putt, cricket, tennis, bowls • Cinema, dancing/discos • Racecourse • Nearby Burns National Heritage Park, Belleisle Park, Rozelle Park, Craig Tara, Heads of Ayr Park.

Special Events: **May:** Ayr Agricultural Show. **June:** Ayr Golf Week. **August:** Flower Show. **September:** Ayr Gold Cup (horse racing).

Tourist Information Centre,
22 Sandgate, Ayr KA7 1BW
0845 2255 121
e-mail: Ayr@visitscotland.com
www.ayrshire-arran.com

Beaches

• **BEACH.** Two and a half miles long, sand and some shingle; promenade and harbour; ample parking. *Beach facilities:* children's playground, crazy golf, boating pond, putting on promenade; cafes; toilets with access.

Children Welcome!

GIRVAN

Family Fun Activities: Swimming pool, golf, putting, tennis, bowls • Boat trips and fishing.

Special Events: **May:** Folk Festival. **June:** Civic Week. **August:** Annual Maidens Harbour Gala. **October:** Folk Festival.

Beaches

• BEACH. One and a half miles long, sandy and some shingle; promenade and harbour, ample parking. *Beach facilities:* children's playground, boating pond; toilets with ♿ access.

LARGS

Family Fun Activities: Swimming pool, sauna/solarium; tennis, putting, squash, golf, bowling, windsurfing, diving. • Vikingar, Kelburn Castle & Country Centre

Special Events: **August:** Regatta Week. **September:** Viking Festival.

Tourist Information Centre,
The Station, Largs
0845 2255 121
e-mail: Largs@visitscotland.com
www.ayrshire-arran.com

Beaches

• BEACH. Shingle and sand; promenade, parking; boating pond; cafes and ice cream kiosks; toilets with ♿ access.

MILLPORT

Family Fun Activities: Organised children's activities • Tennis, pitch and putt, trampolines, golf, riding, cycle hire, bowling, fun fair • Museum, aquarium at Marine Station • The Cathedral of the Isles (smallest cathedral in Britain). Millport is reached by car/passenger ferry from Largs; 10 minute bus ride from ferry slip to town.

Special Events: **July/August:** Country and Western Festival, Cumbrae Weekend.

Beaches

• BEACH. Sand and shingle, rock pools; parking. *Beach facilities:* cafes and shops nearby, toilets, some with ♿ access. *Dog restrictions:* must be kept on lead.

TROON

Family Fun Activities: golf, bowling, tennis, swimming, children's play areas.

Special Events: **June:** Gala Week.

www.ayrshire-arran.com

Beaches

• BEACH. Excellent sandy beach with first-aid and life saving equipment nearby. Toilets.

www.holidayguides.com

The Classified Listing Section
on pages 141-149 is a quick, easy to use summary of the facilities offered by the accommodation featured in this guide.

Scotland

ROTHESAY

Family Fun Activities: Main town on the Isle of Bute easily reached by car/passenger ferry from Wemyss Bay or Colintraive • Pavilion with family variety shows, children's entertainment • Mount Stuart, Isle of Bute Discovery Centre and cinema/theatre, Rothesay Castle, Bute Museum • Putting, tennis, bowling, golf, pony trekking • Leisure Pool with sauna/solarium • Ornamental gardens, castle and museum, walks.

i Isle of Bute Discovery Centre,
Victoria Street, Rothesay,
Isle of Bute PA20 0AH
0845 2255 121
e-mail: Rothesay@visitscotland.com
www.VisitBute.com

FREE AND REDUCED RATE HOLIDAY VISITS!
Don't miss our
Readers' Offer Vouchers
on pages 9-38

ST ANDREWS

Family Fun Activities: Historic University town with 13th century Castle and 12th century Cathedral, St Andrews Museum, University Museum, St Andrews Aquarium, Craigtoun Country Park, East Sands Leisure Centre • Bowling, tennis, putting, water-based sports and (of course) GOLF (British Golf Museum) • Theatre, cinema, arts centre.

i Tourist Information Centre,
70 Market Street, St Andrews KY16 9NU
0845 2255 121
e-mail: Standrews@visitscotland.com
www.standrews.com/fife

Beaches

• **WEST SANDS.** Wide, flat sandy beach. Within walking distance of town centre, ample parking. *Safety and maintenance:* cleaned regularly and patrolled by council staff. *Beach facilities:* catering outlets; toilets. *Dog restrictions:* banned from most of beach in summer months.

• **EAST SANDS.** Sandy beach, just past the harbour; parking. *Safety and maintenance:* cleaned regularly. *Beach facilities:* catering facilities; watersports; toilets. *Dog restrictions:* none.

Fun for all the Family

NORTHERN SCOTLAND

◆ **Anderson's Storybook Glen, Maryculter, near Aberdeen** (01224 732941). Old Woman's Shoe, Pixie Park, Old MacDonald, play park and the Three Bears' House. Waterfalls.

◆ **Archaeolink Prehistory Park, near Insch** (01464 851500). All-weather attraction with events inside and out, exhibition and film theatre, all set in 40 acres.
www.archaeolink.co.uk

◆ **Cawdor Castle, Nairn** (01667 404401). A 14th century Keep, fortified in the 15th century and the 17th century, the massive fortress is set in splendid grounds with nature trails and gardens. Shops, snack bar, picnic area, restaurant and golf course.
www.cawdorcastle.com

◆ **Buckie Drifter Maritime Heritage Centre, Buckie** (01542 8346460. See how the herring industry worked in the past and walk along a re-created 1920's quayside.
www.moray.org/bdrifter

◆ **Eilean Donan Castle, near Kyle of Lochalsh** (01599 555202). Probably the most photographed castle in Scotland, Eilean Donan stands in a romantic and picturesque setting on Loch Duich.
www.eieandonancastle.com

◆ **Glamis Castle, near Forfar**(01307 840393). Childhood home of the Queen Mother and birthplace of Princess Margaret. Visitors have a choice of admission to the Castle/grounds/formal garden/coach house /nature trail/picnic areas, including a children's play area.
www.strathmore-estates.co.uk

◆ **Highland Mysteryworld, Glencoe** (01855 811660). Five fabulous indoor attractions in spectacular setting at foot of Glencoe. Also adventure playground and leisure centre

◆ **Highland Wildlife Park, Kincraig** (01540 651270). Over 250 acres with red deer, European bison, wild horses, roe deer, Soay sheep, Highland cattle, wandering freely amidst magnificent Highland scenery.
www.highlandwildlifepark.org

◆ **Kylerhea Otter Haven, Kylerhea, Isle of Skye** (01320 366322). See otters in their natural habitat and view other wildlife from a spacious hide.

◆ **Landmark Visitor Centre, Carrbridge** (01479 841613). Attractions include tree-top trail, pine forest nature centre, woodland maze and adventure playground with giant slide and aerial walkways.
www.landmark-centre.co.uk

◆ **The Official Loch Ness Monster Exhibition Centre, Drumnadrochit** (01456 450573). Explore the mysteries surrounding the existence (or not!) of Nessie, the world-famous monster.
www.loch-ness-scotland.com

◆ **Timespan Heritage Centre, Helmsdale** (01431 821327). Award-winning heritage centre telling the dramatic story of the Highlands. Landscaped garden with collection of rare herbal medicinal plants.
www.timespan.org.uk

Fun for all the Family

CENTRAL SCOTLAND

◆ **Bannockburn Heritage Centre, near Stirling (01786 812664).** Superb audio visual presentation and magnificent equestrian statue of Robert the Bruce.
www.nts.org.uk/bannockburn

◆ **Blair Drummond Safari & Adventure Park (01786 841456).** Drive through animal reserves, monkey jungle. Pets farm – even a boat safari round chimp island – plus rides, amusements .
www.safari-park.co.uk

◆ **British Golf Museum, St Andrews (01334 460046).** Relive all the history and atmosphere of 500 years of golf. Themed galleries feature the tournaments, players and equipment which today's game.
www.britishgolfmuseum.co.uk

◆ **Deep Sea World, North Queensferry (01383 411880).** An underwater safari beneath the Firth of Forth gives a superb view of thousands of fish as they travel along the longest underwater tunnel in the world.
www.deepseaworld.com

◆ **Falkirk Wheel (08700 500208).** A mechanical marvel, the world's only rotating boatlift used to connect the Forth & Clyde and Union canals.
www.thefalkirkwheel.co.uk

◆ **Frigate Unicorn, Victoria Dock, Dundee (01382 200900).** An 1824 wooden, 46 gun frigate; Britain's oldest ship afloat restored as a floating museum.
www.frigateunicorn.org

◆ **Museum of Transport, Kelvin Hall, Glasgow (0141-287 2720).** The oldest cycle in the world, trams, bikes, trains, horse drawn vehicles, special displays, models and more.
www.seeglasgow.com

◆ **New Lanark, Near Lanark (01555 661345).** An insight into the lives of working men and women in this restored conservation village in an attractive situation by the Falls of Clyde. A World Heritage site.
www.newlanark.org

◆ **Our Dynamic Earth, Edinburgh (0131 550 7800).** Charting the Earth's development over the last 4,500 million years with lots of interactive entertainment for adults and children.
www.dynamicearth.co. uk

◆ **St Andrews Sea Life Aquarium (01334 474786).** Hundreds of different species in displays intended to re-create their natural habitat. Includes playful seals and colourful tropical fish.
www.standrewsaquarium.co.uk

◆ **Scottish Fisheries Museum, Anstruther (01333 310628).** A unique record of Scotland's fishing industry. Museum shop and tearoom. Restored fisherman's cottage.
www.scottish-fisheries-museum.org

◆ **Scottish Deer Centre, Over Rankeilour Farm, near Cupar(01337 810391).** Audio visual show. Outdoor and indoor play areas and the chance to study (and stroke) these beautiful animals at close quarters.

⭐ Fun for all the Family ⭐
SOUTHERN SCOTLAND

◆ **Brodick Castle and Country Park (01770 302202)**. Former seat of the Dukes of Hamilton (now NT) with fine examples of silver, porcelain and paintings. Woodland walks, formal garden; ranger service.
www.nts.org.uk/brodick

◆ **Burns National Heritage Park, Alloway (01292 443700)**. Burns Cottage Museum, Auld Kirk, Tam O' Shanter Experience, Brig O' Doon, Burns Monument and Gardens — all within half a mile of each other.
www.burnsheritagepark.com

◆ **Culzean Castle and Country Park, By Maybole (01655 884455)**. Castle designed by Robert Adam in 1777; park with deer, swans, walled garden, aviary, restaurant and tearoom.
www.nts.org.uk/culzean

◆ **Floors Castle, Kelso (01573 223333)**. Scotland's largest inhabited castle with magnificent collections of tapestries, furniture and porcelain. Gift shop and restaurant.
www.floorscastle.com

◆ **Harestanes Countryside Visitor Centre, Jedburgh (01835 830306)**. Wildlife garden and temporary exhibitions. Games and puzzles, adventure play area, tearoom, gift shop. Woodland walks.

◆ **Kelburn Castle & Country Centre, Fairlie (01475 568204)**. Historic home of the Earls of Glasgow, with beautiful garden walks, tea room, pony trekking, adventure course, children's stockade, pets' corner and The Secret Forest.
www.kelburnecastle.com

◆ **Loudoun Castle Park, Galston (01563 822296)**. Fun for all the family, with amusements and rides (including Britain's largest carousel), castle ruin, animals, aviary, restaurant and gift shop.
www.loudouncastle.co.uk

◆ **Magnum Leisure Centre, Irvine (01294 278381)**. Swimming pool complex, ice rink, sports hall, bowls hall, fitness suite, fast food outlet, theatre/cinema and soft play area.
www.themagnum.co.uk

◆ **Traquair House, Near Innerleithen (01896 830323)**. Oldest inhabited historic mansion in Scotland. Treasures date from 12th century, unique secret staircase to Priest's Room, craft workshop, woodland walks, maze, brewery.

◆ **Thirlestane Castle, Lauder (01578 722430)**. Border country life exhibitions in magnificent castle. Historic toys, woodland walk and picnic areas. Tearoom and gift shop.
www.thirlestanecastle.co.uk

◆ **Vikingar! Largs (01475 689777)**. Let live Viking guides take you on an enthralling multi-media journey back in time to trace the history of the Vikings in Scotland. Also swimming pool, soft play area, cinema/theatre and cafe/bar.
www.vikingar.co.uk

Scotland   131

Palace Hotel
GEORGE STREET, OBAN, ARGYLL PA34 5SB
01631 562294 • www.thepalacehotel.activehotels.com

A small family hotel offering personal supervision situated on Oban's sea front with wonderful views over the Bay, to the Mull Hills beyond. All rooms en suite, with colour TV, tea/coffee making facilities. Non-smoking.

The Palace is an ideal base for a real Highland holiday. By boat you can visit the islands of Kerrera, Coll, Tiree, Lismore, Mull and Iona, and by road Glencoe, Ben Nevis and Inveraray. Fishing, golf, horse riding, sailing, tennis and bowls all nearby. Children and pets welcome. Reductions for children.
Please write or telephone for brochure. Competitive rates.

Catacol Bay Hotel
Catacol, Isle of Arran KA27 8HN

Escape from the pressures of mainland life. Stay awhile by clear shining seas, rocky coast, breathtaking hills and mountains. Comfortable, friendly, small country house hotel where good cooking is our speciality. Extensive bar menu, meals are served from noon until 10pm. Centrally heated. Open all year. Details of Special Breaks and brochure on request. Children and pets welcome.

Tel: 01770 830231 • Fax: 01770 830350
Find us on the web at www.catacol.co.uk • e-mail: catbay@tiscali.co.uk

THE Fife Arms HOTEL
2 The Square, Dufftown, Near Keith AB55 4AD
Tel: 01340 820220 • Fax: 01340 821137
e-mail: fifearmsdufftown@btconnect.com

Welcome to Dufftown, the malt whisky capital of the land of distilleries where, in the centre of the village, the convivial bar of this family-run hotel is a popular meeting place. A range of tempting dishes is on offer in the lounge, including such unusual specialities as Beef and Ostrich. Very reasonably priced bed and breakfast accommodation is available in en suite chalets at the rear of the hotel; all are attractively furnished in pine and are equipped with television and tea and coffee-makers. Good facilities exist for children and disabled guests.   **www.fifearmsdufftown.co.uk**

LOCH LEVEN HOTEL

John & Hilary would like to welcome you to the lovely Loch Leven Hotel, a small, informal, family-run hotel with excellent food and an ideal base to explore this beautiful region. Enjoy the spectacular scenery from the Lochview Restaurant, garden and new decking, or toast yourself by the log fire in the Public Bar, with its inexpensive menu and wonderful selection of malts. Children and pets always welcome.
B&B from £40pp with discounts for Short Breaks.

Tel: 01855 821236
reception@lochlevenhotel.co.uk • www.lochlevenhotel.co.uk
Old Ferry Road, North Ballachulish, Near Fort William PH33 6SA

Scotland

Barfad Farmlands

Three stone cottages set in 80 acres of woodland with beaches and beautiful scenery.

THE CHICKEN COOP • sleeps 2 plus cot. Compact open plan kitchen/dining area, double bedroom, shower/wc.

THE DAIRY • sleeps 4 plus cot and one extra. Large open plan living/dining room with kitchen area, one family room (one double and one single), one single bedroom, sofa bed for one extra. Shower/wc.

THE STABLE • sleeps 4 plus one extra. Spacious open-plan kitchen/living room, one large bedroom, normally 3 single beds, 4 possible. Sofa bed for one extra. Shower, bath, two wcs.

All cottages include colour TV, laundry room (shared), parking, electric heating, linen and towels; electricity extra.

Mrs Barker, Barfad Farm, Tarbert, Loch Fyne, Argyll PA29 6YH
Tel: 01880 820549

The Treehouse

Unique lodge in beautiful woodland setting with views over golf course to Cairngorm mountains.

Comfortable, cosy and well equipped with superb log burning fire. Peaceful, yet only minutes' walk from local amenities. Perfect for an active or relaxing break, with wildlife, woodland walks and cycle tracks nearby. Sleeps 7.

*Pets welcome * Weekly lets and short breaks.*

Phone Mrs Mather on 0131 337 7167
e-mail: fhg@treehouselodge.plus.com
www.treehouselodge.co.uk

CRAIGLEMINE COTTAGE
STB ★★

With a rural location and peaceful atmosphere it's a wonderful place to unwind for a short break or a longer holiday. We have one double/family room, one single/twin room and dining room/lounge. Prices from £22. Evening meals available on request, including vegetarian or other dietary needs. Non- smoking. Off-road parking. Children welcome (under six years free). Pets welcome. An ideal base for walkers, cyclists, golf or touring. We also cater for amateur astronomers - call for details. Whether exploring the history, countryside or unspoilt beaches there is something for everyone. You can be sure of a friendly welcome all year round. Contact us for more details, or visit our website.

Glasserton, Near Whithorn DG8 8NE
Tel: 01988 500594
e-mail: cottage@fireflyuk.net
www.startravel.fireflyinternet.co.uk

Airdeny Chalets - Taynuilt

Situated in 3½ acres of peaceful natural habitat, with its own bluebell wood and a myriad of wildlife. Ideal for children and a 'midge-free zone'!

Three 3-bedroom chalets (STB ★★★★) and four 2-bedroom chalets (STB ★★★), all enjoying spectacular views, own privacy and parking area. Furnished to a very high standard and immaculately maintained by the resident owner.
Ideal for walking, cycling, fishing, bird watching, touring the Western Highlands and Islands, or just relaxing.

Dogs welcome. Assisted wheelchair access. Open all year.
Prices from £250 to £675. Taynuilt 1 mile, Oban 12 miles.
Contact: Jenifer Moffat - 01866 822648
e-mail: jenifer@airdenychalets.co.uk • www.airdenychalets.co.uk

WALES

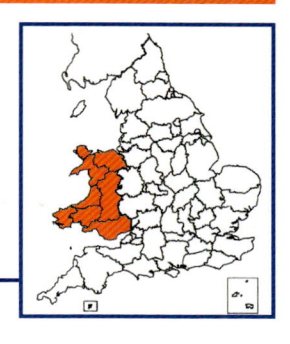

🏖 Best Beaches 🏖

A grand total of 43 beaches in Wales have been awarded the European Blue Flag for 2006, and an impressive number have received Seaside Awards (Resort and Rural Categories). Seaside Awards are given to well-managed beaches which comply with the legal minimum microbiological standards of water quality.

BLUE FLAG BEACHES 2006

- Anglesey
  Benllech, Llanddona, Llanddwyn, Porth Dafarch, Trearddur Bay
- Gwynedd
  Aberdyfi, Barmouth (Abermaw), Abersoch, Pwllheli, Fairbourne, Dinas Dinlle, Criccieth, Tywyn
- North Wales
  Llandudno (North Shore), Llandudno (West Shore), Penmaenmawr
- Carmarthenshire
  Pembrey Country Park
- Ceredigion
  Aberystwyth (North), Aberystwyth (South), Aberporth, Llangrannog, New Quay (Harbour), Borth, Tresaith
- Pembrokeshire
  Broadhaven (North), Dale, Saundersfoot, Lydstep, Tenby (Castle), Tenby (South), Tenby (North), Amroth, St Davids (Whitesands), Poppit Sands, Newgale
- South Wales
  Porthcawl (Rest Bay), Bracelet Bay, Caswell Bay, Port Eynon, Langland Bay Southerndown, Trecco Bay, Barry (Whitmore Bay)

ℹ️ VisitWales
- Tel: 08708 300306
- Fax: 08701 211259
- e-mail: info@visitwales.com
- www.VisitWales.com

Children Welcome!

FREE AND REDUCED RATE HOLIDAY VISITS!
Don't miss our Readers' Offer Vouchers on pages 9-38

Wales

ABERYSTWYTH

Family Fun Activities: Sports and leisure centre, swimming pools, children's playgrounds, parks, promenade, outdoor paddling pool • Narrow gauge railway, electric cliff railway, camera obscura, marina, castle, hill fort, National Library of Wales, theatre, cinema • Nature reserves and forestry centres, farm park, boat trips, coastal paths, cycle path.

i Tourist Information Centre, Terrace Road, Aberystwyth SY23 2AG
01970 612125 • Fax: 01970 626566
aberystwythtic@ceredigion.gov.uk
www.tourism.ceredigion.gov.uk

Beaches

• **BEACH.** Two-award-winning sloping beaches of coarse grey sand and shingle; North Beach fronted by promenade, parking on sea front; South Beach has ample parking. *Safety and maintenance:* water quality on both beaches usually good. Beach Officer/lifeguard usually on duty July/August. *Beach facilities:* rock pools, donkey rides; paddling pool etc on promenade; restaurants and kiosks; toilets. *Dog restrictions:* dogs banned between 1st May and 30th September on North Beach between jetty and Constitution Hill, and on South Beach between Castle headland and first groyne on South Marine Terrace

COLWYN BAY

Family Fun Activities: Welsh Mountain Zoo, Eirias Park with leisure centre, swimming pool, picnic and play areas, boating lake, model yacht pond, indoor tennis centre and skateboarding area • Pier and promenade with cycle track, Puppet Theatre, cricket ground and children's outdoor paddling pool at Rhos-on-Sea • Angling, bowling, golf, walking, watersports • Theatre/cinema with shows all year round.

☆ **Special Events:** **May Bank Holiday:** Bay of Colwyn Promenade Day. **August:** Festive Fridays - every Friday in August.

i Information Centre, Imperial Buildings, Princes Drive, Colwyn Bay
01492 530478
e-mail: colwynbay@nwtic.com
www.colwyn-bay-tourism.co.uk

Beaches

• **BEACH.** Sandy beach with easy access along A55 expressway. *Beach facilities:* kiosks; ♿ toilets operate on National Key system.

Please mention this publication when making enquiries about accommodation featured in these pages

---

See the *Family-Friendly Pubs & Inns* Supplement on pages 150-154 for establishments which really welcome children

Wales

LLANDUDNO

Family Fun Activities: Pier • putting, paddling pool, indoor swimming pool, yacht pond • Alice in Wonderland memorial on West Shore promenade, tramway and cable car to Great Orme Country Park and Visitor Centre, Great Orme Copper Mines, boat trips, Punch & Judy, 10-pin bowling • Llandudno Museum, Alice in Wonderland Visitor Centre, Bodafon Farm Park, Ski & Snowboard Centre with toboggan run • Theatre, art gallery • Victorian shopping centre.

Special Events: **May Bank Holiday:** Victorian Extravaganza. **June:** Gwyl Llandudno Festival - a summer arts festival. **July:** vehicle rally; Fun day, Bodafon Fields; various promenade events. **November:** Celtic Winter Fayre.

Tourist Information Centre, Chapel Street, Llandudno LL30 2UY
01492 876413
e-mail: llandudnotic@conwy.gov.uk
www.llandudno-tourism.co.uk

Beaches

• **NORTH SHORE BEACH.** Two miles long, sand and shingle, naturally sheltered; promenade and pier with amusements etc. *Safety and maintenance:* safe bathing beach. *Beach facilities:* deck chairs, donkey rides; pub and hotels on promenade; ice cream kiosks, snack bars etc nearby; toilets with ♿ access at eastern end.

• **WEST SHORE BEACH.** Sandy beach, one mile long; promenade and parking. *Safety and maintenance:* warning signs (sand banks can be dangerous on incoming tide). *Beach facilities:* children's play area; snack bar.

Children Welcome!

PORTHCAWL

Family Fun Activities: A variety of activities ranging from sports to all the fun of the fair.

Special Events: **February:** Celtic Festival of Wales. **April:** Porthcawl Jazz Festival. **July/August:** Porthcawl Town Carnival; Sea Festival. **September:** Elvis Festival.

Heritage Coast Tourist Information Centre, Old Police Station, John Street, Porthcawl CF36 3DT • 01656 786639
e-mail: porthcawltic@bridgend.gov.uk
www.visitbridgend.com

Beaches

• **BEACHES.** Trecco Bay and Rest Bay offer miles of golden sands; parking and good disabled access. *Beach facilities:* deckchairs; cafes and ice-cream kiosks; toilets nearby in town. *Dog restrictions:* banned in summer from June onwards.

TENBY

Family Fun Activities: Safe, sandy beaches • Leisure centre, amusement arcade, bowls, putting, sailing, pony trekking, golf courses • Pavilion (plays, variety shows, dancing, concerts etc), male voice choir concerts • Museum and art gallery, 15th century Tudor Merchant's House, aquarium, art galleries • The town is pedestrianised during July and August.

Special Events: Air Sea Rescue and Helicopter Displays; Winter and Summer Carnivals, brass bands, Arts Festival.

Information Centre, Tenby
01834 842402
tenby.tic@pembrokeshire.gov.uk

Fun for all the Family

NORTH WALES

◆ **Alice in Wonderland Centre, Llandudno (01492 860082).** Pop down the rabbit hole and see the Alice story come to life in colourful scenes. Souvenir shop. A must for all Lewis Carroll fans.
www.wonderland.co.uk

◆ **Anglesey Sea Zoo, Brynsiencyn (01248 430411).** Meet the fascinating creatures that inhabit the seas and shores around Anglesey; adventure playground, children's activities, shops and restaurants.
www.angleseyseazoo.co.uk

◆ **Electric Mountain Visitor Centre, Llanberis (01286 870636).** Discover the amazing powers of hydro-electricity in an exciting and interactive environment.
www.electricmountain.co.uk

◆ **Knights Cavern, Rhyl (01745 338562).** Spine chilling walk through supernatural, mythological Wales. "Tortures in the Castle" is guaranteed to shiver your timbers!

◆ **Museum of Childhood Memories, Beaumaris (01248 712498).** Over 2000 items in themed rooms will delight and fascinate all ages – from teddy bears to clockwork trains.

◆ **Pili Palas, Anglesey (01248 712474).** Exotic butterflies and birds in natural settings, plus (the children's favourites!) creepy crawlies and reptiles. Picnic area, cafe and adventure playground.
www.pilipalas.co.uk

◆ **Sea Life Centre, Rhyl (01745 344660).** Spectacular underwater tunnel allows you to walk through sharks, stingrays and other sea creatures. Regular talks, feeding displays and demonstrations; gift shop.
www.rhyl.com/sealife

◆ **Sun Centre, Rhyl (01745 344433).** Whatever the weather, it's like an indoor island in the sun. Indoor surfing, water slides – pay once and stay all day.
www.rhylsuncentre.co.uk

◆ **Sygun Copper Mine, Beddgelert (01766 890595).** Stalagmites and stalactites formed from ferrous oxide. Award-winning attraction with underground audio visual tours.
www.syguncoppermine.co.uk

◆ **Welsh Mountain Zoo, Colwyn Bay (01492 532938).** Magnificent animals in natural surroundings, plus Chimpanzee World, Jungle Adventureland and Tarzan Trail, children's farm, etc - a great day out.
www.welshmountainzoo.org

The Classified Listing Section

on pages 141-149 is a quick, easy to use summary of the facilities offered by the accommodation featured in this guide.

Fun for all the Family

MID WALES

◆ **Centre for Alternative Technology, Machynlleth (01654 705950).** A "green" village with displays of sustainable and renewable sources of power eg solar, wind. Energy saving houses, organic gardens, bookshop. Adventure playground, restaurant.
www.cat.org.uk

◆ **Chwarel Hen Slate Caverns, Llanfair, Near Harlech (01766 780247).** Self-guided tours of awesome series of slate caverns – spooky in places, but memorable. Also children's farmyard.

◆ **Felinwynt Rainforest and Butterfly Centre, Rhosmaen, Near Aberporth (01239 810882).** Exotic butterflies flying freely in a hothouse atmosphere amid tropical plants and the taped sounds of a Peruvian rainforest.
www.felinwyntrainforest.co.uk

◆ **Llywernog Silver-Lead Mine, Ponterwyd, Aberystwyth (01970 890620).** Underground tours and miners' trail telling the story of the hunt for gold and silver in the Welsh hills.
www.silverminetours.co.uk

◆ **Portmeirion Italianate Village, Near Penrhyndeudraeth (01766 770000).** The most "un-Welsh" village in Wales, with the atmosphere of a strange, self-contained world. Location of 'The Prisoner' TV series in the mid-60s.
www.portmeirion.wales.com

FREE AND REDUCED RATE HOLIDAY VISITS!
Don't miss our
Readers' Offer Vouchers
on pages 9-38

Wales

☆ Fun for all the Family ☆

SOUTH WALES

◆ **Big Pit, Blaenavon (01495 790311).** Don a miner's helmet and go down a real coal mine with ex-miners as guides. See the stables where the pit ponies were kept.
www.nmgw.ac.uk/bigpit

◆ **Cardiff Castle (029 2087 8100).** Spanning nearly 2000 years of history, the splendidly decorated apartments are set in a magnificent building surrounded by eight-acre grounds.
www.cardiff.gov.uk

◆ **The Dinosaur Experience, Great Wedlock (01834 845272).** Unique Visitor Centre in 33 acre park, with life-size models, dinosaur trail, hands-on activities; restaurant; picnic areas.

◆ **Grove Land, Near Carmarthen (01994 231181).** Indoor and outdoor activities for all the family — laser clay pigeon shoot, bumper boats, fun barn, play area, pony rides and lots more.

◆ **Heron's Brook Animal Park, Narberth (01834 860723).** Set in 30 acres of parkland, where friendly animals roam freely. Feed the rabbits and guinea pigs at Bunny World, enjoy a round of croquet or putting.
www.herons-brook.co.uk

◆ **Llancaiach Fawr Manor, Nelson (01443 412248).** Living museum of the Civil War. Guides in period costume invite visitors to try on clothes, tour the house etc — very much a "hands on" experience.

◆ **Manor House Wild Animal Park, St Florence, Tenby (01646 651201).** Pretty grounds with apes, monkeys, otters, deer and an aquarium plus giant slide, radio-controlled boats and other amusements.
www.manorhousewildanimalpark.co.uk

◆ **Oakwood, Narberth (01834 891373).** There's a whole voyage of discovery just waiting to set sail at Oakwood. With more than 40 rides and attractions set in 80 acres of landscaped gardens and parkland, there are absolutely no constraints on fun!
www.oakwood-leisure.com

◆ **Rhondda Heritage Park, Trehafod (01443 682036).** See the story of Black Gold unfold as you tour the site, set in former working colliery. Underground tour, display, visitor centre, tearoom and gift shop.
www.rhonddaheritagepark.com

◆ **Techniquest, Cardiff (029 2047 5475).** Where science and technology come to life - visitors are actively encouraged to handle the exhibits.
www.tquest.org.uk

◆ **Tredegar House, Newport (01633 815880).** "Upstairs, Downstairs" tour, adventure playground, craft workshops, boating lake – something to interest all the family.

Please mention CHILDREN WELCOME! when enquiring about accommodation featured in this guide

Wales

Come visit us in our beautiful location

- Indoor heated swimming pool
- Lounges with spectacular sea views
- Families welcome
- Snooker room
- Beauty salon
- AA ★★★

Great Value Winter Breaks

Relaxed atmosphere with friendly service

We are located on the mid Wales coast in an idyllic site overlooking the Golf course, sand dunes and sea by the picturesque and historic fishing village of Aberdovey.

For more information on the hotel please call or visit our web site.

TREFEDDIAN HOTEL
ABERDOVEY   LL35 0SB

01654 767 213
www.trefwales.com

WYNNSTAY ARMS HOTEL
Llangollen
Denbighshire
LL20 8PF

Tel: 01978 860710
Fax: 01978 860774
contact@wynnstay-arms.co.uk
www.wynnstay-arms.co.uk

This traditional 17th century coaching inn, with beamed ceilings and many original features, is located in the centre of Llangollen, an ideal base for exploring the local places of interest and scenic countryside.

- Beer garden • Log fires in winter
- Families welcome
- Dogs with well-behaved owners
- Bar snacks daily
- Evening restaurant menu
- Double/twin and family en suite rooms
- En suite bunkhouse accommodation

TYN-Y-GROES HOTEL ~ Accommodation in Snowdonia National Park

16th century coaching inn on the A470 near the village of Ganllwyd overlooking the Mawddach river. Close to Coed-y-Brenin mountain bike centre. Nature trails, walks, fishing (permits issued).

Ganllwyd, Dolgellau LL40 2HN
Tel: 01341 440275 • www.tynygroes.com
e-mail: nephi@tynyg.wanadoo.co.uk

- En suite bedrooms with central heating and TV Cot/high chair available
- Restaurant and dining room. Bar snacks
- Beer garden
- Dogs by arrangement
- Open all year

LLANTEGLOS ESTATE

Charming self-contained Woodland Lodges (sleep up to 6) set in quiet countryside estate. Views over National Parkland and Carmarthen Bay from balconies. Ideal for holidays or shorter breaks in any season. Safe children's play area. Elsewhere on the property, visit our wonderful rustic clubhouse - 'The Wanderer's Rest Inn', with fully licensed bar, roaring fire, food and entertainment. Miles of sandy beaches, many visitor attractions for all ages and rambling trails close by. A warm welcome awaits you. For further details and colour brochure please telephone Tony and Jane Baron.

WTB ★★★★

TONY & JANE BARON, LLANTEGLOS ESTATE, LLANTEG, NEAR AMROTH, PEMBROKESHIRE SA67 8PU • Tel: 01834 831677/831371
e-mail: llanteglosestate@supanet.com • www.llanteglos-estate.com

MADOG'S WELLS • Mid-Wales Holidays

Llanfair Caereinion, Welshpool, Powys SY21 0DE

Beautiful, peaceful valley with lots of wildlife. Three bungalows, wheelchair accessible. Free gas, electricity and linen. Cot and iron also available on request. Games room and children's play area. Daily rates available out of main school holidays. Two three-bedroom bungalows (**WTB ★★★★★**) from £140 to £480. Two-bedroom bungalow (**WTB ★★★**) £100 to £300. Open all year. Farmhouse B&B at £23 pppn.

Contact Michael & Ann Reed for further details • Tel/Fax: 01938 810446
e-mail: info@madogswells.co.uk • www.madogswells.co.uk

Carne Farm

Stone cottage adjoining farmhouse, sleeps six in three bedrooms, also a spacious residential caravan for six with two bedrooms, each with its own garden where children can play safely. In peaceful countryside on 350 acre dairy and sheep farm between Fishguard and Strumble Head, three miles from the sea. Within easy reach of many beaches by car, ideal for walking and bird-watching. No linen supplied. Children welcome. TV, microwave, cots, high chairs. Baby sitting available. You can be sure of a warm welcome and visitors can feed calves and watch the milking.

Contact: Mrs Rosemary Johns

Goodwick, Pembrokeshire SA64 0LB
Tel: 01348 891665

PARC WERNOL PARK • Chwilog, Pwllheli LL53 6SW • 01766 810506

- Panoramic views • Peaceful and quiet
- Ideal for touring Lleyn and Snowdonia
- 4 miles Criccieth and Pwllheli
- 3 miles beach • Cycle route
- Free coarse fishing lake • Safe children's play area
- Games room • Footpaths • Dog exercise field
- Self-catering holidays • 1,2 & 3 bedroom cottages
- 2 and 3 bedroom caravans and chalets
- Colour brochure • Personal attention at all times
- A truly Welsh welcome.

www.wernol.com

CLASSIFIED ACCOMMODATION LISTINGS

This is a brief summary of the facilities available at the accommodation featured in this guide. Please note that not all advertisers supply this information, so some entries are not complete - please contact the proprietors directly for full details.

EXPLANATION OF SYMBOLS

BOARD

- Total number of bedrooms
- Bedrooms with private bath/shower
- Full Board
- Bed/Breakfast/Evening Meal
- Bed/Breakfast
- Children's meals

SELF-CATERING

- Flats/Apartments
- Caravans
- Chalets/Lodges
- Cottages/Houses
- Linen provided
- Linen for hire
- On site shop

GENERAL

- Baby listening
- Cots
- Highchairs
- Laundry facilities
- Indoor play area
- Outdoor play area
- Children's entertainment
- Pets allowed
- Cater for disabled
- Licensed bar
- Live entertainment
- Snack bar/food takeaway
- Indoor heated swimming pool
- Outdoor heated swimming pool
- Jacuzzi
- Solarium
- Tennis courts
- Putting green
- Open all year
- Totally non-smoking

F →2 Child free sharing with parents (eg up to age 2)

R →14 Reductions for children sharing with parents (eg up to age 14)

CORNWALL   Board

CAWSAND • Wringford Down
24 24 [R] ▼ on request

HELSTON • Rocklands
3 2 [R] →14 ▼ £23.00

PADSTOW • Tregea Hotel
8 8 ▼ on request

TRURO • Trenona Farm
4 4 [R] ▼ £25.00 ▲ £38.00

141

CORNWALL — Self-catering

FALMOUTH • Cornish Holiday Cottages
▼ £175
▲ £1650

FOWEY • Fowey Harbour Cottages
▼ on request

HAYLE • St Ives Bay Holiday Park
▼ on request

LAUNCESTON • Bamham Farm Cottages
▼ on request

LISKEARD • Cutkive Wood Holiday Lodges
▼ on request

PADSTOW • Raintree House Holidays
▼ on request

PORT GAVERNE • Green Door Cottages
▼ on request

TRURO • Trenona Farm
▼ £240
▲ £760

SOUTH DEVON — Board

DAWLISH • Langstone Cliff Hotel
66   66
▼ on request

TORQUAY • The Glenorleigh
F → 2   R → 16
15   15
▼ £30.00
▲ £40.00

SOUTH DEVON — Self-Catering

• Farm & Cottage Holidays
▼ on request

• Toad Hall Cottages
▼ on request

ASHBURTON • Parkers Farm Holiday Park
▼ on request

ASHBURTON • Parkers Farm Cottages & Caravans
▼ £135
▲ £600

BRIXHAM • Devoncourt Holiday Flats
▼ on request

DAWLISH • Cofton Country Holidays
▼ £285
▲ £769

HOPE COVE • Sanderlings
▼ £195

NORTH DEVON   Board

BARNSTAPLE • Valley View
R → 12
▼ £20.00

WOOLACOMBE • Woolacombe Bay Hotel
65   65
▼ on request

NORTH DEVON   Self-Catering

BARNSTAPLE • North Hill
▼ £210
▲ £585

COMBE MARTIN • Wheel Farm Country Cottages
▼ on request

LITTLE TORRINGTON • Torridge House Farm Cottages
▼ on request

UMBERLEIGH • Collacott Farm Cottages
▼ on request

WOOLACOMBE • Woolacombe Bay Holiday Parcs
▼ on request

WOOLACOMBE • Woolacombe Bay Hotel Apartments
▼ on request

SOMERSET & WILTSHIRE — Board

STOGUMBER • Wick House — ▼ on request

WESTBURY • Spinney Farmhouse — F→5 — ▼ on request
3

WESTON-SUPER-MARE • Batch Country Hotel — R — ▼ on request
11 11

SOMERSET & WILTSHIRE — Self-Catering

MINEHEAD • St Audries Bay Holiday Club — ▼ on request

HAMPSHIRE & DORSET — Board

BARTON-ON-SEA • Laurel Lodge — ▼ £25.00
3 3

BOURNEMOUTH • Denewood Hotel — ▼ on request
12

CHARMOUTH • Cardsmill Farm Holidays — R→10 — ▼ £24.00
3 3

LULWORTH COVE • Cromwell House — F→2 — R→13 — ▼ on request
17 17

RINGWOOD • High Corner Inn — 2 — ▼ on request
7 7

STUDLAND BAY • Knoll House — R→12 — ▼ on request
80 56

HAMPSHIRE & DORSET — Self-Catering

BRIDPORT • Lancombes House — ▼ on request

BURTON BRADSTOCK • Tamarisk Farm — ▼ £250
▲ £995

WAREHAM • Dormer Cottage
▼ on request

ISLE OF WIGHT — Board

SANDOWN • Fernside Hotel
11 11 BB
▼ on request

SANDOWN • Sandhill Hotel
▼ on request

SHANKLIN • Orchardcroft Hotel
▼ on request

TOTLAND • Frenchman's Cove
10 10 BB
▼ on request

ISLE OF WIGHT — Self-Catering

• Island Cottage Holidays
▼ £139
▲ £1195

RYDE • Hillgrove Park
▼ on request

SHANKLIN • Lyon Court
▼ £275
▲ £760

SUSSEX — Board

HAILSHAM • Longleys Farm Cottage
3 2 BB
▼ £21.00

SUSSEX — Self-Catering

BATTLE • Crowhurst Park
▼ on request

CHIDDINGLY • Pekes
▼ £385
▲ £730

POLEGATE • Polhills
▼ £275

KENT   Board

ASHFORD • Bolden's Wood
🛏 3
[BB]   /🛆\   ⊘   ▼ £25.00

ASHFORD • The Croft Hotel
🛏 27   🍼 27   ⊟   🚼
✖ [BB]   ♫   ♀   ▼ on request

CANTERBURY • Great Field Farm
🛏 3   🍼 3   /🛆\   [R]
   [BB]   ⊘   ▼ £25.00

SEVENOAKS • Bull Hotel
✖ [BB]   ♀   ▼ on request

LONDON & HOME COUNTIES   Board

KINGSTON-UPON-THAMES • Chase Lodge
🛏 11   🍼 11   🍼   ⊟   🚼   🐕   ♀   ▼ on request
🍽 ✖ [BB] 🛌   Ⓐ

LONDON • White Lodge Hotel
🛏 20   🍼 8   🍼   ⊟   🚼
       [BB]   Ⓐ   ▼ on request

LONDON • Gower Hotel
🛏 21   🍼 19
       [BB]   Ⓐ   ▼ on request

LONDON • Athena Hotel
       [BB]   Ⓐ   ▼ on request

LONDON • Queens Hotel
       [BB]   Ⓐ   ▼ on request

LONDON • Barry House Hotel
🛏 18   🍼 15
       [BB]   ▼ on request

EAST ANGLIA   Board

BURWELL • The Meadow House
       [BB]   ⊘   ▼ on request

FRAMLINGHAM • High House Farm
🛏 2   🍼 2   ⊟   🚼   /🛆\
       [BB]   ▼ on request

EAST ANGLIA — Self-Catering

BACTON-ON-SEA • Castaways Holiday Park — ▼ on request

FAKENHAM • Vere Lodge — ▼ on request

KESSINGLAND • Kessingland Cottage — ▼ £95 ▲ £375

SOUTHWOLD • Whitehouse Barns — ▼ £300

MIDLANDS — Board

ASHBOURNE • Dog & Partridge Inn
30 28 — ▼ on request

BUXTON • Alison Park Hotel
17 17 — ▼ on request

GREAT MALVERN • Croft Guest House
5 3 — ▼ on request

ROSS-ON-WYE • Old Kilns — ▼ £20.00

TELFORD • Holiday Inn
150 150 — ▼ on request

TELFORD • International Hotel
101 101 — ▼ on request

NORTH-EAST ENGLAND — Board

BAMBURGH • Mizen Head Hotel — ▼ on request

HALTWHISTLE • Saughy Rigg Farm — ▼ on request

NORTH-EAST ENGLAND — Self-Catering

BISHOP AUCKLAND • Low Lands Farm Cottages
▼ £150
▲ £340

BISHOP THORNTON • Courtyard at Duke's Place
▼ on request

HARTLEPOOL • Ash Vale Holiday Home Park
▼ on request

HEXHAM • Isaac's Cottage
▼ on request

HEXHAM • Moorgair Cottage
▼ on request

WHITBY • Greenhouses Farm Cottages
▼ £220
▲ £585

NORTH-WEST ENGLAND — Board

AMBLESIDE • Rothay Manor
19 19 F→3 R→16
▼ £60.00

LYTHAM ST ANNES • Chadwick Hotel
75 75 F→2 R→12
▼ on request

NANTWICH • Lea Farm
3 2 R
▼ £24.00

ST ANNES • Dalmeny Hotel
128 128 R→16
▼ on request

WINDERMERE • Green Gables
7 7
▼ £23.00
▲ £30.00

NORTH-WEST ENGLAND — Self-Catering

AMBLESIDE • Greenhowe Caravan Park
▼ on request

SCOTLAND   Board

BALLACHULISH • Loch Leven Hotel
🛏 11   🛏 11   🐕   🍷   ▼ £40.00
✕ BB   ♪

CATACOL • Catacol Bay Hotel
🛏 6   🐕   🍷   ▼ on request
✕ BB   ♪

DUFFTOWN • Fife Arms
🛏 6   🛏 6   ♿   🍷   ▼ on request
✕ BB

OBAN • Palace Hotel   F → 2 R → 12
🛏 13 🛏 13   🛏 🪑   🐕   🍷   ▼ on request
       BB

SCOTLAND   Self-Catering

BOAT OF GARTEN • The Treehouse
          🏠   📻   ▼ on request
📑

TARBERT • Barfad Farmlands
          🏡   🛏 📻   ▼ on request
📑

WALES   Board

ABERDOVEY • Trefeddian Hotel   R
🛏 59 🛏 59   🛏 🪑 🎠 ⛱   ⚙ ✏   ♿   🍷   ▼ on request
🍽 ✕ BB ♨   A

DOLGELLAU • Tyn-y-Groes Hotel
                     🛏 🪑   🍷   ▼ on request
✕   BB   A

LLANGOLLEN • Wynnstay Arms
🛏 7   🛏 7   🐕   🍷   ▼ on request
✕   BB   A

WALES   Self-catering

AMROTH • Llanteglos Estate
          🏠   ⛱   🍷   ▼ on request

WELSHPOOL • Madog's Wells
          🏠   🛏 📻 🎠 ⛱   ♿   ▼ on request
📑   A

Family-Friendly Pubs and Inns

Family-Friendly Pubs and Inns

This is a selection of establishments which make an extra effort to cater for parents and children. The majority provide a separate children's menu or they may be willing to serve small portions of main course dishes on request; there are often separate outdoor or indoor play areas where the junior members of the family can let off steam while Mum and Dad unwind over a drink. For more details, please see individual entries under county headings.

NB: Not all establishments featured in this section have an entry in the main section of this guide, but they appear in other FHG publications - see the FHG website www.holidayguides.com.

- half portions
- children's menu
- garden or play area
- baby-changing facilities
- high chairs
- family room

THE CROWN HOTEL
16 High Street, Amersham,
Buckinghamshire HP7 0DH
01494 721541
www.dhillonhotels.co.uk

CROWN & PUNCHBOWL
High Street, Horningsea,
Cambridgeshire CB5 9JG
Tel: 01223 860643
www.cambscuisine.com

COACH HOUSE HOTEL
Flint Cross, Newmarket Road, Near
Melbourn Cambridgeshire SG8 7PN
Tel: 01763 208272
www.coachhousehotel.co.uk

THE DOG INN
Wellbank Lane, Over Peover, Near
Knutsford, Cheshire WA16 8UP
Tel: 01625 861421
www.doginn-overpeover.co.uk

COLEDALE INN
Braithwaite, Near Keswick,
Cumbria CA12 5TN
Tel: 017687 78272
www.coledale-inn.co.uk

Family-Friendly Pubs and Inns

- half portions
- children's menu
- garden or play area
- baby-changing facilities
- high chairs
- family room

BROTHERSWATER INN
Patterdale, Penrith,
Cumbria CA11 0NZ
Tel: 017684 82239
www.sykeside.co.uk

NEW INN HOTEL
High Street, Clovelly, Near
Bideford, Devon EX39 5TQ
Tel: 01237 431303
www.clovelly.co.uk

THE HOOPS INN
Horns Cross, Near Clovelly,
Bideford, Devon EX39 5DL
Tel: 01237 451222
www.hoopsinn.co.uk

WHITE HART HOTEL
Fore Street, Okehampton,
Devon EX20 1HD
Tel: 01837 52730/54514
www.thewhitehart-hotel.com

THE BELL HOTEL
The Quay, Sandwich,
Kent CT13 9EF
Tel: 01304 613388
www.bellhotelsandwich.co.uk

ANGEL & ROYAL HOTEL
4-5 High Street, Grantham,
Lincolnshire NG31 6PN
Tel: 01476 565816
www.angelandroyal.co.uk

THE TALLY HO INN
Aswarby, Near Sleaford,
Lincolnshire NG34 8SA
Tel: 01529 455205
www.tally-ho-aswarby.co.uk

Family-Friendly Pubs and Inns

THE OLD RAM INN
Ipswich Road (A140),
Tivetshall St Mary, Norfolk NR15 2DE
Tel: 01379 676794
www.theoldram.com

THE TOM MOGG INN
Station Road, Burtle,
Near Bridgwater, Somerset TA7 8NU
Tel: 01278 722399
www.tommogg.co.uk

THE CROWN HOTEL
Exford, Exmoor National Park,
Somerset TA24 7PP
Tel: 01643 831554/5
www.crownhotelexmoor.co.uk

LORD POULETT ARMS
High Street, Hinton St George,
Somerset TA17 8SE
Tel: 01460 73149
www.lordpoulettarms.com

THE FOUNTAIN INN
1 St Thomas Street, Wells,
Somerset BA5 2UU
Tel: 01749 672317
www.fountaininn.co.uk

THE CROWN AT WELLS
Market Place, Wells,
Somerset BA5 2RP
Tel: 01749 673457
www.crownatwells.co.uk

THE SIX BELLS
The Green, Bardwell, Bury St
Edmunds, Suffolk IP13 1AW
Tel: 01359 250820
www.sixbellsbardwell.co.uk

WORSLEY ARMS HOTEL
Hovingham, North Yorkshire YO62 4LA
Tel: 01653 628234
www.worsleyarms.com

Family-Friendly Pubs and Inns

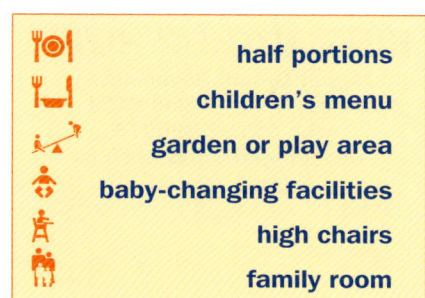

Legend:
- 🍽 half portions
- 🛏 children's menu
- 🛝 garden or play area
- 👶 baby-changing facilities
- 🪑 high chairs
- 👨‍👦 family room

WHITE ROSE HOTEL
Leeming Bar, Northallerton,
North Yorkshire DL7 9AY
Tel: 01677 422707/424941
www.whiterosehotel.co.uk

WHITE SWAN INN
Market Place, Pickering, North
Yorkshire YO18 7AA
Tel: 01751 472288
www.white-swan.co.uk

MURRAY ARMS HOTEL
Gatehouse of Fleet, Castle Douglas,
Kirkcudbrightshire DG7 2HY
Tel: 01557 814207
www.murrayarmshotel.co.uk

LAIRD & DOG HOTEL
5 High Street, Lasswade, Near
Edinburgh, Midlothian EH18 1NA
Tel: 0131 663 9219
www.lairdanddog.btinternet.co.uk

OAK TREE INN
Balmaha, Loch Lomond, G63 0JQ
Tel: 01360 870357
www.oak-tree-inn.co.uk

WATERHOUSE INN
The Square, Balloch Road,
Balloch G83 8LE
Tel: 01389 752120
www.waterhouseinn.co.uk

THE BELLACHROY
Dervaig, Isle of Mull PA75 6QW
Tel: 01688 400314
www.thebellachroy.co.uk

Family-Friendly Pubs and Inns

HUNTER'S MOON INN
Llangattock Lingoed, Near
Abergavenny, NP7 8RR
Tel: 01873 821499
www.hunters-moon-inn.co.uk

KING ARTHUR HOTEL
Higher Green, Reynoldston,
Swansea, South Wales SA31 1AD
Tel: 01792 390775
www.kingarthurhotel.co.uk

Looking for Holiday Accommodation?

FHG
·K·U·P·E·R·A·R·D·

for details of hundreds of
properties throughout the UK
visit our website on

www.holidayguides.com

154

DIRECTORY OF WEBSITE AND E-MAIL ADDRESSES

A quick-reference guide to holiday accommodation with an e-mail address and/or website, conveniently arranged by country and county, with full contact details.

Holiday Parks/Touring & Camping
Cinque Ports Leisure
• website: www.cplholidays.com

•LONDON

B & B
Sohel & Anne Armanios, 67 Rannoch Road, Hammersmith, LONDON W6 9SS
Tel: 020 7385 4904
• website: www.thewaytostay.co.uk

Hotel
Athena Hotel, 110-114 Sussex Gardens, Hyde Park, LONDON W2 1UA
Tel: 020 7706 3866
• e-mail: athena@stavrouhotels.co.uk
• website: www.stavrouhotels.co.uk

Hotel
Barry House Hotel, 12 Sussex Place, Hyde Park, LONDON W2 2TP Tel: 0207 723 7340
• e-mail: hotel@barryhouse.co.uk
• website: www.barryhouse.co.uk

Hotel
Elizabeth Hotel, 37 Eccleston Square, LONDON SW1V 1PB Tel: 020 7828 6812
• e-mail: info@elizabethhotel.com
• website: www.elizabethhotel.com

Hotel
The Elysee Hotel, 25-26 Craven Terrace, LONDON W2 3EL Tel: 020 7402 7633
• e-mail: information@hotelelysee.co.uk
• website: www.hotelelysee.co.uk

Hotel
Gower Hotel, 129 Sussex Gardens, Hyde Park, LONDON W2 2RX
Tel: 020 7262 2262
• e-mail: gower@stavrouhotels.co.uk
• website: www.stavrouhotels.co.uk

Hotel
Lincoln House Hotel, 33 Gloucester Place, Marble Arch, LONDON W1V 8HY
Tel: 0207 486 7630
• e-mail: reservations@lincoln-house-hotel.co.uk
• website: www.lincoln-house-hotel.co.uk

B & B
Manor Court Hotel, 7 Clanricarde Gardens, LONDON W2 4JJ Tel: 020 7792 3361 or 020 7727 5407
• e-mail: enquiries@manorcourthotel.com
• website: www.abc-london.com
    www.123europe-londonhotels.com

Hotel
Queens Hotel, 33 Anson Road, Tufnell Park, LONDON N7 Tel: 020 7607 4725
• e-mail: queens@stavrouhotels.co.uk
• website: www.stavrouhotels.co.uk

•BEDFORDSHIRE

Self-Catering
Bluegate Farm Holiday Cottages
Bluegate Farm, Stanbridge,
LEIGHTON BUZZARD, Beds LU7 9JD
Tel: 01525 210621
• e-mail: enquiries@bluegatecottages.co.uk
• website: www.bluegatecottages.co.uk

Farmhouse / B & B / Self-Catering Cottages
Mrs M. Codd, Highfield Farm,
Tempsford Road, SANDY, Beds SG19 2AQ
Tel: 01767 682332
• e-mail: margaret@highfield-farm.co.uk
• website: www.highfield-farm.co.uk

•BERKSHIRE

Inn
Julie Plastow, The Greyhound,
16 Common Road,
ETON WICK, Berkshire SL4 6JE
Tel: 01753 863 925
• e-mail: thegreyhoundpub@hotmail.com
• website: thegreyhoundetonwick.co.uk

www.holidayguides.com

WEBSITE DIRECTORY

Hotel
Clarence Hotel, 9 Clarence Road, WINDSOR, Berkshire SL4 5AE
Tel: 01753 864436
- e-mail: enquiries@clarence-hotel.co.uk
- website: www.clarence-hotel.co.uk

• BUCKINGHAMSHIRE

B & B / Self-Catering Cottages
Poletrees Farm, Ludgershall Road, Brill, AYLESBURY, Buckinghamshire HP18 9TZ
Tel: 01844 238276
- e-mail: poletrees.farm@virgin.net
- web: www.countryaccom.co.uk/poletrees-farm

• CAMBRIDGESHIRE

B & B
Hilary & Brian Marsh, The Meadow House 2A High Street, BURWELL, Cambridgeshir CB5 0HB Tel: 01638 741 926
- e-mail: hilary@themeadowhouse.co.uk
- website: www.themeadowhouse.co.uk

Guest House
Dykelands Guest House, 157 Mowbray Road, CAMBRIDGE, Cambridgeshire CB1 7SP
Tel: 01223 244300
- website: www.dykelands.com

Self-Catering
Mrs J. Farndale, Cathedral House, 17 St Mary's Street, ELY, Cambridgeshire CB7 4ER
Tel: 01352 662124
- e-mail: farndale@cathedralhouse.co.uk
- website: www.cathedralhouse.co.uk

B & B
Chequer Cottage, 43 Streetly End, HORSEHEATH, Cambridgeshire CB1 6RP
Tel: 01223 891 522
- e-mail: stay@chequercottage.com
- website: www.chequercottage.com

• CHESHIRE

Guest House / Self-Catering
Mrs Joanne Hollins, Balterley Green Farm, Deans Lane, BALTERLEY, near Crewe Cheshire CW2 5QJ Tel: 01270 820 214
- e-mail: greenfarm@balterley.fsnet.co.uk
- website: www.greenfarm.freeserve.co.uk

Guest House
Mitchell's of Chester, 28 Hough Green, CHESTER, Cheshire CH4 8JQ
Tel: 01244 679 004
- e-mail: mitoches@dialstart.net
- website: www.mitchellsofchester.com

Guest House / Self-Catering
Mrs Angela Smith, Mill House and Granary, Higher Wych, MALPAS, Cheshire SY14 7JR
Tel: 01948 780362
- e-mail: angela@videoactive.co.uk
- website: www.millhouseandgranary.co.uk

Farm House / B & B
Jean Callwood, Lea Farm, Wrinehill Road, Wybunbury, NANTWICH, Cheshire CW5 7NS. Tel: 01270 841429
- e-mail: contactus@leafarm.freeserve.co.uk
- website: www.leafarm.co.uk

• CORNWALL

Self-catering
Graham Wright, Guardian House, Barras Street, Liskeard, Cornwall PL14 6AD
Tel: 01579 344080

Self-Catering
Cornish Traditional Cottages, Blisland, BODMIN, Cornwall PL30 4HS
Tel: 01208 821666
- e-mail: info@corncott.com
- website: www.corncott.com

Self-Catering
Mrs Angela Clark, Darrynane Cottages, Darrynane, St Breward, BODMIN, Cornwall PL30 4LZ. Tel: 01208 850885
- e-mail: enquiries@darrynane.co.uk
- website: www.darrynane.com

Self-Catering
Penrose Burden Holiday Cottages, St Breward, BODMIN, Cornwall PL30 4LZ
Tel: 01208 850277 or 01208 850617
- website: www.penroseburden.co.uk

Self-Catering
Trevella, Treveighan, St Teath, BODMIN, Cornwall PL30 3JN
Tel: 01208 850 529
- e-mail: david.trevella@btconnect.com
- website: www.trevellacornwall.co.uk

Readers are requested to mention this FHG guidebook when seeking accommodation

WEBSITE DIRECTORY

Touring Caravan & Camping Park
Budemeadows Touring Park, BUDE, Cornwall EX23 0NA Tel: 01288 361646
- e-mail: **holiday@budemeadows.com**
- website: **www.budemeadows.com**

Self-Catering
Langfield Manor, Broadclose, BUDE, Cornwall EX23 8DP Tel: 01288 352 415
- e-mail: **info@langfieldmanor.co.uk**
- website: **www.langfieldmanor.co.uk**

Guest House
Stratton Gardens, Cot Hill, Stratton, BUDE, Cornwall EX23 9DN Tel: 01288 352500
- e-mail: **moira@stratton-gardens.co.uk**
- website: **www.stratton-gardens.co.uk**

Farm
Mrs Margaret Short, Langaton Farm, Whitstone, Holsworthy, BUDE, Cornwall EX22 6TS Tel: 01288 341 215
- e-mail: **langatonfarm@hotmail.com**
- website: **www.langaton-farm-holidays.co.uk**

Self-Catering Cottage
Lower Kitleigh Cottage, Week St Mary, near BUDE, Cornwall
Contact: Mr & Mrs T. Bruce-Dick, 114 Albert Street, London NW1 7NE
Tel: 0207 485 8976
- e-mail: **timbrucedick@yahoo.co.uk**
- website: **www.tbdarchitects.co.uk**

Hotel
Wringford Down Hotel, Hat Lane, CAWSAND, Cornwall PL10 1LE
Tel: 01752 822287
- e-mail: **a.molloy@virgin.net**
- website: **www.cornwallholidays.co.uk**

Self-Catering
Mineshop Holiday Cottages, CRACKINGTON HAVEN, Bude, Cornwall EX23 0NR Tel: 01840 230338
- e-mail: **info@mineshop.co.uk**
- website: **www.mineshop.co.uk**

Self-Catering
Delamere Holiday Bungalows, DELABOLE, Cornwall
Contact: Mrs J. Snowden Tel: 01895 234144
- website: **www.delamerebungalows.com**

Self-Catering
Cornish Holiday Cottages, Killibrae, West Bay, Maenporth, FALMOUTH, Cornwall TR11 5HP Tel: 01326 250 339
- e-mail: **info@cornishholidaycottages.net**
- website: **www.cornishholidaycottages.net**

Self-Catering
Mr M. Watson, Creekside Holiday Cottages, Strangwith House, Restronguet, FALMOUTH, Cornwall TR11 5ST
Tel: 01326 375972
- e-mail: **martin@creeksidecottages.co.uk**
- website: **www.creeksidecottages.co.uk**

Self-Catering
Colin Kemp, Pantiles,
6 Stracey Road, FALMOUTH, Cornwall TR11 4DW Tel: 01326 211838
- e-mail: **colinkemp@lineone.net**
- website: **www.falmouthapartments.co.uk**

Hotel
Rosemullion Hotel, Gyllyngvase Hill, FALMOUTH, Cornwall TR11 4DF
Tel: 01326 314 690
- e-mail: **gail@rosemullionhotel.demon.co.uk**
- **www.SmoothHound.co.uk/hotels/rosemullion.**

Self-Catering
Mrs K Terry, "Shasta", Carwinion Road, Mawnan Smith, FALMOUTH, Cornwall TR11 5JD Tel: 01326 250775
- e-mail: **katerry@btopenworld.com**
- website: **www.cornwallonline.com**

Guest House
Jenny Lake, Wickham Guest House, 21 Gyllyngvase Terrace, FALMOUTH, Cornwall TR11 4DL Tel: 01326 311140
- e-mail: **enquiries@wickhamhotel.freeserve.co.uk**
- website: **www.wickham-hotel.co.uk**

Self-Catering
Mrs Furniss, Lancrow Farm, near FOWEY, Cornwall PL24 2SA Tel: 01726 814 263
- e-mail: **sarahfurniss@aol.com**
- website: **www.foweyvacations.com**

Caravan & Camping
St Ives Bay Holiday Park, HAYLE, Cornwall TR27 5BH Tel: 0800 317713
- e-mail: **enquiries@stivesbay.co.uk**
- website: **www.stivesbay.co.uk**

Self-Catering
Mrs S. Trewhella, Mudgeon Vean Farm, St Martin, HELSTON, Cornwall TR12 6DB
Tel: 01326 231341
- e-mail: **mudgeonvean@aol.com**
- website: **www.cornwall-online.co.uk/mudgeon-vean/ctb.html**

Self-Catering
Mrs W.J. Morris, Bossava Cottage, LAMORNA, Penzance, Cornwall TR19 6XG
Tel: 01736 732 420
- e-mail: **junekernow@aol.com**
- website: **www.lamornaholidays.com**

WEBSITE DIRECTORY

Hotel / Lodges
Trethorne Golf Club, Kennards House,
LAUNCESTON, Cornwall PL15 8QE
Tel: 01566 86903
- e-mail: jon@trethornegolfclub.com
- website: www.trethornegolfclub.com

Self-Catering Cottages
Swallows & Meadow Cottage, Lower
Dutson Farm, LAUNCESTON,
Cornwall PL15 9SP Tel: 01566 776456
- e-mail: francis.broad@farm-cottage.co.uk
- website: www.farm-cottage.co.uk

Self-Catering
Celia Hutchinson,
Caradon Country Cottages, East Taphouse,
LISKEARD, Cornwall PL14 4NH
Tel: 01579 320355
- e-mail: celia@caradoncottages.co.uk
- website: www.caradoncottages.co.uk

Self-Catering
Mr Lowman, Cutkive Wood Holiday Lodges,
St Ive, LISKEARD, Cornwall PL14 3ND
Tel: 01579 362216
- e-mail: holidays@cutkivewood.co.uk
- website: www.cutkivewood.co.uk

Holiday Home Caravans / Tents & Touring
Mullion Holiday Park, Near Helston, LIZARD,
Cornwall TR12 7LT Tel: 0870 444 0080
- e-mail: bookings@weststarholidays.co.uk
- website: www.weststarholidays.co.uk

Caravan Park
Looe Bay Holiday Park, LOOE,
Cornwall PL13 1NX Tel: 0870 444 0080
- e-mail: bookings@weststarholidays.co.uk
- website: www.weststarholidays.co.uk

Self-Catering
Mr P. Brumpton, Talehay Holiday Cottages,
Pelynt, Near LOOE, Cornwall PL13 2LT
Tel: 01503 220252
- e-mail: paul@talehay.co.uk
- website: www.talehay.co.uk

Self-Catering
Tremaine Green Country Cottages,
Tremaine Green, Pelynt, Near LOOE,
Cornwall PL13 2LT. Tel: 01503 220333
- e-mail: stay@tremainegreen.co.uk
- website: www.tremainegreen.co.uk

Self-Catering
Mr & Mrs Holder, Valleybrook Holidays,
Peakswater, Lansallos, LOOE,
Cornwall PL13 2QE Tel: 01503 220493
- e-mail: admin@valleybrookholidays.co.uk
- website: www.valleybrookholidays.co.uk

Self-Catering Cottages
Wringworthy Cottages, LOOE, Cornwall
PL13 1PR Tel: 01503 240 685
- e-mail: pets@wringworthy.co.uk
- website: www.wringworthy.co.uk

Self-Catering
St Anthony Holidays, St Anthony,
MANACCAN, Helston, Cornwall TR12 6JW
Tel: 01326 231357
- e-mail: info@stanthony.co.uk
- website: www.stanthony.co.uk

Hotel
Blue Bay Hotel, Trenance, MAWGAN
PORTH, Cornwall TR8 4DA
Tel: 01637 860324
- e-mail: hotel@bluebaycornwall.co.uk
- website: www.bluebaycornwall.co.uk

B & B
Mrs Dawn Rundle, Lancallan Farm,
MEVAGISSEY, St Austell,Cornwall PL26
6EW Tel: 01726 842 284
- e-mail: dawn@lancallan.fsnet.co.uk
- website: www.lancallanfarm.co.uk

B & B
Mr & Mrs M. Limer, Alicia, 136 Henver Road,
NEWQUAY, Cornwall TR7 3EQ
Tel: 01637 874328
- e-mail: aliciaguesthouse@mlimer.fsnet.co.uk
- website: www.alicia-guesthouse.co.uk

Guest House
Pensalda Guest House, 98 Henver Road,
NEWQUAY, Cornwall TR7 3BL
Tel: 01637 874 601
- e-mail: karen_pensalda@yahoo.co.uk±
- website: www.pensalda-guesthouse.co.uk

Hotel
St George's Hotel, 71 Mount Wise,
NEWQUAY, Cornwall TR7 2BP
Tel: 01637 873010
- e-mail: enquiries@stgeorgeshotel.free-online.co.uk
- website: www.st-georges-newquay.co.uk

Caravan & Camping / Self-Catering
Quarryfield Caravan & Camping Park,
Crantock, NEWQUAY, Cornwall
Contact: Mrs A. Winn, Tretherras, Newquay,
Cornwall TR7 2RE
Tel: 01637 872 792
- website: www.quarryfield.co.uk

Hotel
Tregea Hotel, 16-18 High Street, PADSTOW,
Cornwall PL28 8BB Tel: 01841 532 455
- e-mail: info@tregea.co.uk
- website: www.tregea.co.uk

WEBSITE DIRECTORY

B & B
Mrs Owen, Penalva Private Hotel, Alexandra Road, PENZANCE, Cornwall TR18 4LZ
Tel: 01736 369 060
- website: www.penalva.co.uk

Holiday Park
Perran Sands Holiday Park, PERRANPORTH, Cornwall TR6 0AQ Tel: 01872 573742
- website: www.touringholidays.co.uk

Hotel / Inn
Cornish Arms, Pendoggett, PORT ISAAC, Cornwall PL30 3HH Tel: 01208 880263
- e-mail: info@cornisharms.com
- website: www.cornisharms.com

Guest House
Mrs E. Neal, Tamarind, 12 Shrubberies Hill, PORTHLEVEN, Cornwall TR13 9EA
Tel: 01326 574303
- e-mail: lizzybenzimra@hotmail.com
- www.web-direct.co.uk/porthleven/tamarind.html

Hotel
Rosevine Hotel, Porthcurnick Beach, PORTSCATHO, Near St Mawes, Cornwall TR2 5EW Tel: 01872 580206
- e-mail: info@rosevine.co.uk
- website: www.rosevine.co.uk

Caravan & Camping
Globe Vale Holiday Park, Radnor, REDRUTH, Cornwall TR16 4BH Tel: 01209 891183
- e-mail: info@globevale.co.uk
- website: www.globevale.co.uk

Hotel
Penventon Park Hotel, West End, REDRUTH, Cornwall TR15 1TE Tel: 01209 20 3000
- e-mail: enquiries@penventon.com
- website: www.penventon.com

Caravan & Camping
Wheal Rose Caravan & Camping Park, Scorrier, REDRUTH, Cornwall TR16 5DD
Tel: 01209 891496
- e-mail: whealrose@aol.com
- website: www.whealrosecaravanpark.co.uk

Guest House
Mrs Merchant, Woodpeckers, RILLA MILL, Callington, Cornwall PL17 7NT
Tel: 01579 363717
- e-mail: alison.merchant@virgin.net
- website: www.woodpeckersguesthouse.co.uk

Hotel
The Beacon Country House Hotel, Goonvrea Road, ST AGNES, Cornwall TR5 0NW Tel:01872 552 318
- e-mail: info@beaconhotel.co.uk
- website: www.beaconhotel.co.uk

Caravan & Camping / Holiday Park
Chiverton Park, Blackwater, ST AGNES, Cornwall TR4 8HS Tel: 01872 560667
- e-mail: info@chivertonpark.co.uk
- website: www.chivertonpark.co.uk

Hotel / Inn
Driftwood Spars Hotel, Trevaunance Cove, ST AGNES, Cornwall TR5 0RT
Tel: 01872 552428/553323
- website: www.driftwoodspars.com

Hotel / B & B
Penkerris, Penwinnick Road, ST AGNES, Cornwall TR5 0PA Tel: 01872 552262
- e-mail: info@penkerris.co.uk
- website: www.penkerris.co.uk

Guest House
Mr Gardener, The Elms, 14 Penwinnick Road, ST AUSTELL, Cornwall PL25 5DW
Tel: 01726 74981
- website: www.edenbb.co.uk

Farmhouse
Mrs Diana Clemes, Tregilgas Farm, Gorran, ST AUSTELL, Cornwall PL26 6ND
Tel: 01726 842342
- e-mail: dclemes88@aol.com

Self-Catering
Big-Picture Holiday Apartments, ST IVES, Cornwall Tel: 07803 129918
- e-mail: sarah@bigpictureholidays.co.uk
- website: www.bigpictureholidays.co.uk

Self-Catering
R.G. Pontefract, The Links Holiday Flats, Church Lane, Lelant, ST IVES, Cornwall TR26 3HY Tel: 01736 753326
- e-mail: jackpontefract@aol.com

Guest House
Angela & Barrie Walker, Rivendell, 7 Porthminster Terrace, ST IVES, Cornwall TR26 2DQ Tel: 01736 794923
- e-mail: rivendellstives@aol.com
- website: www.rivendell-stives.co.uk

Self-Catering
Sandbank Holidays, ST IVES BAY, Hayle, St Ives, Cornwall TR27 5BL
Tel: 01736 752594
- website: www.sandbank-holidays.com

Self-Catering
Mr & Mrs C.W. Pestell, Hockadays, Tregenna, Near Blisland, ST TUDY, Cornwall PL30 4QJ Tel: 01208 850146
- e-mail: holidays@hockadaysholidaycottages.co.uk
- website: www.hockadaysholidaycottages.co.uk

WEBSITE DIRECTORY

Self-Catering
Mrs R. Reeves, Polstraul, Trewalder,
Delabole, ST TUDY, Cornwall PL33 9ET
Tel: 01840 213 120
* e-mail: aandr.reeves@virgin.net
* website: www.maymear.co.uk

Self-Catering
Mrs Susan Tanzer, Trewithian Farm,
ST WENN, Bodmin, Cornwall PL30 5PH
Tel: 01208 895 181
* e-mail: trewithian@hotmail.co.uk
* www.cornwall-online.co.uk/trewithianfarm

Self-Catering
Mrs Sandy Wilson, Salutations, Atlantic
Road, TINTAGEL, Cornwall PL34 0DE
Tel: 01840 770287
* e-mail: sandyanddave@tinyworld.co.uk
* website: www.salutationstintagel.co.uk

Touring Caravan Park
Summer Valley Touring Park, Shortlanesend,
TRURO, Cornwall TR4 9DW
Tel: 01872 277878
* e-mail: res@summervalley.co.uk
* website: www.summervalley.co.uk

Farm / B & B / Self-Catering Cottages
Mrs P. Carbis. Trenona Farm Holidays, Ruan
High Lanes, TRURO, Cornwall TR2 5JS
Tel: 01872 501339
* e-mail: info@trenonafarmholidays.co.uk
* website: www.trenonafarmholidays.co.uk

Farm
Pengelly Farmhouse, Pengelly Farm,
Burlawn, WADEBRIDGE, Cornwall PL27 7LA
Tel: 01208 814 217
* e-mail: hodgepete@hotmail.com
* website: www.pengellyfarm.co.uk

•CUMBRIA

Inn
The Britannia Inn, Elterwater, AMBLESIDE,
Cumbria LA22 9HP Tel: 015394 37210
* e-mail: info@britinn.co.uk
* website: www.britinn.co.uk

Hotel
Crow How Country House, Rydal Road,
AMBLESIDE, Cumbria LA22 9PN
Tel: 015394 32193
* e-mail: stay@crowhowcountryhouse.co.uk
* website: www.crowhowcountryhouse.co.uk

Caravan Park
Greenhowe Caravan Park, Great Langdale,
AMBLESIDE, Cumbria LA22 9JU
Tel: 015394 37231
* e-mail: enquiries@greenhowe.com
* website: www.greenhowe.com

Hotel / Guest House
Ian & Helen Burt, The Old Vicarage,
Vicarage Road, AMBLESIDE, Cumbria
LA22 9DH. Tel: 015394 33364
* e-mail: info@oldvicarageambleside.co.uk
* website: www.oldvicarageambleside.co.uk

B & B
Broom House, Long Martin, APPLEBY-IN-
WESTMORLAND, Cumbria CA16 6JP
Tel: 01768 361 318
* website: www.broomhouseappleby.co.uk

Guest House
Barbara & Derick Cotton, Glebe House,
Bolton, APPLEBY-IN-WESTMORLAND,
Cumbria CA16 6AW Tel: 01768 361125
* e-mail: derick.cotton@btinternet.com
* website: www.glebeholidays.co.uk

B & B
Sharon Moore, Annisgarth B & B, 48 Craig
Walk, BOWNESS-ON-WINDERMERE,
Cumbria LA23 2JT Tel: 015394 43866
* website: www.annisgarth.co.uk

Self-Catering
Lakelovers, Belmont House, Lake Road,
BOWNESS-ON-WINDERMERE,
Cumbria LA23 3BJ Tel: 015294 88855
* e-mail: bookings@lakelovers.co.uk
* website: www.lakelovers.co.uk

Self-Catering / Farm
Mrs J. M. Almond, Irton House Farm,
Isel, COCKERMOUTH, Cumbria CA13 9ST
Tel: 017687 76380
* e-mail: almond@farmersweekly.net
* website: www.irtonhousefarm.com

B & B
Mosser Heights, Mosser, COCKERMOUTH,
Cumbria CA13 0SS Tel: 01900 822644
* e-mail: AmandaVickers@aol.com

Guest House
Rose Cottage Guest House, Lorton Road,
COCKERMOUTH, Cumbria CA13 9DX
Tel: 01900 822189
* website: www.rosecottageguest.co.uk

B & B
Birkhow Cottage, ESKDALE, Cumbria
Contact: Sally Tel: 017687 76836
* e-mail: sally@hollinhead.co.uk

www.holidayguides.com

WEBSITE DIRECTORY

Guest House
Mr & Mrs J. D. Bromage, Forest How Guest House, ESKDALE GREEN, Cumbria CA19 1TR
Tel: 019467 23201
- website: www.foresthow.co.uk

Holiday Park
Lakeland Leisure Park, Moor Lane, Flookburgh, Near GRANGE-OVER-SANDS, Cumbria LA11 7LT Tel: 01539 558556
- website: www.touringholidays.co.uk

Farm / Self-Catering
Mr P. Brown, High Dale Park Farm, High Dale Park, Salterthwaite, Ulverston, GRIZEDALE FOREST, Cumbria LA12 8LJ
Tel: 01229 860226
- e-mail: peter@lakesweddingmusic.com
- www.lakesweddingmusic.com/accomm

Self-Catering Cottages
Hideaways, The Square, HAWKSHEAD, Cumbria LA22 0NZ Tel: 015394 42435
- e-mail: bookings@lakeland-hideaways.co.uk
- website: www.lakeland-hideaways.co.uk

Hotel
Ivy House Hotel, Main Street, HAWKSHEAD, Cumbria LA22 0NS Tel: 015394 36204
- e-mail: ivyhousehotel@btinternet.com
- website: www.ivyhousehotel.com

Self-Catering
Keswick Cottages, 8 Beechcroft, Braithwaite, KESWICK, Cumbria CA12 5RS
Tel: 017687 78555
- e-mail: info@keswickcottages.co.uk
- website: www.keswickcottages.co.uk

Guest House
Rickerby Grange Guest House, Portinscale, KESWICK, Cumbria CA12 5RH
Tel: 017687 72344
- e-mail: stay@rickerbygrange.co.uk
- website: www.rickerbygrange.co.uk

Self-Catering
Mrs S.J. Bottom, Crossfield Cottages, KIRKOSWALD, Penrith, Cumbria CA10 1EU
Tel: 01768 898711
- e-mail: info@crossfieldcottages.co.uk
- website: www.crossfieldcottages.co.uk

Self-Catering
Routen House & Little Paddock, LAKE DISTRICT, Cumbria
Contact: Mrs J. Green Tel: 01604 626383
- e-mail: joanne@routenhouse.co.uk
- website: www.routenhouse.co.uk

Farm
Esthwaite How Farmhouse, NEAR SAWREY, Ambleside, Cumbria LA22 0LB
Tel: 01539 436 450
- e-mail: elizabeth@esthwaitehow.co.uk
- website: www.esthwaitehow.co.uk

B & B
Mr Bell, Albany House, 5 Portland Place, PENRITH, Cumbria CA11 7QN
Tel: 01768 863072
- e-mail: info@albany-house.org.uk
- website: www.albany-house.org.uk

Guest House
Blue Swallow Guest House,
11 Victoria Road, PENRITH, Cumbria CA11 8HR Tel: 01768 866335
- e-mail: blueswallow@tiscali.co.uk
- website: www.blueswallow.co.uk

Self-Catering
Mr & Mrs Iredale, Carrock Cottages, Carrock House, Hutton Roof, PENRITH, Cumbria CA11 0XY Tel: 01768 484111
- e-mail: info@carrockcottages.co.uk
- website: www.carrockcottages.co.uk

Self-Catering
Mark Cowell, Church Court Cottages, Gamblesby, PENRITH, Cumbria CA10 1HR
Tel: 01768 881682
- e-mail: markcowell@tiscali.co.uk
- website: www.gogamblesby.co.uk

B & B
Greenah Crag, Troutbeck, PENRITH, Cumbria CA11 0SQ Tel: 017684 83233
- e-mail: greenahcrag@lineone.net
- website: www.greenahcrag.co.uk

Golf Club
Seascale Golf Club, The Banks, SEASCALE, Cumbria CA20 1QL Tel: 01946 728202
- e-mail: seascalegolfclub@btconnect.com
- website: www.seascalegolfclub.co.uk

Self-Catering / Caravan & Camping
Tanglewood Caravan Park, Causeway Head, SILLOTH-ON-SOLWAY, Cumbria CA7 4PE
Tel: 016973 31253
- e-mail: tanglewoodcaravanpark@hotmail.com
- website: www.tanglewoodcaravanpark.co.uk

Hotel
Golf Hotel, SILLOTH-ON-SOLWAY, Cumbria CA7 4AB Tel: 016973 31438
- e-mail: golf.hotel@virgin.net
- website: www.golfhotelsilloth.co.uk

Self-Catering / Caravan
Fell View Holidays, Glenridding,
Penrith, ULLSWATER, Cumbria CA11 0PJ
Tel: 01768 482342; Evening: 01768 867420
- e-mail: enquiries@fellviewholidays.com
- website: www.fellviewholidays.com

B & B / Self-Catering
Barbara Murphy, Land Ends Country Lodge,
Watermillock, Near Penrith, ULLSWATER,
Cumbria CA11 0NB Tel: 01768 486438
- e-mail: infolandends@btinternet.com
- website: www.landends.co.uk

Guest House
Fir Trees Guest House, Lake Road,
WINDERMERE, Cumbria LA23 2EQ
Tel: 015394 42272
- e-mail: enquiries@fir-trees.com
- website: www.fir-trees.com

Guest House
Green Gables, 37 Broad Street,
WINDERMERE LA23 2AB Tel: 015394 43886
- e-mail: greengables@fsbdial.co.uk
  info@greengablesguesthouse.co.uk

Guest House
Josette & Mark Bayley,
Holly-Wood Guest House, Holly Road,
WINDERMERE, Cumbria LA23 2AF
Tel: 015394 42219
- e-mail: info@hollywoodguesthouse.co.uk
- website: www.hollywoodguesthouse.co.uk

Guest House
Meadfoot Guest House, New Road,
WINDERMERE, Cumbria LA23 2LA
Tel: 015394 42610
- website: www.meadfoot-guesthouse.co.uk

•DERBYSHIRE

B & B
Compton House, 27-31 Compton,
ASHBOURNE, Derbyshire DE6 1BX
Tel: 01335 343100
- e-mail: enquiries@comptonhouse.co.uk
- website: www.comptonhouse.co.uk

B & B
Mrs M Harris, The Courtyard,
Dairy House Farm, Alkmonton, Longford,
ASHBOURNE, Derbyshire DE6 3DG
Tel: 01335 330187
- e-mail: michael@dairyhousefarm.org.uk
- website: www.dairyhousefarm.org.uk

Inn
The Dog & Partridge Country Inn,
Swinscoe, ASHBOURNE, Derbyshire
DE6 2HS Tel: 01335 343183
- e-mail: info@dogandpartridge.co.uk
- website: www.dogandpartridge.co.uk

B & B
Mrs A.M. Whittle, Stone Cottage,
Green Lane, Clifton, ASHBOURNE,
Derbyshire DE6 2BL Tel: 01335 343377
- e-mail: info@stone-cottage.fsnet.co.uk
- website: www.stone-cottage.fsnet.co.uk

B&B
Mrs J. Salisbury, Turlow Bank, Hognaston,
ASHBOURNE, Derbyshire DE6 1PW
Tel: 01335 370299
- e-mail: turlowbank@w3z.co.uk
- website: www.turlowbank.co.uk

Self-Catering
P. Skemp, Cotterill Farm,
BIGGIN-BY-HARTINGTON, Buxton,
Derbyshire SK17 0DJ Tel: 01298 84447
- e-mail: enquiries@cotterillfarm.co.uk
- website: www.cotterillfarm.co.uk

Hotel
Biggin Hall Hotel, Biggin-by-Hartington,
BUXTON, Derbyshire SK17 0DH
Tel: 01298 84451
- e-mail: enquiries@bigginhall.co.uk
- website: www.bigginhall.co.uk

Guest House
Mr & Mrs Hyde, Braemar Guest House,
10 Compton Road, BUXTON,
Derbyshire SK17 9DN Tel: 01298 78050
- e-mail: buxtonbraemar@supanet.com
- website:
www.cressbrook.co.uk/buxton/braemar

Self-Catering
Mrs Gillian Taylor, Priory Lea Holiday Flats,
50 White Knowle Road, BUXTON,
Derbyshire SK17 9NH Tel: 01298 23737
- e-mail: priorylea@tiscali.co.uk
- website:
www.cressbrook.co.uk/buxton/priorylea

Self-Catering
Mr R. D. Hollands, Wheeldon Trees Farm,
Earl Sterndale, BUXTON, Derbyshire
SK17 0AA Tel: 01298 83219
- e-mail: hollands@easterndale.fsnet.co.uk
- website: www.wheeldontreesfarm.co.uk

WEBSITE DIRECTORY

Hotel
Charles Cotton Hotel, Hartington,
Near BUXTON, Derbyshire SK17 0AL
Tel: 01298 84229
- e-mail: info@charlescotton.co.uk
- website: www.charlescotton.co.uk

Caravan & Camping Park
Newhaven Caravan & Camping Park,
Newhaven, NEAR BUXTON,
Derbyshire SK17 0DT Tel: 01298 84300
- website: www.newhavencaravanpark.com

Farm / B & B
Mrs Catherine Dicken, Bonehill Farm, Etwall Road, Mickleover, DERBY,
Derbyshire DE3 0DN Tel: 01332 513553
- website: www.bonehillfarm.co.uk

Farm / Self-Catering
J. Gibbs, Wolfscote Grange, HARTINGTON,
Near Buxton, Derbyshire SK17 0AX
Tel: 01298 84342
- e-mail: wolfscote@btinternet.com
- website: www.wolfscotegrangecottages.co.uk

Guest House
Ivy House Farm, Stanton-by-Bridge, NEAR MELBOURNE, Derby, Derbyshire DE73 7HT
Tel: 01332 863152
- e-mail: mary@guesthouse.fsbusiness.co.uk
- website: www.ivy-house-farm.com

Self-Catering
Angela Kellie, Shatton Hall Farm, Bamford, Hope Valley, PEAK DISTRICT,
Derbyshire S33 0BG Tel: 01433 620635
- e-mail: ahk@peakfarmholidays.co.uk
- website: www.peakfarmholidays.co.uk

•DEVON

Self-Catering
Farm & Cottage Holidays, DEVON
Tel: 01237 479698
- e-mail: enquiries@farmcott.co.uk
- website: www.holidaycottages.co.uk

Self-Catering
Helpful Holidays, Mill Street, Chagford,
DEVON TQ13 8AW Tel: 01647 433593
- e-mail: help@helpfulholidays.com
- website: www.helpfulholidays.com

Self-Catering
Toad Hall Cottages, DEVON
Tel: 01548 853089 (24 Hours)
- e-mail: thc@toadhallcottages.com
- website: www.toadhallcottages.com

Self-Catering
Robin & Wren Cottages,
ASHBURTON, Devon
Contact: Mrs M. Phipps, Newcott Farm,
Poundsgate, Newton Abbot TQ13 7PD
Tel: 01364 631421
- e-mail: enquiries@newcott-farm.co.uk
- website: www.newcott-farm.co.uk

B & B
The Durant Arms, ASHPRINGTON, Totnes,
Devon TQ9 7UP Tel: 01803 732240
- e-mail: info@thedurantarms.com
- website: www.thedurantarms.com

Self-Catering
Braddon Cottages, ASHWATER, Beaworthy,
Holsworthy, Devon Tel: 01409 211350
- e-mail: holidays@braddoncottages.co.uk
- website: www.braddoncottages.co.uk

B & B / Self-Catering
Mrs S.J. Avis, Lea Hill, Membury,
AXMINSTER, Devon EX13 7AQ
Tel: 01404 881881
- e-mail: reception@leahill.co.uk
- website: www.leahill.co.uk

Self-Catering
North Devon Holiday Homes,
19 Cross Street, BARNSTAPLE,
Devon EX31 1BD Tel: 01271 376322
- e-mail: info@northdevonholidays.co.uk
- website: www.northdevonholidays.co.uk

Farm / B & B
Jenny Cope, North Down Farm B & B,
Pyncombe Lane, Wiveliscombe,
BARNSTAPLE, Devon TA4 2BL
Tel: 01984 623730
- e-mail: jennycope@tiscali.co.uk
- website: www.north-down-farm.co.uk

Hotel
Sandy Cove Hotel, Combe Martin Bay,
BERRYNARBOR, Devon EX34 9SR
Tel: 01271 882243/882888
- website: www.sandycove-hotel.co.uk

B & B / Self-Catering
Mr & Mrs Lewin, Lake House Cottages
and B&B, Lake Villa, BRADWORTHY,
Devon EX22 7SQ Tel: 01409 241962
- e-mail: info@lakevilla.co.uk
- website: www.lakevilla.co.uk

Caravan & Camping
Berry Barton Caravan Park, BRANSCOMBE,
Seaton, Devon EX12 3BD Tel: 01297 680208
- email: berrybarton@amserve.com
- website: www.berrybarton.co.uk

WEBSITE DIRECTORY

Self-Catering / Organic Farm
Little Comfort Farm Cottages,
Little Comfort Farm, BRAUNTON,
North Devon EX33 2NJ Tel: 01271 812414
- e-mail: **info@littlecomfortfarm.co.uk**
- website: **www.littlecomfortfarm.co.uk**

Self-Catering
Marsdens Cottage Holidays, 2 The Square,
BRAUNTON, Devon EX33 2JB
Tel: 01271 813777
- e-mail: **holidays@marsdens.co.uk**
- website: **www.marsdens.co.uk**

Self-Catering
Devoncourt Holiday Flats, Berryhead Road,
BRIXHAM, Devon TQ5 9AB
Tel: 01803 853748
- website: **www.devoncourt.info**

Guest House
Woodlands Guest House, Parkham Road,
BRIXHAM, South Devon TQ5 9BU
Tel: 01803 852040
- e-mail: **woodlandsbrixham@btinternet.com**
- website: **www.dogfriendlyguesthouse.co.uk**
  www.woodlandsdevon.co.uk

Self-Catering / B & B / Caravans
Mrs Gould, Bonehayne Farm, COLYTON,
Devon EX24 6SG
Tel: 01404 871416/871396
- e-mail: **gould@bonehayne.co.uk**
- website: **www.bonehayne.co.uk**

Self-Catering
Watermouth Cove Cottages,
Watermouth, Near COMBE MARTIN,
Devon EX34 9SJ Tel: 0870 2413168
- e-mail: **stay@coastalvalleyhideaways.co.uk**
- website: **www.coastalvalleyhideaways.co.uk**

Holiday Park
Manleigh Holiday Park,
Rectory Road, COMBE MARTIN,
Devon EX34 0NS Tel: 01271 883353
- e-mail: **info@manleighpark.co.uk**
- website: **www.manleighpark.co.uk**

B & B
Miss Audrey Isaac, Crowborough,
Georgeham, Braunton, CROYDE,
Devon EX33 1JZ Tel: 01271 891005
- website: **www.crowboroughfarm.co.uk**

Self-Catering
Mrs S.R. Ridalls, The Old Bakehouse,
7 Broadstone, DARTMOUTH, Devon TQ6 9NR
Tel: 01803 834585
- e-mail: **ridallsleisure@aol.com**
- website: **www.oldbakehousedartmouth.co.uk**

Self-Catering
Watermill Cottages, Higher North Mill,
Hansel, DARTMOUTH, Devon TQ6 0LN
Tel: 01803 770219
- e-mail: **graham@hanselpg.freeserve.co.uk**
- website: **www.watermillcottages.co.uk**

Farm B & B
Mrs Karen Williams, Stile Farm, Starcross,
EXETER, Devon EX6 8PD Tel: 01626 890268
- e-mail: **info@stile-farm.co.uk**
- website: **www.stile-farm.co.uk**

Self-Catering
The Independent Traveller, The Bury,
Thorverton, EXETER, Devon EX5 5NT
Tel: 01392 860 807
- e-mail: **help@gowithit.co.uk**
- website: **www.gowithit.co.uk**

Holiday Park
Devon Cliffs Holiday Park, Sandy Bay,
EXMOUTH, Devon EX8 5BT
Tel: 01395 226226
- website: **www.touringholidays.co.uk**

Hotel
Devoncourt Hotel, Douglas Avenue,
EXMOUTH, Devon EX8 2EX
Tel: 01395 272277
- website: **www.devoncourt.com**

Caravan & Camping
Mrs Megan Daglish, Tamarstone Farm,
Bude Road, Pancrasweek, HOLSWORTHY,
Devon EX22 7JT
Tel: 01288 381734
- e-mail: **pets@tamarstone.co.uk**
- website: **www.tamarstone.co.uk**

Hotel / Guest House
St Brannocks House, St Brannocks Road,
ILFRACOMBE, Devon EX34 8EQ
Tel: 01271 863873
- e-mail: **barbara@stbrannockshotel.co.uk**
- website: **www.stbrannockshotel.co.uk**

Farm / B & B
Venn Farm, Ugborough, IVYBRIDGE,
Devon PL21 0PE Tel: 01364 73240
- e-mail: **info@vennfarm.co.uk**
- website: **www.vennfarm.co.uk**

www.holidayguides.com

WEBSITE DIRECTORY

Self-Catering
Beachdown Holiday Bungalows,
Beachdown House, Challaborough Bay,
KINGSBRIDGE, South Devon
Tel: 01548 810089
• e-mail: enquiries@beachdown.co.uk or
           petswelcome@beachdown.co.uk
• website: www.beachdown.co.uk

Hotel
Alford House Hotel, Alford Terrace,
LYNTON, Devon EX35 6AT
Tel: 01598 752359
• e-mail: enquiries@alfordhouse.co.uk
• website: www.alfordhouse.co.uk

Caravan Park
Pennymoor Caravan Park, MODBURY,
Near Ivybridge, Devon PL21 0SB
Tel: 01548 830542 or 01548 830020
• e-mail: enquiries@pennymoor-camping.co.uk
• website: www.pennymoor-camping.co.uk

Guest House
The Smugglers Rest Inn, North Morte Road,
MORTEHOE, North Devon EX34 7DR
Tel: 01271 870891
• e-mail: info@smugglersmortehoe.co.uk
• website: www.smugglersmortehoe.co.uk

Farm B & B
Mrs T.M. Merchant, Great Sloncombe Farm,
MORETONHAMPSTEAD, Newton Abbot,
Devon TQ13 8QF Tel: 01647 440595
• e-mail: hmerchant@sloncombe.freeserve.co.uk
• website: www.greatsloncombefarm.co.uk

Hotel
Riversford Hotel, Limers Lane, NORTHAM,
Bideford, Devon EX39 2RG
Tel: 01237 474239
• e-mail: riversford@aol.com
• website: www.riversford.co.uk

Self-Catering
Crab Cottage, NOSS MAYO, South Devon
Tel: 01425 471 372
• website: www.crab-cottage.co.uk

Farm Guest House
Mrs Ann Forth, Fluxton Farm,
OTTERY ST MARY, Devon EX11 1RJ
Tel: 01404 812818
• website: www.fluxtonfarm.co.uk

Self-Catering
Mr & Mrs Dillon, Boswell Farm Cottages,
Sidford, Near SIDMOUTH, Devon EX10 0PP
Tel: 01395 514162
• e-mail: dillon@boswell-farm.co.uk
• website: www.boswell-farm.co.uk

Caravan & Camping
Harford Bridge Holiday Park, Peter Tavy,
TAVISTOCK, Devon PL19 9LS
Tel: 01822 810349
• e-mail: enquiry@harfordbridge.co.uk
• website: www.harfordbridge.co.uk

Farm / B & B
Mary & Roger Steer, Rubbytown Farm,
Gulworthy, TAVISTOCK, Devon PL19 8PA
Tel: 01822 832493
• e-mail: jimmy.steer@virgin.net
• website: www.rubbytown-farm.co.uk

Guest House
Mrs Arnold, The Mill, Lower Washfield,
TIVERTON, Devon EX16 9PD
Tel: 01884 255297
• e-mail: arnold5@washfield.freeserve.co.uk
• website: www.washfield.freeserve.co.uk

Hotel
Heathcliff House Hotel, 16 Newton Road,
TORQUAY, Devon TQ2 5BZ
Tel: 01803 211580
• e-mail: heathcliffhouse@btconnect.com
• website: www.heathcliffhousehotel.co.uk

Hotel
The Aveland Hotel, Babbacombe, TORQUAY,
Devon TQ1 3PT Tel: 01803 326622
• e-mail: avelandhotel@aol.com
• website: www.avelandhotel.co.uk

Hotel
Grosvenor House Hotel, Falkland Road,
TORQUAY, Devon TQ2 5JP
Tel: 01803 294110
• e-mail: fhg@grosvenorhousehotel.co.uk
• website: www.grosvenorhousehotel.co.uk

Self-Catering
Mrs H. Carr, Sunningdale Apartments,
11 Babbacombe Downs Road, TORQUAY,
Devon TQ1 3LF Tel: 01803 325786
• e-mail: allancarr@yahoo.com
• website: www.sunningdaleapartments.co.uk

Self-Catering
West Pusehill Farm Cottages,
West Pusehill Farm, Pusehill,
WESTWARD HO!, Devon EX39 5AH
Tel: 01237 475638 or 01237 474622
• e-mail: info@wpfcottages.co.uk
• website: www.wpfcottages.co.uk

www.holidayguides.com

WEBSITE DIRECTORY

Golf Club
Royal North Devon Golf Club, Golf Links Road, WESTWARD HO!, Devon EX39 1HD
Tel: 01237 473817
- e-mail: info@royalnorthdevongolfclub.co.uk
- website: www.royalnorthdevongolfclub.co.uk

Caravan & Camping
North Morte Farm Caravan & Camping Park, Mortehoe, WOOLACOMBE, Devon EX34 7EG. Tel: 01271 870381
- e-mail: info@northmortefarm.co.uk
- website: www.northmortefarm.co.uk

Self-Catering
David Mallet, Dartmoor Country Holidays, Bedford Bridge, Horrabridge, YELVERTON, Devon PL20 7RY Tel: 01822 852651
- website: www.dartmoorcountryholidays.co.uk

• DORSET

Self-catering
Dorset Coastal Cottages, The Manor House, Winfrith Newburgh, Dorchester, Dorset DT2 8JR Tel: 0800 980 4070
- e-mail: hols@dorsetcoastalcottages.com
- website: www.dorsetcoastalcottages.com

Self-Catering
Dorset Cottage Holidays
Tel: 01929 553443
- e-mail: enq@dhcottages.co.uk
- website: www.dhcottages.co.uk

Inn
The Anvil Inn, Salisbury Road, Pimperne, BLANDFORD, Dorset DT11 8UQ
Tel: 01258 453431
- e-mail: theanvil.inn@btconnect.com
- website: www.anvilinn.co.uk

Self-Catering
Iona Holiday Flat, 71 Sea Road, BOURNEMOUTH, Dorset BH5 1BG
Contact: Andrew Hooper
Tel: 01202 460517 or 07967 027025
- e-mail: hoops2@ntlworld.com
- website: www.ionaholidayflat.co.uk

Guest House
Cransley Hotel, 11 Knyveton Road, East Cliff, BOURNEMOUTH, Dorset BH1 3QG
Tel: 01202 290067
- e-mail: info@cransley.com
- website: www.cransley.com

Hotel
Southbourne Grove Hotel, 96 Southbourne Road, BOURNEMOUTH, Dorset BH6 3QQ
Tel: 01202 420 503
- e-mail: neil@pack1462.freeserve.co.uk

Hotel
White Topps, 45 Church Road, Southbourne, BOURNEMOUTH, Dorset B46 4BB Tel: 01202 428868
- e-mail: thedoghotel@aol.com
- website: www.whitetopps.co.uk

Guest House
Hazel & Keith Ingram, Woodside Hotel, 29 Southern Road, Southbourne, BOURNEMOUTH, Dorset BH6 3SR
Tel: 01202 427213
- e-mail: enquiries@woodsidehotel.co.uk
- website: www.woodsidehotel.co.uk

Inn
The Fox & Hounds Inn, Duck Street, CATTISTOCK, Dorchester, Dorset DT2 0JH
Tel: 01300 320 444
- e-mail: info@foxandhoundsinn.com
- website: www.foxandhoundsinn.com

Hotel
The Queens Armes Hotel, The Street, CHARMOUTH, Dorset DT6 6QF
Tel: 01297 560339
- e-mail: darkduck@btconnect.com
- website: www.queensarmeshotel.co.uk

Golf Club
Parley Court Golf Course Ltd, Parley Green Lane, Hurn, CHRISTCHURCH, Dorset
Tel: 01202 591600
- e-mail: info@parleygolf.co.uk
- website: www.parleygolf.co.uk

Looking for holiday accommodation?
for details of hundreds of properties throughout the UK including comprehensive coverage of all areas of Scotland try:
www.holidayguides.com

WEBSITE DIRECTORY

Guest House
Church View Guest House, Winterbourne Abbas, DORCHESTER, Dorset DT2 9LS
Tel: 01305 889 296
• e-mail: stay@churchview.co.uk
• website: www.churchview.co.uk

Caravan Park
Giants Head Caravan & Camping Park, Old Sherborne Road, Cerne Abbas, DORCHESTER, Dorset DT2 7TR
Tel: 01300 341242
• e-mail: holidays@giantshead.co.uk
• website: www.giantshead.co.uk

Farm / Self-Catering
Tamarisk Farm, West Bexington, DORCHESTER, Dorset DT2 9DF
Tel: 01308 897784
• e-mail: holidays@tamariskfarm.com
• website: www.tamariskfarm.com

Hotel
Cromwell House Hotel, LULWORTH COVE, Dorset BH20 5RJ
Tel: 01929 400253
• e-mail: catriona@lulworthcove.co.uk
• website: www.lulworthcove.co.uk

Self-Catering
Westover Farm Cottages, Wootton Fitzpaine, Near LYME REGIS, Dorset DT6 6NE
Tel: 01297 560451/561395
• e-mail: wfcottages@aol.com
• website: www.westoverfarmcottages.co.uk

Holiday Park
Rockley Park Holiday Park, Hamworthy, POOLE, Dorset BH15 4LZ
Tel: 01202 679393
• website: www.touringholidays.co.uk

Holiday Park
Sandford Holiday Park, Holton Heath, POOLE, Dorset BH16 6JZ
Tel: 0870 444 0080
• e-mail: bookings@weststarholidays.co.uk
• website: www.weststarholidays.co.uk

Farm / Self-Catering
White Horse Farm, Middlemarsh, SHERBORNE, Dorset DT9 5QN
Tel: 01963 210222
• e-mail: enquiries@whitehorsefarm.co.uk
• website: www.whitehorsefarm.co.uk

Hotel
The Knoll House, STUDLAND BAY, Dorset BH19 3AW Tel: 01929 450450
• e-mail: info@knollhouse.co.uk
• website: www.knollhouse.co.uk

Hotel
The Limes Hotel, 48 Park Road, SWANAGE, Dorset BH19 2AE Tel: 01929 422664
• e-mail: info@limeshotel.net
• website: www.limeshotel.net

B & B
Fairway Bed and Breakfast, 7A Demoulham Road, SWANAGE, Dorset BH19 1NR
Tel: 01929 423 367
• e-mail: rita@ritawaller.plus.com
• website: www.swanagefairway.co.uk

Farm/ Guest House/ Caravan & Camping
Luckford Wood House, East Stoke, WAREHAM, Dorset BH20 6AW
Tel: 01929 463098/07888 719002
• e-mail: info@luckfordleisure.co.uk
• website: www.luckfordleisure.co.uk

Guest House/ Self-Catering
Glenthorne Castle Cove, 15 Old Castle Road, WEYMOUTH, Dorset DT4 8QB
Tel: 01305 777281
• e-mail: info@glenthorne-holidays.co.uk
• website: www.glenthorne-holidays.co.uk

Holiday Park
Littlesea Holiday Park, Lynch Lane, WEYMOUTH, Dorset DT4 9DT
Tel: 01305 774414
• website: www.touringholidays.co.uk

B & B
Mrs Karina Hill, Pebble Villa, Enkworth Road, Preston, WEYMOUTH, Dorset DT3 6JT Tel: 01305 837 469
• e-mail: stay@pebblevilla.co.uk
• website: www.weymouthbedandbreakfast.net

Holiday Park
Seaview & Weymouth Bay Holiday Parks, Preston, WEYMOUTH, Dorset DT3 6D2
Tel: 01305 833037
• website: www.touringholidays.co.uk

•DURHAM

Self-Catering Cottages
Low Lands Farm, Lowlands, Cockfield, BISHOP AUCKLAND, Durham DL13 5AW
Tel: 01388 718251
• e-mail: info@farmholidaysuk.com
• website: www.farmholidays.com

Hotel
The Teesdale Hotel, MIDDLETON-IN-TEESDALE, Durham DL12 0QG
Tel: 01833 640264
• e-mail: john@teesdalehotel.co.uk
• website: www.teesdalehotel.co.uk

Farm / Self-Catering Cottage
Frog Hall Cottage, Herdship Farm, Harwood Inn, TEESDALE, Durham DL12 0YB
Tel: 01833 622215
- e-mail: kath.herdship@btinternet.com
- website: www.herdship.co.uk

Hotel
Ivesley Equestrian Centre, Ivesley, WATERHOUSES, Durham DH7 9HB
Tel: 0191 373 4324
- e-mail: ivesley@msn.com
- website: www.ridingholidays-ivesley.co.uk

•ESSEX

B & B / Self-Catering
Mrs B. Lord, Pond House, Earls Hall Farm, CLACTON-ON-SEA, Essex CO16 8BP
Tel: 01255 820458
- e-mail: brenda_lord@farming.co.uk
- website: www.earlshallfarm.info

Farm
Rye Farm, Rye Lane, COLCHESTER, Essex, CO2 0JL Tel: 01206 734 350
- e-mail: peter@buntingp.fsbusiness.co.uk
- website: www.buntingp.fsbusiness.co.uk

•GLOUCESTERSHIRE

Hotel
Chester House Hotel, Victoria Street, BOURTON-ON-THE-WATER, Gloucs GL54 2BU Tel: 01451 820286
- e-mail: info@chesterhousehotel.com
- website: www.chesterhousehotel.com

Farmhouse B & B
Box Hedge Farm B & B, Box Hedge Farm Lane, Coalpit Heath, BRISTOL, Gloucs BS36 2UW Tel: 01454 250786
- e-mail: marilyn@bed-breakfast-bristol.com
- website: www.bed-breakfast-bristol.com

Lodge
Thornbury Golf Centre, Bristol Road, Thornbury, BRISTOL, Gloucs BS35 3XL
Tel: 01454 281144
- e-mail: info@thornburygc.co.uk
- website: www.thornburygc.co.uk

B & B
Mrs C. Hutsby, Holly House, Ebrington, CHIPPING CAMPDEN, Gloucs GL55 6NL
Tel: 01386 593213
- e-mail: hutsbybandb@aol.com
- website: www.hollyhousebandb.co.uk

B & B
Mrs Z.I. Williamson, Kempsford Manor, Kempsford, Near FAIRFORD, Gloucs GL7 4EQ Tel: 01285 810131
- e-mail: ipek@kempsfordmanor.co.uk
- website: www.kempsfordmanor.co.uk

B & B
Anthea & Bill Rhoton, Hyde Crest, Cirencester Road, MINCHINHAMPTON, Gloucs GL6 8PE.
Tel: 01453 731631
- e-mail: anthea@hydecrest.demon.co.uk
- website: www.hydecrest.co.uk

B & B
Mrs F.J. Adams, Aston House, Broadwell, MORETON-IN-MARSH, Gloucs GL56 0TJ
Tel: 01451 830475
- e-mail: fja@netcomuk.co.uk
- website: www.astonhouse.net

Self-Catering
Richard Drinkwater, Rose's Cottage, The Green, Broadwell, MORETON-IN-MARSH, Gloucs GL56 0UF
Tel: 01451 830007
- e-mail: richard.drinkwater@ukonline.co.uk

Self-Catering
Orion Holidays, Cotswold Water Park, Gateway Centre, Lake 6, Spine Road, SOUTH CERNEY, Gloucs GL7 5TL
Tel: 01285 861839
- e-mail: bookings@orionholidays.com
- website: www.orionholidays.com

B & B
Mrs Wendy Swait, Inschdene, Atcombe Road, SOUTH WOODCHESTER, Stroud, Gloucs GL5 5EW
Tel: 01453 873254
- e-mail: swait@inschdene.co.uk
- website: www.inschdene.co.uk

Farmhouse B & B
Robert Smith, Corsham Field Farmhouse, Bledington Road, STOW-ON-THE-WOLD, Gloucs GL54 1JH. Tel: 01541 831750
- e-mail: farmhouse@corshamfield.co.uk
- website: www.corshamfield.co.uk

B & B
The Limes, Evesham Road, STOW-ON-THE-WOLD, Gloucs GL54 1EN
Tel: 01451 830034 or 01451 831056
- e-mail: thelimes@zoom.co.uk

www.holidayguides.com

WEBSITE DIRECTORY

Farm / Self-Catering
Mrs Anne Meadows, Home Farm, Bredons Norton, TEWKESBURY, Gloucs GL20 7HA
Tel: 01684 772 332
- e-mail: info@meadowshomefarm.co.uk
- website: www.meadowshomefarm.co.uk

Hotel / Golf Club
Tewkesbury Park Hotel, Golf & Country Club, Lincoln Green lane, TEWKESBURY, Gloucs GL20 7DN Tel: 0870 609 6101
- e-mail: tewkesburypark@corushotels.com
- website: www.tewkesburypark.co.uk

•HAMPSHIRE

B & B
Mrs Arnold-Brown, Hilden B&B, Southampton Road, Boldre, BROCKENHURST, Hampshire SO41 8PT Tel: 01590 623682
- website: www.newforestbandb-hilden.co.uk

Campsite
Lower Tye Campsite, Copse Lane, HAYLING ISLAND, Hampshire
Tel: 02392 462479
- e-mail: lowertye@aol.com
- website: www.haylingcampsites.co.uk

Holiday Park
Hayling Island Holiday Park, Manor Road, HAYLING ISLAND, Hampshire PO11 0QS
Tel: 0870 444 0800
- e-mail: bookings@weststarholidays.co.uk
- website: www.weststarholidays.co.uk

B & B
Mrs P. Ellis, Efford Cottage, Everton, LYMINGTON, Hampshire SO41 0JD
Tel: 01590 642315
- e-mail: effordcottage@aol.com
- website: www.effordcottage.co.uk

B & B
Mr & Mrs Farrell, Honeysuckle House, 24 Clinton Road, LYMINGTON, Hampshire SO41 9EA Tel: 01590 676435
- e-mail: skyblue@beeb.net

Hotel
Bramble Hill Hotel, Bramshaw, Near LYNDHURST, New Forest, Hampshire SO43 7JG Tel: 02380 813165
- website: www.bramblehill.co.uk

Hotel
Crown Hotel, High Street, LYNDHURST, Hampshire SO43 7NF Tel: 023 8028 2922
- e-mail: reception@crownhotel-lyndhurst.co.uk
- website: www.crownhotel-lyndhurst.co.uk

Caravans for Hire
Downton Holiday Park, Shorefield Road, MILFORD-ON-SEA, Hampshire SO41 0LH
Tel: 01425 476131/01590 642515
- e-mail: info@downtonholidaypark.co.uk
- website: www.downtonholidaypark.co.uk

Self Catering
Gorse Cottage, Balmer Lawn Road, Brockenhurst, NEW FOREST, Hampshire
Contact: Mr J. Gilbert Tel: 0870 3210020
- e-mail: info@ gorsecottage.co.uk
- website: www.gorsecottage.co.uk

Hotel
Woodlands Lodge Hotel, Bartley Road, Woodlands, NEW FOREST, Southampton Hampshire SO40 7GN Tel: 023 8029 2257
- e-mail: reception@woodlands-lodge.co.uk
- website: www.woodlands-lodge.co.uk

B & B / Guest House
Michael & Maureen Burt, Fraser House, Salisbury Road, Blashford, RINGWOOD (NEW FOREST), Hampshire BH24 3PB
Tel: 01425 473958
- e-mail: mail@fraserhouse.net
- website: www.fraserhouse.net

Guest House
Mrs Thelma Rowe, Tiverton B & B, 9 Cruse Close, SWAY, Hampshire SO41 6AY
Tel: 01590 683092
- e-mail: ronrowe@talk21.com
- website: www.tivertonnewforest.co.uk

•HEREFORDSHIRE

Hotel
Hedley Lodge, Belmont Abbey, HEREFORD, Herefordshire HR2 9RZ Tel: 01432 374747
- e-mail: hedley@belmontabbey.org.uk
- website: www.hedleylodge.com

Self-catering
Mrs Williams, Radnor's End, Huntington, KINGTON, Herefordshire HR5 3NZ
Tel: 01544 370289
- e-mail: enquiries@the-rock-cottage.co.uk
- website: www.the-rock-cottage.co.uk

B&B
Mrs E. Godshall, Moor Court Farm, Stretton Grandison, Near LEDBURY, Herefordshire HR8 2TP Tel: 01531 670408
- website: www.moorcourtfarm.co.uk

Farm B&B
Marian Drzymalski, Thatch Close, Llangrove, ROSS-ON-WYE, Herefordshire HR9 6EL Tel: 01989 770300
- e-mail: info@thatchclose.co.uk
- website: www.thatchclose.co.uk

•ISLE OF WIGHT

Self-Catering
Island Cottage Holidays, ISLE OF WIGHT Tel: 01929 480080
- e-mail: enq@islandcottageholidays.com
- website: www.islandcottageholidays.com

Caravan Park
Hillgrove Park, Field Lane, St Helens, RYDE, Isle of Wight PO33 1UT Tel: 01983 872802
- e-mail: holidays@hillgrove.co.uk
- website: www.hillgrove.co.uk

Guest House
Mrs V. Hudson, Strang Hall, Uplands Road, TOTLAND, Isle of Wight PO39 0DZ Tel: 01983 753189
- e-mail: strang_hall@hotmail.com
- website: www.strang-hall.co.uk

•KENT

Self-Catering Cottages
Garden Of England
Contact: The Mews Office, 189a High Street, Tonbridge, KENT TN9 1BX Tel: 01732 369168
- e-mail: holidays@gardenofenglandcottages.co.uk
- website: www.gardenofenglandcottages.co.uk

Self-Catering Cottages
Fairhaven Holiday Cottages, KENT Tel: 01208 821255
- website: www.fairhaven-holidays.co.uk

Guest House
S. Twort, Heron Cottage, Biddenden, ASHFORD, Kent TN27 8HH. Tel: 01580 291358
- e-mail: susantwort@hotmail.com
- website: www.heroncottage.info

Farm B & B
Alison & Jim Taylor, Boldens Wood, Fiddling Lane, Stowting, FOLKESTONE, Ashford, Kent TN25 6AP Tel: 01303 812011
- e-mail: StayoverNight@aol.com
- website: www.countrypicnics.com

Hotel
Collina House Hotel, 5 East Hill, TENTERDEN, Kent TN30 6RL Tel: 01580 764852/764004
- e-mail: enquiries@collinahousehotel.co.uk
- website: www.collinahousehotel.co.uk

•LANCASHIRE

Hotel
The Chadwick Hotel, South Promenade, LYTHAM ST ANNES, Lancashire FY8 1NS Tel: 01253 720061
- e-mail: sales@thechadwickhotel.com
- website: www.thechadwickhotel.com

Self-Catering
Don-Ange Holiday Apartments, 29 Holmfield Road, BLACKPOOL, Lancashire FY2 9TB Tel: 01253 355051
- e-mail: donange@msn.com
- website: www.donange.cjb.net

Holiday Park
Marton Mere Holiday Village, Mythop Road, BLACKPOOL, Lancashire FY4 4XN Tel: 01253 767544
- website: www.touringholidays.co.uk

•LEICESTERSHIRE & RUTLAND

Golf Club
Birstall Golf Club, Station Road, BIRSTALL, Leicestershire LE4 3BB Tel: 0116 267 4322
- e-mail: sue@birstallgolfclub.co.uk
- website: www.birstallgolfclub.co.uk

Guest House
Richard & Vanessa Peach, The Old Rectory, 4 New Road, Belton In Rutland,OAKHAM, Rutland LE15 9LE Tel: 01572 717279
- e-mail: bb@iepuk.com
- website: www.theoldrectorybelton.co.uk

•LINCOLNSHIRE

Self-Catering
S. Jenkins, Grange Farm Riding School Holiday Cottages, Waltham Road, BARNOLDBY-LE-BECK, Grimsby, Lincolnshire DN37 0AR Tel: 01472 822216
- e-mail: sueuk4000@netscape.net
- website: www.grangefarmcottages.com

www.holidayguides.com

WEBSITE DIRECTORY

Caravan & Camping
The White Cat Caravan & Camping Park,
Shaw Lane, Old Leake, BOSTON,
Lincolnshire PE22 9LQ Tel: 01205 870121
- e-mail: kevin@klannen.freeserve.co.uk
- website: www.whitecatpark.com

Hotel
Branston Hall Hotel, BRANSTON,
Lincolnshire LN4 1PD Tel: 01522 793305
- e-mail: info@branstonhall.com
- website: www.branstonhall.com

Holiday Park
Thorpe Park Holiday Centre,
CLEETHORPES, North East Lincolnshire
DN35 0PW Tel: 01472 813395
- website: www.touringholidays.co.uk

Self-Catering / Caravans
Woodland Waters, Willoughby Road,
Ancaster, GRANTHAM,
Lincolnshire NG31 3RT Tel: 01400 230888
- e-mail: info@woodlandwaters.co.uk
- website: www.woodlandwaters.co.uk

Farm B & B
Mrs C.E. Harrison, Baumber Park, Baumber,
HORNCASTLE, Lincolnshire LN9 5NE
Tel: 01507 578235
- e-mail: baumberpark@amserve.com
- website: www.baumberpark.com

Holiday Park
Golden Sands Holiday Park, Quebec Road,
MABLETHORPE, Lincolnshire LN12 1QJ
Tel: 01507 477871
- website: www.touringholidays.co.uk

Farmhouse B & B
S Evans, Willow Farm, Thorpe Fendykes,
SKEGNESS, Lincolnshire PE24 4QH
Tel: 01754 830316
- e-mail: willowfarmhols@aol.com
- website: www.willowfarmholidays.co.uk

•MERSEYSIDE

Guest House
Holme Leigh Guest House, 93 Woodcroft
Road, Wavertree, LIVERPOOL,
Merseyside L15 2HG Tel: 0151 734 2216
- e-mail: info@homeleigh.com
- website: www.holmeleigh.com

Readers are requested to mention this FHG guide when seeking accommodation

•NORFOLK

Self-Catering
Sand Dune Cottages, Tan Lane,
CAISTER-ON-SEA, Great Yarmouth,
Norfolk NR30 5DT Tel: 01493 720352
- e-mail: sand.dune.cottages@amserve.net
- website: www.eastcoastlive.co.uk/sites/sanddunecottages.php

Farmhouse B & B
Mrs M. Ling, The Rookery, Wortham, DISS,
Norfolk IP22 1RB. Tel: 01379 783236
- e-mail: russell.ling@ukgateway.net
- www.avocethosting.co.uk/rookery/home.htm

Self-Catering
Idyllic Cottages at Vere Lodge,
South Raynham, FAKENHAM,
Norfolk NR21 7HE Tel: 01328 838261
- e-mail: major@verelodge.co.uk
- website: www.idylliccottages.co.uk

Holiday Park
Wild Duck Holiday Park, Howards Common,
Belton, GREAT YARMOUTH,
Norfolk NR31 9NE Tel: 01493 780268
- website: www.touringholidays.co.uk

Self-Catering
Blue Riband Holidays, HEMSBY,
Great Yarmouth, Norfolk NR29 4HA
Tel: 01493 730445
- website: www.BlueRibandHolidays.co.uk

Farm
Little Abbey Farm, Low Road, Pentney,
KING'S LYNN, Norfolk PE32 1JF
Tel: 01760 337348
- e-mail: enquiries@littleabbeyfarm.co.uk
- website: www.littleabbeyfarm.co.uk

B & B
Dolphin Lodge, 3 Knapton Road, Trunch,
NORTH WALSHAM, Norfolk NR28 0QE
Tel: 01263 720961
- e-mail: dolphin.lodge@btopenworld.com
- website: www.dolphinlodges.net

Hotel
Elderton Lodge Hotel, THORPE MARKET,
Cromer, Norfolk NR11 8TZ
Tel: 01263 833547
- e-mail: enquiries@eldertonlodge.co.uk
- website: www.eldertonlodge.co.uk

Self-Catering
Mr & Mrs Castleton, Poppyland Holiday
Cottages, The Green, THORPE MARKET,
Norfolk NR11 8AJ Tel: 01263 833219
- e-mail: poppylandjc@netscape.net
- website: www.poppyland.com

WEBSITE DIRECTORY

Self-Catering
Winterton Valley Holidays, WINTERTON-ON-SEA/CALIFORNIA, Norfolk
Contact: 15 Kingston Avenue, Caister-on-Sea NR30 5ET Tel: 01493 377175
- e-mail: info@wintertonvalleyholidays.co.uk
- website: www.wintertonvalleyholidays.co.uk

• NORTHAMPTONSHIRE

Farmhouse B&B
Mrs B. Hawkins, Pear Tree Farm, Aldwincle, KETTERING, Northants NN14 3EL
Tel: 01832 720614
- e-mail: beverley@peartreefarm.net
- website: www.peartreefarm.net

• NORTHUMBERLAND

Self-Catering
Mrs M. Thompson, Heritage Coast Holidays, 6G Greensfield Court, ALNWICK, Northumberland NE66 2DE
Tel: 01665 604935
- e-mail: info@heritagecoastholidays.com
- website: www.heritagecoastholidays.com

Self-Catering Cottages
Buston Farm Holiday Cottages, Low Buston Hall, Warkworth, ALNWICK, Morpeth, Northumberland NE65 0XY
Tel: 01665 714805
- e-mail: jopark@farming.co.uk
- website: www.buston.co.uk

Hotel
The Blue Bell Hotel, Market Place, BELFORD, Northumberland NE70 7NE
Tel: 01668 213543
- e-mail: bluebel@globalnet.co.uk
- website: www.bluebellhotel.com

Self-Catering
Swinhoe Farmhouse, BELFORD, Northumberland NE70 7LJ
Tel: 016682 13370
- e-mail: valerie@swinhoecottages.co.uk
- website: www.swinhoecottages.co.uk

Hotel / Self-Catering
Riverdale Hall Hotel, BELLINGHAM, Northumberland NE48 2JT
Tel: 01434 220254
- e-mail: reservations@riverdalehallhotel.co.uk
- website: www.riverdalehallhotel.co.uk

Self-Catering
2, The Courtyard, BERWICK-UPON-TWEED
Contact: J. Morton, 1, The Courtyard, Church Street, Berwick-upon-Tweed TD15 1EE
Tel: 01289 308737
- e-mail: jvm@patmosphere.uklinux.net
- website: www.berwickselfcatering.co.uk

Hotel
The Cobbled Yard Hotel, 40 Walkergate, BERWICK-UPON-TWEED, Northumberland TD15 1DJ Tel: 01289 308407
- e-mail: cobbledyardhotel@berwick35.fsnet.co.uk
- website: www.cobbledyardhotel.com

B & B
Friendly Hound Cottage, Ford Common, BERWICK-UPON-TWEED, Northumberland TD15 2QD Tel: 01289 388554
- e-mail: friendlyhound@aol.com
- website: www.friendlyhoundcottage.co.uk

Holiday Park
Haggerston Castle Holiday Park, Beal, Near BERWICK-UPON-TWEED, Northumberland TD15 2PA Tel: 01289 381333
- website: www.touringholidays.co.uk

B & B / Farm / Camping
Mrs S. Maughan, Greencarts Farm, Near Humshaugh, HEXHAM, Northumberland NE46 4BW Tel: 01434 681320
- e-mail: sandra@greencarts.co.uk
- website: www.greencarts.co.uk

Self-Catering
Burradon Farm Cottages & Houses, Burradon Farm, Cramlington, NEWCASTLE-UPON-TYNE, Northumberland NE23 7ND
Tel: 0191 2683203
- e-mail: judy@burradonfarm.co.uk
- website: www.burradonfarm.co.uk

Self-Catering Cottages
Lorbottle Holiday Cottages, THROPTON, Northumberland
Contact: Leslie & Helen Far, Lorbottle, West Steads, Thropton, Near Morpeth, Northumberland NE65 7JT
Tel: 01665 574672
- e-mail: stay@lorbottle.com
- website: www.lorbottle.com

Please mention this publication when making enquiries about accommodation featured in these pages

Guest House / B & B
Mrs M. Halliday, Beck'n'Call, Birling West Cottage, WARKWORTH, Northumberland NE65 0XS Tel: 01665 711653
- e-mail: beck-n-call@lineone.net
- website: www.beck-n-call.co.uk

• NOTTINGHAMSHIRE

Farm / B & B
Mrs D. Hickling, Woodside Farm, Long Lane, BARKESTONE-LE-VALE, Nottinghamshire NG13 0HQ Tel: 01476 870336
- e-mail: hickling-woodside@supanet.com
- website: www.woodsidebandb.co.uk

Visitor Attraction
White Post Farm Centre, FARNSFIELD, Nottinghamshire NG22 8HL
Tel: 01623 882977
- website: www.whitepostfarmcentre.co.uk

• OXFORDSHIRE

Self-Catering
Cottage in the Country Cottage Holidays Tukes Cottage, 66 West Street, Chipping Norton, Oxfordshire OX7 5ER
Tel: 0870 027 5930
- e-mail: enquiries@cottageinthecountry.co.uk
- website: www.cottageinthecountry.co.uk

Self-Catering Cottages
Grange Farm Country Cottages, Grange Farm Estates, Godington, BICESTER, Oxfordshire OX27 9AF Tel: 01869 278 778
- e-mail: info@grangefarmcottages.co.uk
- website: www.grangefarmcottages.co.uk

Leisure Park
Cotswold Wildlife Park, BURFORD, Oxfordshire OX18 4JN Tel: 01993 823006
- website: www.cotswoldwildlifepark.co.uk

B & B
The Old Bakery, Skirmett, Near HENLEY-ON-THAMES, Oxfordshire RG9 6TD
Tel: 01491 410716
- e-mail: lizzroach@aol.com

Guest House
The Bungalow, Cherwell Farm, Mill Lane, Old Marston, OXFORD,
Oxfordshire OX3 0QF Tel: 01865 557171
- e-mail: ros.bungalowbb@btinternet.com
- www.cherwellfarm-oxford-accomm.co.uk

Guest House
Nanford Guest House, 137 Iffley Road, OXFORD, Oxfordshire, OX4 1EJ
Tel: 01865 244743
- e-mail: b.cronin@btinternet.com
- website: www.nanfordguesthouse.com

B & B
Fords Farm, Ewelme, WALLINGFORD, Oxfordshire OX10 6HU Tel: 01491 839272
- e-mail: fordsfarm@callnetuk.com
- www.country-accom.co.uk/fords-farm/

Guest House
Mrs Elizabeth Simpson, Field View, Wood Green, WITNEY, Oxfordshire OX28 1DE
Tel: 01993 705485
- e-mail: bandb@fieldview-witney.co.uk
- website: www.fieldview-witney.co.uk

B & B
Mr & Mrs N. Hamilton, Gorselands Hall, Boddington Lane, North Leigh,
between WOODSTOCK and WITNEY, Oxfordshire OX29 6PU Tel: 01993 882292
- e-mail: hamilton@gorselandshall.com
- website: www.gorselandshall.com

• SHROPSHIRE

Golf Club / Self-Catering Cottages
Cleobury Mortimer Golf Club, Wyre Common, CLEOBURY MORTIMER, Kidderminster, Worcestershire DY14 8HQ
Tel: 01299 271112
- e-mail: enquiries@cleoburygolfclub.com
- website: www.cleoburygolfclub.com

• SHROPSHIRE

Guest House
Ron & Jenny Repath, Meadowlands, Lodge Lane, Frodesley, DORRINGTON, Shropshire SY5 7HD Tel: 01694 731350
- e-mail: meadowlands@talk21.com
- website: www.meadowlands.co.uk

Self-Catering
Clive & Cynthia Prior, Mocktree Barns Holiday Cottages, Leintwardine, LUDLOW, Shropshire SY7 0LY Tel: 01547 540441
- e-mail: mocktreebarns@care4free.net
- website: www.mocktreeholidays.co.uk

B & B / Self-Catering
Mrs E. Purnell, Ravenscourt Manor, Woofferton, LUDLOW, Shropshire SY8 4AL
Tel: 01584 711905
- e-mail: elizabeth@ravenscourtmanor.plus.com
- website: www.internet-tsp.co.uk/ravenscourt
  www.cottagesdirect.com

WEBSITE DIRECTORY

Inn / Hotel
The Four Alls Inn, Woodseaves,
MARKET DRAYTON, Shropshire TF9 2AG
Tel: 01630 652995
• e-mail: inn@thefouralls.com
• website: www.thefouralls.com

Farmhouse / B & B
Sambrook Manor, Sambrook, NEWPORT,
Shropshire TF10 8AL Tel: 01952 550406
• website: www.sambrookmanor.com

B & B
The Mill House, High Ercall, TELFORD,
Shropshire TF6 6BE Tel: 01952 770394
• e-mail: mill-house@talk21.com
• website: www.ercallmill.co.uk

• SOMERSET

Self-Catering
The Pack Horse, ALLERFORD, Near Porlock,
Somerset TA24 8HW Tel: 01643 862475
• e-mail: holidays@thepackhorse.net
• website: www.thepackhorse.net

B&B
Mrs C. Bryson, Walton Villa, 3 Newbridge
Hill, BATH, Somerset BA1 3PW
Tel: 01225 482792
• e-mail: walton.villa@virgin.net
• website: www.walton.izest.com

B & B / Self-Catering
Mrs P. Foster, Pennsylvania Farm, Newton-
St-Loe, NEAR BATH, Somerset BA2 9JD
Tel: 01225 314912
• website: www.pennsylvaniafarm.co.uk

Inn
The Talbot 15th Century Coaching Inn,
Selwood Street, Mells, Near BATH,
Somerset BA11 3PN Tel: 01373 812254
• e-mail: roger@talbotinn.com
• website: www.talbotinn.com

Farm Guest House / Self-Catering
Jackie & David Bishop, Toghill House Farm,
Freezing Hill, Wick, Near BATH,
Somerset BS30 5RT. Tel: 01225 891261
• e-mail: accommodation@toghillhousefarm.com
• website: www.toghillhousefarm.co.uk

Self-Catering / Caravans
Beachside Holiday Park, Coast Road,
BREAN, Somerset TA8 2QZ
Tel: 01278 751346
• e-mail: enquiries@beachsideholidaypark.co.uk
• website: www.beachsideholidaypark.co.uk

Self-Catering
Westward Rise Holiday Park, South Road,
BREAN, Burnham-on-Sea, Somerset TA8 2RD
Tel: 01278 751310
• e-mail: westwardrise@breansands.freeserve.co.uk
• website: www.breansands.freeserve.co.uk

Farmhouse / Self-Catering
Josephine Smart, Leigh Farm, Old Road,
Pensford, NEAR BRISTOL, Somerset
BS39 4BA Tel: 01761 490281
• website: www.leighfarm.co.uk

Holiday Park
Burnham-On-Sea Holiday Village, Marine
Drive, BURNHAM-ON-SEA,
Somerset TA8 1LA Tel: 01278 783391
• website: www.touringholidays.co.uk

Farm / Self-Catering Cottages
Mrs Wendy Baker, Withy Grove Farm, East
Huntspill, NEAR BURNHAM-ON-SEA,
Somerset TA9 3NP Tel: 01278 784471
• website: www.withygrovefarm.co.uk

Farm / B & B
Mrs C. Bacon, Honeydown Farm,
Seaborough Hill, CREWKERNE,
Somerset TA18 8PL Tel: 01460 72665
• e-mail: c.bacon@honeydown.co.uk
• website: www.honeydown.co.uk

Guest House
Mrs M. Rawle, Winsbere House,
64 Battleton, DULVERTON, Somerset
TA22 9HU Tel: 01398 323278
• e-mail: info@winsbere.co.uk
• website: www.winsbere.co.uk

Inn
Exmoor White Horse Inn, Exford,
EXMOOR, Somerset TA24 7PY
Tel: 01643 831229
• e-mail: user@exmoor-whitehouse.co.uk
• website: www.exmoor-whitehorse.co.uk

Farm Self-Catering & Camping
Westermill Farm, Exford, EXMOOR,
Somerset TA24 7NJ
Tel: 01643 831216 or 01643 831238
• e-mail: fhg@westermill.com
• website: www.westermill.com

Farm Self-Catering
Jane Styles, Wintershead Farm,
Simonsbath, EXMOOR, Somerset TA24 7LF
Tel: 01643 831222
• e-mail: wintershed@yahoo.co.uk
• website: www.wintershead.co.uk

www.holidayguides.com

WEBSITE DIRECTORY

B & B / Half-Board / Self-Catering / Towing Pitches
St Audries Bay Holiday Club, West Quantoxhead, MINEHEAD, Somerset TA4 4DY Tel: 01984 632515
• e-mail: mrandle@staudriesbay.co.uk
• website: www.staudriesbay.co.uk

Self-Catering
Wood Dairy, Wood Lane, NORTH PERROTT, Somerset TA18 7TA Tel: 01935 891532
• e-mail: liz@acountryretreat.co.uk
• website: www.acountryretreat.co.uk

Self-Catering Cottages
Knowle Farm, West Compton, SHEPTON MALLET, Somerset BA4 4PD
Tel: 01749 890482
• website: www.knowle-farm-cottages.co.uk

Guest House / B & B
Blorenge House, 57 Staplegrove Road, TAUNTON, Somerset TA1 1DG
Tel: 01823 283005
• e-mail: enquiries@blorengehouse.co.uk
• website: www.blorengehouse.co.uk

Guest House
The Old Mill, Netherclay, Bishop's Hull, TAUNTON, Somerset TA1 5AB
Tel: 01823 289732
• website: www.theoldmillbandb.co.uk

Self-Catering
Mrs J Greenway, Woodlands Farm, Bathealton, TAUNTON, Somerset TA4 2AH
Tel: 01984 623271
• website: www.woodlandsfarm-holidays.co.uk

B & B
G. Clark, Yew Tree Farm, THEALE, Near Wedmore, Somerset BS28 4SN
Tel: 01934 712475
• e-mail: yewtreefarm@yewtreefarmbandb.co.uk
• website: www.yewtreefarmbandb.co.uk

Self-Catering
Croft Holiday Cottages, 2 The Croft, Anchor Street, WATCHET, Somerset TA23 0BY
Tel: 01984 631121
• e-mail: croftcottages@talk21.com
• website: www.cottagessomerset.com

B&B
Cricklake Farm, Bartlett Bridge, Cocklake, WEDMORE, Somerset BS28 4HH
Tel: 01934 712736
• e-mail: info@cricklakefarm.co.uk
• website: www.cricklakefarm.co.uk

Guest House
Infield House, 36 Portway, WELLS, Somerset BA5 2BN Tel: 01749 670989
• e-mail: infield@talk21.com
• website: www.infieldhouse.co.uk

B & B
Susan Crane, Birdwood House, Bath Road, WELLS, Somerset BA5 3EW
Tel: 01749 679250
• website: www.birdwood-bandb.co.uk

Farm / B & B
Mrs Sheila Stott, "Lana", Hollow Farm, Westbury-Sub-Mendip, NEAR WELLS, Somerset BA5 1HH Tel: 01749 870635
• e-mail: sheila@stott2366.freeserve.co.uk

Mrs H.J. Millard, Double-Gate B&B Ltd, Godney, WELLS, Somerset BA5 1RX
Tel: 01458 832217
• e-mail: doublegatefarm@aol.com
• website: www.doublegatefarm.com

Hotel / Self-Catering
Francesca Day, Timbertop Aparthotel, 8 Victoria Park, WESTON-SUPER-MARE, Somerset BS23 2HZ
Tel: 01934 631178 or 01934 424348
• e-mail: stay@aparthoteltimbertop.com
• website: www.aparthoteltimbertop.com

•STAFFORDSHIRE

Caravan & Camping / Holiday Park
The Star Caravan & Camping Park, Star Road, Cotton, Near ALTON TOWERS Staffordshire ST10 3DW
Tel: 01538 702219
• website: www.starcaravanpark.co.uk

Farm B & B / Self-Catering
Mrs M. Hiscoe-James, Offley Grove Farm, Adbaston, ECCLESHALL, Staffordshire ST20 0QB. Tel: 01785 280205
• e-mail: accom@offleygrovefarm.freeserve.co.uk
• website: www.offleygrovefarm.co.uk

Self-catering
The Raddle Log Cabins, Quarry Bank, Hollington, Near Tean, STOKE-ON-TRENT, Staffordshire ST10 4HQ Tel: 01889 507278
•e-mail: peter@logcabin.co.uk
•website: www.logcabin.co.uk

Guest House
Mrs Griffiths, Prospect House Guest House, 334 Cheadle Road, Cheddleton, LEEK, Staffordshire ST13 7BW Tel: 01782 550639
• e-mail: prospect@talk21.com
• website: www.prospecthouseleek.co.uk

Readers are requested to mention this FHG guide when seeking accommodation

WEBSITE DIRECTORY

•SUFFOLK

Guest House
Kay Dewsbury, Manorhouse, The Green, Beyton, BURY ST EDMUNDS, Suffolk IP30 9AF
Tel: 01359 270960
• e-mail: manorhouse@beyton.com
• website: www.beyton.com

Self-catering
Rede Hall Farm Park, Rede,
BURY ST EDMUNDS, Suffolk IP29 4UG
Tel: 01284 850695
• e-mail: oakley@soils.fsnet.co.uk
• website: www.redehallfarmpark.co.uk

Self-Catering
Mr & Mrs D. Cole, The Close, Middlegate Barn, DUNWICH, Suffolk IP17 3DP
Tel: 01728 648741
• e-mail: middlegate@aol.com

Self-Catering
Mr P. Havers, Athelington Hall, Norham, EYE, Suffolk IP21 5EJ Tel: 01728 628233
• e-mail: peter@logcabinholidays.co.uk
• website: www.logcabinholidays.co.uk

Guest House
The Grafton Guest House, 13 Sea Road, FELIXSTOWE, Suffolk IP11 2BB
Tel: 01394 284881
• e-mail: info@grafton-house.com
• website: www.grafton-house.com

B & B / Self-Catering
Mrs Sarah Kindred, High House Farm, Cransford, Woodbridge, FRAMLINGHAM, Suffolk IP13 9PD Tel: 01728 663461
• e-mail: b&b@highhousefarm.co.uk
• website: www.highhousefarm.co.uk

Self-Catering
Kessingland Cottages, Rider Haggard Lane, KESSINGLAND, Suffolk.
Contact: S. Mahmood,
156 Bromley Road, Beckenham,
Kent BR3 6PG Tel: 020 8650 0539
• e-mail: jeeptrek@kjti.freeserve.co.uk
• website: www.k-cottage.co.uk

Farm / Guest House
Sweffling Hall Farm, Sweffling, SAXMUNDHAM, Suffolk IP17 2BT
Tel: 01728 663644
• e-mail: stephenmann@suffolkonline.net
• website: www.swefflinghallfarm.co.uk

Self-Catering
Southwold Self-Catering Properties.
H.A. Adnams, 98 High Street,
SOUTHWOLD, Suffolk IP18 6DP
Tel: 01502 723292
• e-mail: haadnams_lets@ic24.net
• website: www.haadnams

Self-Catering Cottage
Anvil Cottage, WOODBRIDGE, Suffolk
Contact: Mr & Mrs R. Blake, IA Moorfield Road, Woodbridge, Suffolk IP12 4JN
Tel: 01394 382 565
• e-mail: robert@blake4110.fsbusiness.co.uk

Self-Catering
Windmill Lodges Ltd, Redhouse Farm, Saxtead, WOODBRIDGE, Suffolk IP13 9RD
Tel: 01728 685338
• e-mail: holidays@windmilllodges.co.uk
• website: www.windmilllodges.co.uk

•SURREY

Guest House
The Lawn Guest House, 30 Massetts Road, Horley, GATWICK, Surrey RH6 7DF
Tel: 01293 775751
• e-mail: info@lawnguesthouse.co.uk
• website: www.lawnguesthouse.co.uk

Hotel
Chase Lodge Hotel, 10 Park Road, Hampton Wick, KINGSTON-UPON-THAMES, Surrey KT1 4AS. Tel: 020 8943 1862
• e-mail: info@chaselodgehotel.com
• website: www.chaselodgehotel.com
         www.surreyhotels.com

•EAST SUSSEX

Self-Catering
"Pekes", CHIDDINGLY, East Sussex
Contact: Eva Morris, 124 Elm Park Mansions, Park Walk, London SW10 0AR
Tel: 020 7352 8088
• e-mail: pekes.afa@virgin.net
• website: www.pekesmanor.com

Guest House
Ebor Lodge, 71 Royal Parade, EASTBOURNE, East Sussex BN22 7AQ
Tel: 01323 640792
• e-mail: info@eborlodge.co.uk
• website: www.eborlodge.co.uk

www.holidayguides.com

Self-Catering Cottages
Caburn Cottages, Ranscombe Farm, GLYNDE, Lewes, East Sussex BN8 6AA
Tel: 01273 858062
• e-mail: enquiries@caburncottages.co.uk
• website: www.caburncottages.co.uk

Guest House / Self-Catering
Longleys Farm Cottage, Harebeating Lane, HAILSHAM, East Sussex BN27 1ER
Tel: 01323 841227
• e-mail: longleysfarmcottagebb@dsl.pipex.com
• website: www.longleysfarmcottage.co.uk

Hotel
Grand Hotel, Grand Parade, St. Leonards, HASTINGS, East Sussex TN38 0DD
Tel: 01424 428510
• e-mail: petermann@grandhotelhastings.co.uk
• website: www.grandhotelhastings.co.uk

Bed & Breakfast
Barbara Martin, Little Saltcote, 22 Military Road, RYE, East Sussex TN31 7NY
Tel: 01797 223210
• e-mail: info@littlesaltcote.co.uk
• website: www.littlesaltcote.co.uk

Hotel
Rye Lodge Hotel, Hilders Cliff, RYE, East Sussex TN31 7LD Tel: 01797 223838
• e-mail: chris@ryelodge.co.uk
• website: www.ryelodge.co.uk

B & B
Jeake's House, Mermaid Street, RYE, East Sussex TN31 7ET
Tel: 01797 222828
• e-mail: stay@jeakeshouse.com
• website: www.jeakeshouse.com

Hotel
Flackley Ash Hotel & Restaurant, Peasmarsh, Near RYE, East Sussex TN31 6YH. Tel: 01797 230651
• e-mail: enquiries@flackleyashhotel.co.uk
• website: www.flackleyashhotel.co.uk

• WEST SUSSEX

B & B
Mrs Vicki Richards, Woodacre, Arundel Road, Fontwell, ARUNDEL, West Sussex BN18 0QP Tel: 01243 814301
• e-mail: wacrebb@aol.com
• website: www.woodacre.co.uk

B & B
Broxmead Paddock, Broxmead Lane, Bolney, HAYWARDS HEATH, West Sussex RH17 5RG
Tel: 01444 881458
• e-mail: broxmeadpaddock@hotmail.com
• website: www.broxmeadpaddock.eclipse.co.uk

Self-Catering
Mrs M. W. Carreck, New Hall Holiday Flat and Cottage, New Hall Lane, Small Dole, HENFIELD, West Sussex BN5 9YJ
Tel: 01273 492546
• website: www.newhallcottage.co.uk

Touring Park
Warner Touring Park, Warner Lane, SELSEY, West Sussex PO20 9EL Tel: 01243 604499
• website: www.bunnleisure.co.uk

Guest House
Manor Guest House, 100 Broadwater Road, WORTHING, West Sussex BN14 8AN
Tel: 01903 236028
• e-mail: stay@manorworthing.com
• website: www.manorworthing.com

•WARWICKSHIRE

Guest House / B & B
Julia & John Downie, Holly Tree Cottage, Pathlow, STRATFORD-UPON-AVON, Warwickshire CV37 0ES Tel: 01789 204461
• e-mail: john@hollytree-cottage.co.uk
• website: www.hollytree-cottage.co.uk

Guest House
The Croft, Haseley Knob, WARWICK, Warwickshire CV35 7NL Tel: 01926 484447
• e-mail: david@croftguesthouse.co.uk
• website: www.croftguesthouse.co.uk

•WEST MIDLANDS

Hotel
Featherstone Farm Hotel, New Road, Featherstone, WOLVERHAMPTON, West Midlands WV10 7NW Tel: 01902 725371
• e-mail: info@featherstonefarm.co.uk
• website: www.featherstonefarm.co.uk

Readers are requested to mention this FHG guide when seeking accommodation

WEBSITE DIRECTORY

•WILTSHIRE

Guest House
Alan & Dawn Curnow, Hayburn Wyke Guest House, 72 Castle Road, SALISBURY, Wiltshire SP1 3RL Tel:01722 412627
• e-mail: hayburn.wyke@tinyonline.co.uk
• website: www.hayburnwykeguesthouse.co.uk

•WORCESTERSHIRE

Farmhouse / B & B
The Barn House, BROADWAS ON TEME, Worcestershire WR6 5NS Tel: 01886 888733
• e-mail: info@barnhouseonline.co.uk
• website: www.barnhouseonline.co.uk

Guest House
Ann & Brian Porter, Croft Guest House, Bransford, GREAT MALVERN, Worcester, Worcestershire WR6 5JD Tel: 01886 832227
• e-mail: hols@crofthousewr6.fsnet.co.uk
• website: www.croftguesthouse.com

Self-Catering Cottages
Rochford Park, TENBURY WELLS, Worcestershire WR15 8SP
Tel: 01584 781 372
• e-mail: cottages@rochfordpark.co.uk
• website: www.rochfordpark.co.uk

•NORTH YORKSHIRE

Self-Catering
Recommended Cottage Holidays, Eastgate House, Pickering, NORTH YORKSHIRE
Tel: 01751 475547
• website: www.recommended-cottages.co.uk

Farmhouse B & B
Mrs Julie Clarke, Middle Farm, Woodale, COVERDALE, Leyburn,
North Yorkshire DL8 4TY Tel: 01969 640271
• e-mail: j-a-clarke@amserve.com
• www.yorkshirenet.co.uk/stayat/middlefarm

Holiday Park
Blue Dolphin Holiday Park, Gristhorpe Bay, FILEY, North Yorkshire YO14 9PU
Tel: 01723 515155
• website: www.touringholidays.co.uk

Holiday Park
Primrose Valley Holiday Park, Primrose Valley, NEAR FILEY, North Yorkshire YO14 9RF Tel: 01723 513771
• website: www.touringholidays.co.uk

Holiday Park
Reighton Sands Holiday Park, Reighton Gap, NEAR FILEY, North Yorkshire YO14 9SH • Tel: 01723 890476
• website: www.touringholidays.co.uk

Farmhouse B&B
Mr & Mrs Richardson, Egton Banks Farmhouse, GLAISDALE, Whitby, North Yorkshire YO21 2QP Tel: 01947 897289
e-mail: egtonbanksfarm@agriplus.net
•website: www.egtonbanksfarm.agriplus.net

Country Inn
The Foresters Arms, Main Street, GRASSINGTON, Near Skipton,
North Yorkshire BD23 5AA
Tel: 01756 752349
• e-mail: theforesters@totalise.co.uk
• website: www.forestersarmsgrassington.co.uk

Caravan & Camping
Bainbridge Ings Caravan & Camping Site, HAWES, North Yorkshire DL8 3NU
Tel: 01969 667354
• e-mail: janet@bainbridge-ings.co.uk
• website: www.bainbridge-ings.co.uk

Hotel
Stone House Hotel, Sedbusk, HAWES, Wensleydale, North Yorkshire DL8 3PT
Tel: 01969 667571
• e-mail: daleshotel@aol.com
• website: www.stonehousehotel.com

Guest House
The New Inn Motel, Main Street, HUBY, York, North Yorkshire YO61 1HQ
Tel: 01347 810219
• enquiries@newinnmotel.freeserve.co.uk
• website: www.newinnmotel.co.uk

Guest House
Mr B.L.F. Martin, The Old Star, West Witton, LEYBURN, North Yorkshire DL8 4LU
Tel: 01969 622949
• e-mail: enquiries@theoldstar.com
• website: www.theoldstar.com

Self-Catering
Abbey Holiday Cottages, MIDDLESMOOR. 12 Panorama Close, Pateley Bridge, Harrogate, North Yorkshire HG3 5NY
Tel: 01423 712062
• e-mail: abbeyholiday.cottages@virgin.net
• website: www.abbeyholidaycottages.co.uk

B & B
Banavie, Roxby Road, Thornton-Le-Dale, PICKERING, North Yorkshire YO18 7SX
Tel: 01751 474616
• e-mail: info@banavie.co.uk
• website: www.banavie.uk.com

WEBSITE DIRECTORY

Guest House / Self-Catering
Sue & Tony Hewitt, Harmony Country Lodge,
80 Limestone Road, Burniston,
SCARBOROUGH, North Yorkshire
YO13 0DG Tel: 0800 2985840
- e-mail: mail@harmonylodge.net
- website: www.harmonylodge.net

B & B
Beck Hall, Malham, SKIPTON, North
Yorkshire BD23 4DJ Tel: 01729 830332
- e-mail: simon@beckhallmalham.com
- website: www.beckhallmalham.com

Inn
Gamekeepers Inn, Long Ashes Park,
Threshfield, NEAR SKIPTON, North
Yorkshire BD23 5PN Tel: 01756 752434
- e-mail: info@gamekeeperinn.co.uk
- website: www.gamekeeperinn.co.uk

Self-Catering
Mrs Jones, New Close Farm, Kirkby Malham,
SKIPTON, North Yorkshire BD23 4DP
Tel: 01729 830240
- brendajones@newclosefarmyorkshire.co.uk
- website: www.newclosefarmyorkshire.co.uk

Self-Catering
Allaker in Coverdale, WEST SCRAFTON,
Near Leyburn, North Yorkshire
Contact Mr A. Cave Tel: 020 8567 4862
- e-mail: ac@adriancave.com
- website: www.adriancave.com/allaker

Guest House
Ashford Guest House, 8 Royal Crescent,
WHITBY, North Yorkshire YO21 3EJ
Tel: 01947 602138
- e-mail: info@ashfordguesthouse.co.uk
- website: www.ashfordguesthouse.co.uk

Self-Catering
Mrs Jill McNeil, Swallow Holiday Cottages,
Long Leas Farm, Hawsker, WHITBY, North
Yorkshire YO22 4LA Tel: 01947 603790
- e-mail: jillian@swallowcottages.co.uk
- website: www.swallowcottages.co.uk

Self-Catering
Mr J.N. Eddleston,
Greenhouses Farm Cottages,
Greenhouses Farm, Lealholm,
Near WHITBY, North Yorkshire YO21 2AD
Tel: 01947 897486
- e-mail: n_eddleston@yahoo.com
- www.greenhouses-farm-cottages.co.uk

Self-Catering
The Old Granary & Copper Cottage,
Ravenhill Farm, Dunsley, NEAR WHITBY,
North Yorkshire YO21 3TJ
Tel: 01947 893331
- e-mail: jackie.richardson6@btopenworld.com

Self-Catering
White Rose Holiday Cottages,
NEAR WHITBY, North Yorkshire
Contact: Mrs J. Roberts, 5 Brook Park,
Sleights, Near Whitby, North Yorkshire
YO21 1RT Tel: 01947 810763
- e-mail: enquiries@whiterosecottages.co.uk
- website: www.whiterosecottages.co.uk

Guest House
Mrs J.M. Wood, Ascot House,
80 East Parade, YORK, North Yorkshire
YO31 7YH Tel: 01904 426826
- e-mail: admin@ascothouseyork.com
- website: www.ascothouseyork.com

Self-Catering Cottages
The Grange Farm Holiday Cottages,
Bishop Wilton, York, North Yorkshire
YO42 1SA Tel: 01759 369500
- e-mail: richarddavy@supanet.com
- website: www.thegrangefarm.com

Guest House / Self-Catering
Mr Gary Hudson, Orillia House, 89 The
Village, Stockton on Forest, YORK, North
Yorkshire YO3 9UP Tel: 01904 400600
- e-mail: info@orilliahouse.co.uk
- website: www.orilliahouse.co.uk

Guest House / Camping
Mrs Jeanne Wilson, Robeanne House,
Driffield Lane, Shiptonthorpe, YORK, North
Yorkshire YO43 3PW Tel: 01430 873312
- e-mail: robert@robeanne.freeserve.com
- website: www.robeannehouse.co.uk

Guest House
St George's, 6 St George's Place, YORK,
North Yorkshire YO24 1DR
Tel: 01904 625056
- e-mail: sixstgeorg@aol.com
- website: http://members.aol.com/sixstgeorg/

FHG Guides

publish a large range of well-known accommodation guides. We will be happy to send you details or you can use the order form at the back of this book.

WEBSITE DIRECTORY

Self-Catering
Mr N. Manasir, York Lakeside Lodges, Moor Lane, YORK, North Yorkshire YO24 2QU
Tel: 01904 702346
* e-mail: neil@yorklakesidelodges.co.uk
* website: www.yorklakesidelodges.co.uk

•SOUTH YORKSHIRE

Golf Club
Sandhill Golf Club, Middlecliffe Lane, Little Houghton, BARNSLEY, South Yorkshire S72 0HW Tel: 01226 753444
* e-mail: vwistow@sandhillgolfclub.co.uk
* website: www.sandhillgolfclub.co.uk

B & B
Padley Farm Bed & Breakfast, Dungworth Green, Bradfield, SHEFFIELD, South Yorkshire S6 6HE Tel: 01142 851427
* e-mail: info@padleyfarm.co.uk
* website: www.padleyfarm.co.uk

•WEST YORKSHIRE

Farm / B & B / Self-Catering Cottages
Currer Laithe Farm, Moss Carr Road, Long Lee, KEIGHLEY, West Yorkshire BD21 4SL
Tel: 01535 604387
* website: www.currerlaithe.co.uk

FHG
·K·U·P·E·R·A·R·D·

Please mention this publication when making enquiries about accommodation featured in these pages

•SCOTLAND

Self-Catering Cottages
Islands & Highlands Cottages, Bridge Road, Portree, Isle of Skye, SCOTLAND IV51 9ER
Tel: 01478 612123
* website: www.islands-and-highlands.co.uk

•ABERDEEN, BANFF & MORAY

Hotel
Banchory Lodge Hotel, BANCHORY, Kincardineshire AB31 5HS
Tel: 01330 822625
* e-mail: enquiries@banchorylodge.co.uk
* website: www.banchorylodge.co.uk

B & B
Davaar B & B, Church Street, DUFFTOWN, Moray, AB55 4AR Tel: 01340 820464
* e-mail: davaar@cluniecameron.co.uk
* website: www.davaardufftown.co.uk

Self-catering
Newseat & Kirklea, FRASERBURGH, Aberdeenshire.
Contact: Mrs E.M. Pittendrigh, Kirktown, Tyrie, Fraserburgh AB43 7DQ. Tel: 01346 541231
•e-mail: pittendrigh@supanet.com

Golf Club
Moray Golf Club, Stotfield Road, LOSSIEMOUTH, Moray IV31 6QS
Tel: 01343 812018
* e-mail: secretary@moraygolf.co.uk
* website: www.moraygolf.co.uk

Self-Catering
Val & Rob Keeble, Lighthouse Cottages, RATTRAY HEAD, Peterhead, Aberdeenshire AB42 3HB Tel: 01346 532236
* e-mail: enquiries@rattrayhead.net
* website: www.rattrayhead.net

Self-Catering
Simon Pearse, Forglen Cottages, Forglen Estate, TURRIFF, Aberdeenshire AB53 4JP Tel: 01888 562918
* e-mail: reservations@forglen.co.uk
* website: www.forglen.co.uk

•ARGYLL & BUTE

Self-Catering
Ardtur Cottages, APPIN, Argyll PA38 4DD
Tel: 01631 730223
* e-mail: pery@btinternet.com
* website: www.selfcatering-appin-scotland.com

WEBSITE DIRECTORY

Inn
Mr D. Fraser, Cairndow Stagecoach Inn,
CAIRNDOW, Argyll PA26 8BN
Tel: 01499 600286
- e-mail: cairndowinn@aol.com
- website: www.cairndow.com

Self-Catering
Catriona O'Keeffe, Blarghour Farm Cottages,
Blarghour Farm, By DALMALLY,
Argyll PA33 1BW Tel: 01866 833246
- e-mail: blarghour@btconnect.com
- website: www.self-catering-argyll.co.uk

Guest House / Self-Catering
Rockhill Guesthouse & Self-Catering
Cottages, DALMALLY, Argyll PA33 1BH
Tel: 01866 833218
- website: www.rockhill@lochawe.co.uk

Hotel
West End Hotel, West Bay, DUNOON,
Argyll PA23 7HU Tel: 01369 702907
- e-mail: mike@westendhotel.com
- website: www.westendhotel.com

Self-Catering
B & M Phillips, Kilbride Croft, Balvicar,
ISLE OF SEIL, Argyll PA34 4RD
Tel: 01852 300475
- e-mail: kilbridecroft@aol.com
- website: www.kilbridecroft.co.uk

Self-Catering
Robin Malcolm, Duntrune Castle,
KILMARTIN, Argyll PA31 8QQ
Tel: 01546 510283
- website: www.duntrune.com

Caravans
Caolasnacon Caravan Park, KINLOCHLEVEN,
Argyll PH50 4RJ Tel: 01855 831279
- e-mail: caolasnacon@hotmail.com
- website: www.kinlochlevencaravans.com

Self-Catering
Castle Sween Bay (Holidays) Ltd, Ellary,
LOCHGILPHEAD, Argyll PA31 8PA
Tel: 01880 770232
- e-mail: info@ellary.com
- website: www.ellary.com

Self-Catering
Linda Battison,
Cologin Country Chalets & Lodges,
Lerags Glen, OBAN, Argyll PA34 4SE
Tel: 01631 564501
- e-mail: info@cologin.co.uk
- website: www.cologin.co.uk

Self-Catering
Colin Mossman, Lagnakeil Lodges,
Lerags, OBAN, Argyll PA34 4SE
Tel: 01631 562746
- e-mail: info@lagnakeil.co.uk
- website: www.lagnakeil.co.uk

Self-Catering
Mrs Barker, Barfad Farm, TARBERT,
Loch Fyne, Argyll PA29 6YH
Tel: 01880 820549
- e-mail: vbarker@hotmail.com
- website: www.tarbertlochfyne.com

Golf Club
Taynuilt Golf Club, TAYNUILT, Argyll
PA35 1JE Tel: 01866 822429
- website: www.taynuiltgolfclub.co.uk

•AYRSHIRE & ARRAN

Caravan Park
Laggan House Leisure Park, BALLANTRAE,
Near Girvan, Ayrshire KA26 0LL
Tel: 01465 831229
- e-mail: lhlp@lagganhouse.co.uk
- website: www.lagganhouse.co.uk

Farmhouse / B & B
Mrs Nancy Cuthbertson, West Tannacrieff,
Fenwick, KILMARNOCK, Ayrshire KA3 6AZ
Tel: 01560 600258
- e-mail: westtannacrieff@btopenworld.com
- website: www.smoothhound.co.uk/hotels/
westtannacrieff.html

Farmhouse B&B/Caravan & Camping
Mrs M. Watson, South Whittlieburn Farm,
Brisbane Glen, LARGS, Ayrshire KA30 8SN
Tel: 01475 675881
- largsbandb@southwhittlieburnfarm.freeserve.co.uk
- www.SmoothHound.co.uk/hotels/whittlie.html
  www.ukcampsite.co.uk

Self-Catering
Bradan Road, TROON, Ayrshire
Contact: Mr Ward Brown
Tel: 07770 220830
- e-mail: stay@bradan.info
- website: www.bradan.info

•BORDERS

Self-Catering
The Old Barn, High Letham,
BERWICK-UPON-TWEED.
Contact: Richard & Susan Persse,
High Letham Farmhouse, High Letham,
Berwick-upon-Tweed, Borders TD15 1UX
Tel: 01289 306585
- e-mail: r.persse-highl@amserve.com
- website: www.oldbarnhighletham.co.uk

Self-Catering
Wauchope Cottages, BONCHESTER BRIDGE, Hawick, Borders TD9 9TG
Tel: 01450 860630
• e-mail: wauchope@btinternet.com
• website: www.wauchopecottages.co.uk

Self-Catering / Caravan & Camping
Neuk Farm Cottages & Chesterfield Caravan Park, Neuk Farmhouse, COCKBURNSPATH, Berwickshire TD13 5YH Tel: 01368 830459
• e-mail: info@chesterfieldcaravanpark.co.uk
• website: www.chesterfieldcaravanpark.co.uk

Guest House
Ferniehirst Mill Lodge, JEDBURGH, Borders TD8 6PQ Tel: 01835 863279
• e-mail: ferniehirstmill@aol.com
• website: www.ferniehirstmill.co.uk

Self-Catering
Mill House Cottage, JEDBURGH. Contact: Mrs A. Fraser, Overwells, Jedburgh, Borders TD8 6LT
Tel: 01835 863020
• e-mail: abfraser@btinternet.com
• website: www.overwells.co.uk

Hotel
George & Abbotsford Hotel, High Street, MELROSE, Borders TD6 9PD
Tel: 01896 822308
• e-mail: enquiries@georgeandabbotsford.co.uk
• website: www.georgeandabbotsford.co.uk

Farm B & B/ Self Catering / Inn
Mrs J. P. Copeland, Bailey Mill, Bailey, NEWCASTLETON, Roxburghshire TD9 0TR
Tel: 01697 748617
• e-mail: pam@baileymill.fsnet.co.uk
• www.baileycottages/riding/racing.com

Self-Catering
Mrs C. M. Kilpatrick, Slipperfield House, WEST LINTON, Peeblesshire EH46 7AA
Tel: 01968 660401
• e-mail: cottages@slipperfield.com
• website: www.slipperfield.com

•DUMFRIES & GALLOWAY

Hotel
Hetland Hall Hotel, CARRUTHERSTOWN, Dumfries & Galloway DG1 4JX
Tel: 01387 840201
• e-mail: info@hetlandhallhotel.co.uk
• website: www.hetlandhallhotel.co.uk

Farm
Celia Pickup, Craigadam, CASTLE DOUGLAS, Kirkcudbrightshire DG7 3HU Tel: 01556 650233
• website: www.craigadam.com

Self-Catering
Rusko Holidays, Gatehouse of Fleet, CASTLE DOUGLAS, Kirkcudbrightshire DG7 2BS Tel: 01557 814215
• e-mail: info@ruskoholidays.co.uk
• website: www.ruskoholidays.co.uk

B & B
Langlands Bed & Breakfast, 8 Edinburgh Road, DUMFRIES DG1 1JQ
Tel: 01387 266549
• e-mail: langlands@tiscali.co.uk
• website: www.langlands.info

Farm / Camping & Caravans / Self-Catering
Barnsoul Farm Holidays, Barnsoul Farm, Shawhead, DUMFRIES, Dumfriesshire
Tel: 01387 730249
• e-mail: barnsouldg@aol.com
• website: www.barnsoulfarm.co.uk

Guest House
Kirkcroft Guest House, Glasgow Road, GRETNA GREEN, Dumfriesshire DG16 5DU
Tel: 01461 337403
• e-mail: info@kirkcroft.co.uk
• website: www.kirkcroft.co.uk

B & B
June Deakins, Annandale House, MOFFAT, Dumfriesshire DG10 9SA
Tel: 01683 221460
• e-mail: june@annandalehouse.com
• website: www.annandalehouse.com

Camping & Touring Site
Drumroamin Farm Camping and Touring Site, 1 South Balfern, Kirkinner, NEWTON STEWART, Wigtownshire DG8 9DB
Tel: 01988 840613 or 077524 71456
• e-mail: lesley.shell@btinternet.com
• website: www.drumroamin.co.uk

Caravan Park
Whitecairn Caravan Park, Glenluce, NEWTON STEWART, Wigtownshire DG8 0NZ Tel: 01581 300267
• e-mail: enquiries@whitecairncaravans.co.uk
• website: www.whitecairncaravans.co.uk

• DUNBARTONSHIRE

Self-Catering
Inchmurrin Island Self-Catering Holidays, Inchmurrin Island, LOCH LOMOND, Dunbartonshire G63 0JY Tel: 01389 850245
• e-mail: scotts@inchmurrin-lochlomond.com
• website: www.inchmurrin-lochlomond.com

www.holidayguides.com

WEBSITE DIRECTORY 183

•EDINBURGH & LOTHIANS

B & B
Cruachan B&B, 78 East Main Street,
BLACKBURN, By Bathgate, West Lothian
EH47 7QS Tel: 01506 655221
- e-mail: cruachan.bb@virgin.net
- website: www.cruachan.co.uk

B & B
Mrs Kay, Blossom House, 8 Minto Street,
EDINBURGH EH9 1RG Tel: 0131 667 5353
- e-mail: blossom_house@hotmail.com
- website: www.blossomguesthouse.co.uk

Guest House
Kenvie Guest House, 16 Kilmaurs Road,
EDINBURGH EH16 5DA Tel: 0131 6681964
- e-mail: dorothy@kenvie.co.uk
- website: www.kenvie.co.uk

Guest House
International Guest House, 37 Mayfield
Gardens, EDINBURGH EH9 2BX
Tel: 0131 667 2511
- e-mail: intergh1@yahoo.co.uk
- website: www.accommodation-edinburgh.com

B & B
McCrae's B&B, 44 East Claremont Street,
EDINBURGH EH7 4JR Tel: 0131 556 2610
- e-mail: mccraes.bandb@lineone.net
- http://website.lineone.net/~mccraes.bandb

Holiday Park
Seton Sands Holiday Village, LONGNIDDRY,
East Lothian EH32 0QF Tel: 01875 813333
- website: www.touringholidays.co.uk

Self-Catering / Caravan & Camping
Drummohr Caravan Park, Levenhall,
MUSSELBURGH, East Lothian EH21 8JS
Tel: 0131 6656867
- e-mail: bookings@drummohr.org
- website: www.drummohr.org

•FIFE

Hotel
The Lundin Links Hotel, Leven Road,
LUNDIN LINKS, Fife KY8 6AP
Tel: 01333 320207
- e-mail: info@lundin-links-hotel.co.uk
- website: www.lundin-links-hotel.co.uk

Self-Caterting
Balmore, 3 West Road, NEWPORT-ON-TAY,
Fife DD6 8HH Tel: 01382 542274
- e-mail: allan.ramsay@ukgateway.net
- website: www.thorndene.co.uk

Self-Catering
Kingask Cottages, Kingask House,
ST ANDREWS, Fife KY16 8PN
Tel: 01334 472011
- e-mail: info@kingask-cottages.co.uk
- website: www.kingask-cottages.co.uk

B & B
Mrs Duncan, Spinkstown Farmhouse,
ST ANDREWS, Fife KY16 8PN
Tel: 01334 473475
- e-mail: anne@spinkstown.com
- website: www.spinkstown.com

•GLASGOW & DISTRICT

B & B
Mrs P. Wells, Avenue End B & B, 21 West
Avenue, Stepps, GLASGOW G33 6ES
Tel: 0141 7791990
- website: www.avenueend.co.uk

•HIGHLANDS

Accommodation in the HIGHLANDS.
- website: www.Aviemore.com

Self-Catering
Linda Murray, 29 Grampian View,
AVIEMORE, Inverness-shire PH22 1TF
Tel: 01479 810653
- e-mail: linda.murray@virgin.net
- website: www.cairngorm-bungalows.co.uk

Self-Catering
Pink Bank Chalets, Dalfaber Road,
AVIEMORE, Inverness-shire PH22 1PX
Tel: 01479 810000
- e-mail: pinebankchallets@btopenworld.com
- website: www.pinebankchalets.co.uk

Self Catering / Caravans
Speyside Leisure Park, Dalfaber Road,
AVIEMORE, Inverness-shire PH22 1PX
Tel: 01479 810236
- e-mail: fhg@speysideleisure.com
- website: www.speysideleisure.com

Self-Catering
The Treehouse, BOAT-OF-GARTEN,
Highlands
Contact: Mrs Mather Tel: 0131 337 7167
- e-mail: fhg@treehouselodge.plus.com
- website: www.treehouselodge.co.uk

Guest House
Mrs Lynn Benge, The Pines Country House,
Duthil, CARRBRIDGE, Inverness-shire
PH23 3ND Tel: 01479 841220
- e-mail: lynn@thepines-duthil.co.uk
- website: www.thepines-duthil.fsnet.co.uk

Hotel
The Clan MacDuff Hotel, Achintore Road,
FORT WILLIAM PH33 6RW
Tel: 01397 702341
- e-mail: reception@clanmacduff.co.uk
- website: www.clanmacduff.co.uk

Hotel
Invergarry Hotel, INVERGARRY,
Inverness-shire PH35 4HJ Tel: 01809 501206
- e-mail: info@invergarryhotel.co.uk
- website: www.invergarryhotel.co.uk

Self-Catering
Invermoriston Holiday Chalets,
INVERMORISTON, Glenmoriston,
Inverness, Inverness-shire IV63 7YF
Tel: 01320 351254
- website: www.invermoriston-holidays.com

Caravan & Camping
Auchnahillin Caravan & Camping Park,
Daviot East, INVERNESS, Inverness-shire
IV2 5XQ Tel: 01463 772286
- e-mail: info@auchnahillin.co.uk
- website: www.auchnahillin.co.uk

Self-Catering
Mrs A MacIver, The Sheiling, Achgarve,
LAIDE, Ross-shire IV22 2NS
Tel: 01445 731487
- e-mail: stay@thesheilingholidays.com
- website: www.thesheilingholidays.com

Self-Catering
Wildside Highland Lodges, Whitebridge,
By LOCH NESS, Inverness-shire IV2 6UN
Tel: 01456 486373
- e-mail: info@wildsidelodges.com
- website: www.wildsidelodges.com

B & B / Self-Catering Chalets
D.J. Mordaunt, Mondhuie, NETHY BRIDGE,
Inverness-shire PH25 3DF Tel: 01479 821062
- e-mail: david@mondhuie.com
- website: www.mondhuie.com

Self-Catering
Crubenbeg Holiday Cottages,
NEWTONMORE, Inverness-shire PH20 1BE
Tel: 01540 673566
- e-mail: enquiry@crubenbeg.com
- website: www.crubenbeg.com

Self-Catering
Mr A. Urquhart, Crofters Cottages,
15 Croft, POOLEWE, Ross-shire IV22 2JY
Tel: 01445 781268
- e-mail: croftcottages@btopenworld.com
- website: www.croftcottages.btinternet.co.uk

Hotel
Whitebridge Hotel, WHITEBRIDGE,
Inverness IV2 6UN Tel: 01456 486226
- e-mail: info@whitebridgehotel.co.uk
- website: www.whitebridgehotel.co.uk

•LANARKSHIRE

Self-Catering
Carmichael Country Cottages,
Carmichael Estate Office, Westmains,
Carmichael, BIGGAR, Lanarkshire ML12 6PG
Tel: 01899 308336
- e-mail: chiefcarm@aol.com
- website: www.carmichael.co.uk/cottages

Guest House
Blairmains Guest House, Blairmains,
HARTHILL, Lanarkshire ML7 5TJ
Tel: 01501 751278
- e-mail: heather@blairmains.freeserve.co.uk
- website: www.blairmains.co.uk

•PERTH & KINROSS

Self-Catering
Loch Tay Lodges, Remony, Acharn,
ABERFELDY, Perthshire PH15 2HR
Tel: 01887 830209
- e-mail: remony@btinternet.com
- website: www.lochtaylodges.co.uk

Hotel
Lands of Loyal Hotel, ALYTH, Perthshire
PH11 8JQ Tel: 01828 633151
- e-mail: info@landsofloyal.com
- website: www.landsofloyal.com

Self-Catering
Laighwood Holidays, Laighwood,
Butterstone, BY DUNKELD,
Perthshire PH8 0HB Tel: 01350 724241
- e-mail: holidays@laighwood.co.uk
- website: www.laighwood.co.uk

Self-catering
East Cottage, Roro Estate, GLEN LYON.
Contact: E. Thompson LLP, 76 Overhaugh
Street, Galashiels TD1 1DP
Tel: 01896 751300
- e-mail: Galashiels@edwin-thompson.co.uk

WEBSITE DIRECTORY

B & B
Brochanach, 43 Fingal Road, KILLIN, Perthshire FK21 8XA Tel: 01567 820028
• e-mail: alifer@msn.com
• website: www.s-h-systems.co.uk/hotels/brochanach.html

Self-Catering
Gill Hunt, Wester Lix Cottage, Wester Lix, KILLIN, Perthshire FK21 8RD
Tel: 01567 820990
• e-mail: gill@westerlix.net
• website: www.westerlix.net

Hotel
Balrobin Hotel, Higher Oakfield, PITLOCHRY, Perthshire PH16 5HT Tel: 01796 472901
• e-mail: info@balrobin.co.uk
• website: www.balrobin.co.uk

Guest House
Jacky & Malcolm Catterall, Tulloch, Enochdhu, By Kirkmichael, PITLOCHRY, Perthshire PH10 7PW Tel: 01250 881404
• e-mail: maljac@tulloch83.freeserve.co.uk
• website: www.maljac.com

B & B
Mrs Ann Guthrie, Newmill Farm, STANLEY, Perthshire PH1 4QD Tel: 01738 828281
• e-mail: guthrienewmill@sol.co.uk
• website: www.newmillfarm.co.uk

B & B / Self-Catering
Ardoch Lodge, STRATHYRE, Near Callander FK18 8NF Tel: 01877 384666
• e-mail: ardoch@btinternet.com
• website: www.ardochlodge.co.uk

•STIRLING & TROSSACHS

Camping & Caravan Park
Riverside Caravan Park, Dollarfield, DOLLAR, Clackmannanshire FK14 7LX
Tel: 01259 742896
• e-mail: info@riverside-caravanpark.co.uk
• website: www.riverside-caravanpark.co.uk

Guest House
Croftburn Bed & Breakfast, Croftamie, DRYMEN, Loch Lomond G63 0HA
Tel: 01360 660796
• e-mail: enquiries@croftburn.co.uk
• website: www.croftburn.co.uk

•SCOTTISH ISLANDS•SKYE

Hotel & Restaurant
Royal Hotel, Bank Street, PORTREE, Isle of Skye IV51 9BU Tel: 01478 612585
• e-mail: info@royal-hotel-skye.com
• website: www.royal-hotel-skye.com

•WALES

Self-Catering
Quality Cottages, Cerbid, Solva, HAVERFORDWEST, Pembrokeshire SA62 6YE Tel: 01348 837871
• website: www.qualitycottages.co.uk

•ANGLESEY & GWYNEDD

Self-Catering / Caravan Park
Mrs A. Skinner, Ty Gwyn, Rhyduchaf, BALA, Gwynedd LL23 7SD Tel: 01678 521267
• e-mail: richard.skin@btinternet.com

Caravan & Camping Site
Glanllyn Lakeside Caravan & Camping Park, Llanuwchllyn, BALA, Gwynedd LL23 7ST
Tel: 01678 540227
• e-mail: info@glanllyn.com
• website: www.glanllyn.com

Caravan Park
Parc Caerelwan, Talybont, BARMOUTH, Gwynedd LL43 2AX Tel: 01341 247236
• e-mail: parc@porthmadog.co.uk
• website: www.porthmadog.co.uk/parc/

Country House
Sygun Fawr Country House, BEDDGELERT, Gwynedd LL55 4NE Tel: 01766 890258
• e-mail: sygunfawr@aol.com
• website: www.sygunfawr.co.uk

Holiday Park
Greenacres Holiday Park, Black Rock Sands, Morfa Bychan, Porthmadog, CAERNARFON, Gwynedd LL49 9YF Tel: 01766 512781
• website: www.touringholidays.co.uk

Self-Catering / Caravans
Plas-y-Bryn Chalet Park, Bontnewydd, CAERNARFON, Gwynedd LL54 7YE
Tel: 01286 672811
• www.plasybrynholidayscaernarfon.co.uk

Self-Catering within a Castle
BrynBras Castle, Llanrug, Near CAERNARFON, Gwynedd LL55 4RE
Tel: 01286 870210
• e-mail: holidays@brynbrascastle.co.uk
• website: www.brynbrascastle.co.uk

www.holidayguides.com

WEBSITE DIRECTORY

Self-Catering
Mrs A. Jones, Rhos Country Cottages, Betws Bach, Ynys, CRICCIETH, Gwynedd LL52 0PB Tel: 01758 720047
- e-mail: cottages@rhos.freeserve.co.uk
- website: www.rhos-cottages.co.uk

Caravan & Chalet Park/ Self-Catering
Parc Wernol Parc, Chwilog, Pwllheli, Near CRICCIETH, Gwynedd LL53 6SW Tel: 01766 810506
- e-mail: catherine@wernol.com
- website: www.wernol.com

Guest House
Mrs M. Bamford, Ivy House, Finsbury Square, DOLGELLAU, Gwynedd LL40 1RF. Tel: 01341 422535
- e-mail: marg.bamford@btconnect.com
- website: www.ukworld.net/ivyhouse

Guest House
Fron Deg Guest House, LLanfair, HARLECH, Gwynedd LL46 2RB Tel: 01766 780448
- website: www.bedandbreakfast-harlech.co.uk

Caravan & Camping
Mr John Billingham, Islawrffordd Caravan Park, Tal-y-Bont, MERIONETH, Gwynedd LL43 2BQ Tel: 01341 247269
- e-mail: info@islawrffordd.co.uk
- website: www.islawrffordd.co.uk

Golf Club
Anglesey Golf Club Ltd, Station Road, RHOSNEIGR, Anglesey LL64 5QX Tel: 01407 811127 ext 2
- e-mail: info@theangleseygolfclub.com
- website: www.angleseygolfclub.co.uk

•NORTH WALES

Hotel
Fairy Glen Hotel, Beaver Bridge, BETWS-Y-COED, Conwy, North Wales LL24 0SH Tel: 01690 710269
- e-mail: fairyglen@youe.fsworld.co.uk
- website: www.fairyglenhotel.co.uk

Country House
Hafod Country House, Trefrin, Llanrwst, CONWY VALLEY, North Wales LL27 0RQ Tel: 01492 640029
- e-mail: hafod@breathemail.net
- website: www.hafod-house.co.uk

Guest House
The Park Hill / Gwesty Bryn Parc, Llanrwst Road, Betws-y-Coed, CONWY, North Wales LL24 0HD Tel: 01690 710540
- e-mail: welcome@park-hill.co.uk
- website: www.park-hill.co.uk

Guest House
Sychnant Pass House, Sychnant Pass Road CONWY, North Wales LL32 8BJ Tel: 01492 596868
- e-mail: bre@sychnant-pass-house.co.uk
- website: www.sychnant-pass-house.co.uk

Golf Club
Denbigh Golf Club, Henllan Road, DENBIGH, North Wales LL16 5AA Tel: 01745 816669
- e-mail: denbighgolfclub@aol.com
- website: www.denbighgolfclub.co.uk

Golf Club
North Wales Golf Club, 72 Bryniau Road, West Shore, LLANDUDNO, North Wales LL30 2DZ Tel:01492 875325 or 01492 876878
- e-mail: golf@nwgc.freeserve.co.uk
- website: www.northwalesgolfclub.co.uk

Hotel / Inn
The Golden Pheasant Country Hotel & Inn, Llwynmawr, Glyn Ceiriog, Near LLANGOLLEN, North Wales LL20 7BB Tel: 01691 718281
- e-mail: goldenpheasant@micro-plus-web.net
- website: goldenpheasanthotel.co.uk

Self-Catering Cottages
Glyn Uchaf, Conwy Old Road, PENMAENMAWR, North Wales LL34 6YS Tel: 01492 623737
- e-mail: john@baxter6055.freeserve.co.uk
- website: www.glyn-uchaf.co.uk

Holiday Park
Presthaven Sands Holiday Park, Gronaut, PRESTATYN, North Wales LL19 9TT Tel: 01745 856471
website: www.touringholidays.co.uk

•CARMARTHENSHIRE

Self-Catering
Maerdy Cottages, Taliaris, LLANDEILO, Carmarthenshire SA19 7BD Tel: 01550 777448
- e-mail: mjones@maerdyholidaycottages.co.uk
- website: www.maerdyholidaycottages.co.uk

WEBSITE DIRECTORY

• CEREDIGION

Holiday Village
Gilfach Holiday Village, Llwyncelyn, Near ABERAERON, Ceredigion SA46 0HN
Tel: 01545 580288
- e-mail: info@stratfordcaravans.co.uk
- website: www.selfcateringholidays.com
          www.stratfordcaravans.co.uk

• PEMBROKESHIRE

Farm Self-Catering
Holiday House, BROAD HAVEN, Pembrokeshire.
Contact: L.E. Ashton, 10 St Leonards Road, Thames Ditton, Surrey KT7 0RJ
Tel: 020 8398 6249
- e-mail: lejash@aol.com
- website: www.33timberhill.com

Hotel / Guest House
Ivybridge, Drim Mill, Dyffryn, Goodwick, FISHGUARD, Pembrokeshire SA64 0JT
Tel: 01348 875366
- e-mail: ivybridge@cwcom.net
- website: www.ivybridge.cwc.net

Caravans & Camp Site
Brandy Brook Caravan & Camping Site, Rhyndaston, Hayscastle, HAVERFORDWEST, Pembrokeshire SA62 5PT
Tel: 01348 840272
- e-mail: f.m.rowe@btopenworld.com

Farmhouse B & B
Mrs Jen Patrick, East Hook Farm, Portfield Gate, HAVERFORDWEST, Pembrokeshire SA62 3LN
Tel: 01437 762211
- e-mail: jen.patrick@easthookfarmhouse.co.uk
- website: www.easthookfarmhouse.co.uk

Inn
The Dial Inn, Ridgeway Road, LAMPHEY, Pembroke, Pembrokeshire SA71 5NU
Tel: 01646 672426
- e-mail: info@dialinn.co.uk

Hotel
Trewern Arms Hotel, Nevern, NEWPORT, Pembrokeshire SA42 0NB
Tel: 01239 820395
- e-mail: info@trewern-arms-pembrokeshire.co.uk
- www.trewern-arms-pembrokeshire.co.uk

Self-catering
Ffynnon Ddofn, ST DAVIDS, Pembrokeshire.
Contact: Mrs B. Rees White, Brick House Farm, Burnham Road, Woodham Mortimer, Maldon, Essex CM9 6SR
Tel: 01245 224611
- website: www.ffynnonddofn.co.uk

Self-Catering
T. M. Hardman, High View, Catherine Street, ST DAVIDS, Pembrokeshire SA62 6RJ
Tel: 01437 720616
- e-mail: enquiries@stnbc.co.uk
- website: www.stnbc.co.uk

Farm Guest House
Mrs Morfydd Jones,
Lochmeyler Farm Guest House, Llandeloy, Pen-y-Cwm, Near SOLVA, St Davids, Pembrokeshire SA62 6LL
Tel: 01348 837724
- e-mail: stay@lochmeyler.co.uk
- website: www.lochmeyler.co.uk

Holiday Park
Kiln Park Holiday Centre, Marsh Road, TENBY, Pembrokeshire SA70 7RB
Tel: 01834 844121
- website: www.touringholidays.co.uk

• POWYS

Farm
Caebetran Farm, Felinfach, BRECON, Powys LD3 0UL Tel: 01874 754460
- e-mail: hazelcaebetran@aol.com
- website: caebetranfarmhousebedandbreakfastwales.com

Guest House
Maeswalter, Heol Senni, Near BRECON, Powys LD3 8SU Tel: 01874 636629
- e-mail: joy@maeswalter.fsnet.co.uk
         bb@maeswalter.co.uk
- website: www.maeswalter.co.uk

Self-Catering
Mrs Jones, Penllwyn Lodges, GARTHMYL, Powys SY15 6SB
Tel: 01686 640269
- e-mail: daphne.jones@onetel.net
- website: www.penllwynlodges.co.uk

Readers are requested to mention this FHG guidebook when seeking accommodation

WEBSITE DIRECTORY

B & B
Annie McKay, Hafod-y-Garreg, Erwood, Builth Wells, Near HAY-ON-WYE, Powys LD2 3TQ
Tel: 01982 560400
• website: www.hafodygarreg.co.uk

Hotel & Restaurant
Lasswade Country House Hotel & Restaurant, Station Road, LLANWRTYD WELLS, Powys LD5 4RW Tel: 01591 610515
• e-mail: info@lasswadehotel.co.uk
• website: www.lasswadehotel.co.uk

Self-Catering
Oak Wood Lodges, Llwynbaedd, RHAYADER, Powys LD6 5NT
Tel: 01597 811422
• e-mail: info@oakwoodlodges.co.uk
• website: www.oakwoodlodges.co.uk

Self-Catering
Ann Reed, Madog's Wells, Llanfair Caereinion, WELSHPOOL, Powys SY21 0DE
Tel: 01938 810446
• e-mail: madogswells@btinternet.com
• website: www.madogswells.co.uk

•SOUTH WALES

Narrowboat Hire
Castle Narrowboats, Church Road Wharf, Gilwern, Monmouthshire NP7 0EP
Tel: 01873 832340
• info@castlenarrowboats.co.uk
• website: www.castlenarrowboats.co.uk

Guest House / Self-Catering Cottages
Mrs Norma James, Wyrloed Lodge, Manmoel, BLACKWOOD, Caerphilly, South Wales NP12 0RN Tel: 01495 371198
• e-mail: norma.james@btinternet.com
• website: www.btinternet.com/~norma.james/

Self-Catering
Cwrt-y-Gaer, Wolvesnewton, CHEPSTOW, Monmouthshire NP16 6PR Tel: 01291 650700
• e-mail: johnllewellyn11@btinternet.com
• website: www.cwrt-y-gaer.co.uk

Hotel
Culver House Hotel, Port Eynon, GOWER, Swansea, South Wales SA3 1NN
Tel: 01792 390755
• e-mail: stay@culverhousehotel.co.uk
• website: www.culverhousehotel.co.uk

Guest House
Rosemary & Derek Ringer, Church Farm Guest House, Mitchel Troy, MONMOUTH, South Wales NP25 4HZ Tel: 01600 712176
• e-mail: info@churchfarmguesthouse.eclipse.co.uk
• website: www.churchfarmmitcheltroy.co.uk

Golf Club
St Mellons Golf Club, ST MELLONS, Cardiff, South Wales Tel: 01633 680408
• e-mail: stmellons@golf2003.fs.co.uk
• website: www.stmellonsgolfclub.co.uk

Hotel
Egerton Grey Country House Hotel, Porthkerry, Barry, VALE OF GLAMORGAN, South Wales CF62 3BZ Tel: 01446 711666
• e-mail: info@egertongrey.co.uk
• website: www.egertongrey.co.uk

•IRELAND

Self-Catering Cottages
Imagine Ireland
Tel: 0870 112 77 32
• e-mail: info@imagineireland.com
• website: www.imagineireland.com

CO. CLARE

Self-Catering
Ballyvaughan Village & Country Holiday Homes, BALLYVAUGHAN.
Contact: George Quinn, Frances Street, Kilrush, Co. Clare Tel: 00 353 65 9051977
• e-mail: sales@ballyvaughan-cottages.com
• website: www.ballyvaughan-cottages.com

•CHANNEL ISLANDS
GUERNSEY

Self-Catering Apartments
Swallow Apartments, La Cloture, L'Ancresse, GUERNSEY Tel: 01481 249633
• e-mail: swallowapt@aol.com
• website: www.swallowapartments.com

www.holidayguides.com

Index of towns and sections

Please also refer to Contents page 3

Aberdovey	WALES	Kessingland	EAST ANGLIA
Ambleside	NORTH WEST ENGLAND	Kingsbridge	SOUTH DEVON
Arlington	SUSSEX	Kingston upon Thames	LONDON & HOME COUNTIES
Ashbourne	MIDLANDS		
Ashburton	SOUTH DEVON	Launceston	CORNWALL
Ashford	KENT	Liskeard	CORNWALL
Bacton-on-Sea	EAST ANGLIA	Little Torrington	NORTH DEVON
Ballachulish	SCOTLAND	Llangollen	WALES
Bamburgh	NORTH EAST ENGLAND	Llanteg	WALES
Barnstaple	NORTH DEVON	London	LONDON & HOME COUNTIES
Barton on Sea	HAMPSHIRE & DORSET	Lulworth Cove	HAMPSHIRE & DORSET
Battle	SUSSEX	Lytham St Annes	NORTH WEST ENGLAND
Bishop Auckland	NORTH EAST ENGLAND	Minehead	SOMERSET & WILTSHIRE
Boat of Garten	SCOTLAND	Oban	SCOTLAND
Bournemouth	HAMPSHIRE & DORSET	Padstow	CORNWALL
Bridport	HAMPSHIRE & DORSET	Port Gaverne	CORNWALL
Brixham	SOUTH DEVON	Pwllheli	WALES
Burton Bradstock	HAMPSHIRE & DORSET	Ringwood	HAMPSHIRE & DORSET
Burwell	EAST ANGLIA	St Annes	NORTH WEST ENGLAND
Buxton	MIDLANDS	St Helens	ISLE OF WIGHT
Canterbury	KENT	Sevenoaks	KENT
Catacol	SCOTLAND	Shanklin	ISLE OF WIGHT
Cawsand	CORNWALL	South Molton	NORTH DEVON
Charmouth	HAMPSHIRE & DORSET	Southwold/Walberswick	EAST ANGLIA
Chiddingly	SUSSEX	Stogumber	SOMERSET & WILTSHIRE
Combe Martin	NORTH DEVON	Studland Bay	HAMPSHIRE & DORSET
Dawlish	SOUTH DEVON	Tarbert	SCOTLAND
Dolgellau	WALES	Taynuilt	SCOTLAND
Dufftown	SCOTLAND	Telford	MIDLANDS
Exeter	SOUTH DEVON	Torquay	SOUTH DEVON
Fakenham	EAST ANGLIA	Totland	ISLE OF WIGHT
Falmouth	CORNWALL	Truro	CORNWALL
Farnsfield	MIDLANDS	Umberleigh	NORTH DEVON
Fowey	CORNWALL	Wareham	HAMPSHIRE & DORSET
Framlingham	EAST ANGLIA	Warminster	SOMERSET & WILTSHIRE
Goodwick	WALES	Welshpool	WALES
Great Malvern	MIDLANDS	Weston-super-Mare	SOMERSET & WILTSHIRE
Hailsham	SUSSEX	Whitby	NORTH EAST ENGLAND
Haltwhistle	NORTH EAST ENGLAND	Whithorn	SCOTLAND
Hartlepool	NORTH EAST ENGLAND	Windermere	NORTH WEST ENGLAND
Hayle	CORNWALL	Woolacombe Bay	NORTH DEVON
Helston	CORNWALL	Wrotham	KENT
Hereford	MIDLANDS	Wybunbury	NORTH WEST ENGLAND
Hexham	NORTH EAST ENGLAND		

Ratings & Awards

For the first time ever the AA, VisitBritain, VisitScotland, and the Wales Tourist Board will use a single method of assessing and rating serviced accommodation. Irrespective of which organisation inspects an establishment the rating awarded will be the same, using a common set of standards, giving a clear guide of what to expect. The RAC is no longer operating an Hotel inspection and accreditation business.

Accommodation Standards: Star Grading Scheme

Using a scale of 1-5 stars the objective quality ratings give a clear indication of accommodation standard, cleanliness, ambience, hospitality, service and food, This shows the full range of standards suitable for every budget and preference, and allows visitors to distinguish between the quality of accommodation and facilities on offer in different establishments. All types of board and self-catering accommodation are covered, including hotels, B&Bs, holiday parks, campus accommodation, hostels, caravans and camping, and boats.

The more stars, the higher level of quality

★★★★★
exceptional quality, with a degree of luxury

★★★★
excellent standard throughout

★★★
very good level of quality and comfort

★★
good quality, well presented and well run

★
acceptable quality; simple, practical, no frills

VisitBritain and the regional tourist boards, **enjoyEngland.com, VisitScotland** and **VisitWales**, and **the AA** have full details of the grading system on their websites

National Accessible Scheme

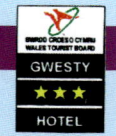

If you have particular mobility, visual or hearing needs, look out for the National Accessible Scheme. You can be confident of finding accommodation or attractions that meet your needs by looking for the following symbols.

Typically suitable for a person with sufficient mobility to climb a flight of steps but would benefit from fixtures and fittings to aid balance

Typically suitable for a person with restricted walking ability and for those that may need to use a wheelchair some of the time and can negotiate a maximum of three steps

Typically suitable for a person who depends on the use of a wheelchair and transfers unaided to and from the wheelchair in a seated position. This person may be an independent traveller

Typically suitable for a person who depends on the use of a wheelchair in a seated position. This person also requires personal or mechanical assistance (eg carer, hoist).

191

OTHER FHG TITLES FOR 2007

FHG Guides Ltd have a large range of attractive holiday accommodation guides for all kinds of holiday opportunities throughout Britain. They also make useful gifts at any time of year. Our guides are available in most bookshops and larger newsagents but we will be happy to post you a copy direct if you have any difficulty. POST FREE for addresses in the UK. We will also post abroad but have to charge separately for post or freight.

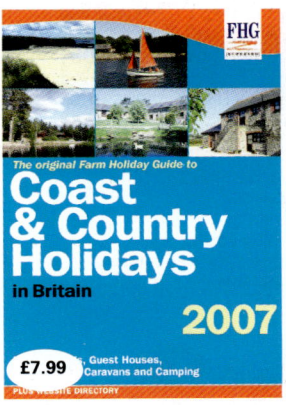

The original Farm Holiday Guide to **COAST & COUNTRY HOLIDAYS** in England, Scotland, Wales and Channel Islands. Board, Self-catering, Caravans/Camping, Activity Holidays.

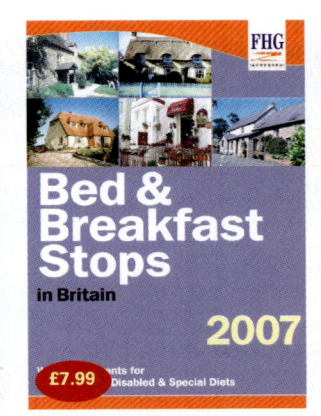

BED AND BREAKFAST STOPS
Over 1000 friendly and comfortable overnight stops. Non-smoking, Disabled and Special Diets Supplements.

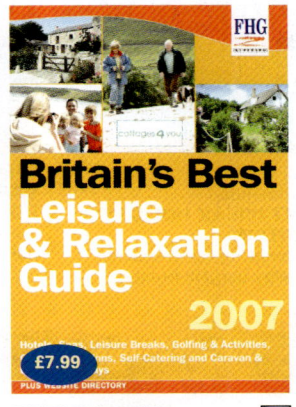

BRITAIN'S BEST LEISURE & RELAXATION GUIDE
A quick-reference general guide for all kinds of holidays.

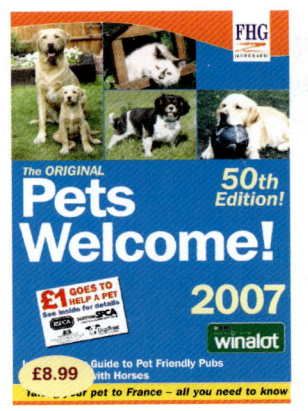

The Original **PETS WELCOME!**
The bestselling guide to holidays for pet owners and their pets.

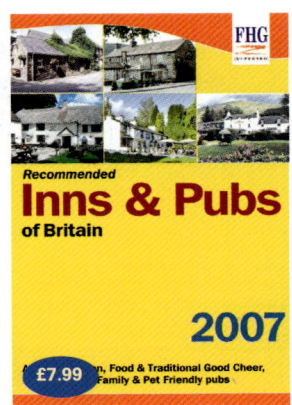

Recommended **INNS & PUBS** of Britain
Including Pubs, Inns and Small Hotels.

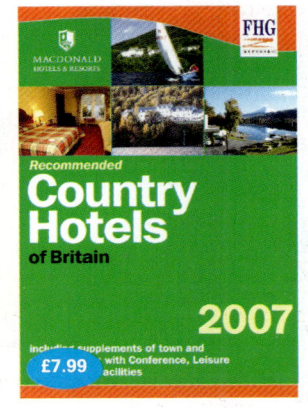

Recommended **COUNTRY HOTELS** of Britain
Including Country Houses, for the discriminating.

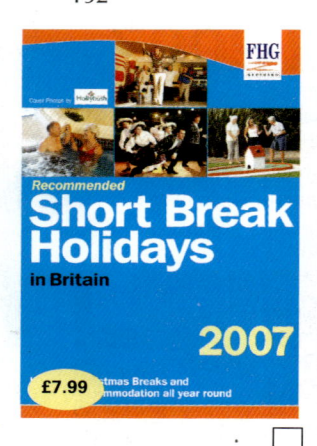

Recommended SHORT BREAK HOLIDAYS IN BRITAIN
"Approved" accommodation for quality bargain breaks.

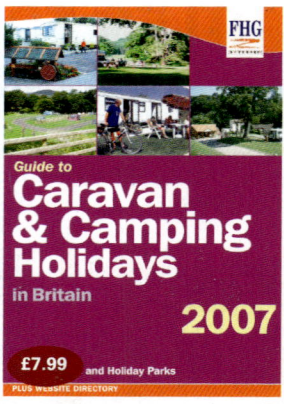

The FHG Guide to CARAVAN & CAMPING HOLIDAYS,
Caravans for hire, sites and holiday parks and centres.

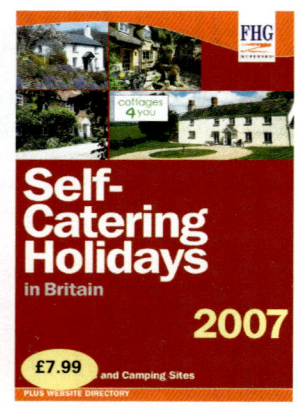

SELF-CATERING HOLIDAYS
in Britain
Over 1000 addresses throughout for self-catering and caravans in Britain.

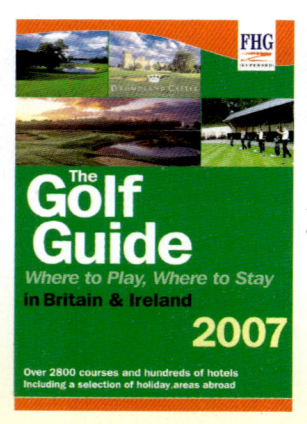

The GOLF GUIDE –
Where to play   Where to stay
In association with GOLF MONTHLY. Over 2800 golf courses in Britain with convenient accommodation. Holiday Golf in France, Portugal, Spain, USA, South Africa and Thailand.

£9.99

Tick your choice above and send your order and payment to

**FHG Guides Ltd. Abbey Mill Business Centre
Seedhill, Paisley, Scotland PA1 1TJ
TEL: 0141- 887 0428 • FAX: 0141- 889 7204
e-mail: admin@fhguides.co.uk**

Deduct 10% for 2/3 titles or copies; 20% for 4 or more.

Send to: NAME..

ADDRESS ....

....

....

POST CODE ....

I enclose Cheque/Postal Order for £ ....

SIGNATURE..DATE ....

Please complete the following to help us improve the service we provide.
How did you find out about our guides?

☐ Press   ☐ Magazines   ☐ TV/Radio   ☐ Family/Friend   ☐ Other